NELLIE MELBA

The greatest Australian prima donna. She began her study of music in the Presbyterian College, Melbourne, where she was born in 1865, and made her debut in Brussels, 1877. She has since toured the world in opera. Her popular encore is "Annie Laurie"—Heart Songs, p. 301.

GERALDINE FARRAR

A famous young American prima donna. She was born in Melrose, Massachusetts,
and while in her teens made her debut at the Royal Opera House, Berlin, as
*Marguerite* in "Faust." Since 1906 she has been a member of the Metropolitan
Opera Company, New York. Her popular encore is "Kathleen Mavourneen"—
Heart Songs, p. 376.

Contributed by 25,000 People

# HEART
# SONGS

## 𝔇ear to the American 𝔓eople

And by them Contributed in the Search for Treasured Songs
Initiated by the

## NATIONAL MAGAZINE

CLEARFIELD

Originally published
Boston, Massachusetts, 1909

Reprinted, with a new Introduction, for
Clearfield Company, Inc. by
Genealogical Publishing Co., Inc.
Baltimore, Maryland
1997

International Standard Book Number: 0-8063-4737-6

*Made in the United States of America*

# INTRODUCTION

In 1905 when Joe Mitchell Chapple undertook to compile a book of the favorite songs of the American people, he was inspired by *Heart Throbs*, a selection of America's favorite prose and verse that he published in 1906. Indeed, the song collection was but the second entry in a series of heart-themed efforts he produced during the first two decades of the twentieth century. Subsequent books included *Heart Letters* (1912) and *Heart Chord* (1915); he also produced a Heart Throb series of movies.[1] Exactly how successful these volumes and films were is uncertain; however, it is clear that they did not have the lasting appeal of *Heart Songs*, which underwent a major reprinting in 1938 and is still avidly sought in used book shops by those interested in American musical literature.

Who was the man responsible for promoting this collection? Multi-talented Joseph Mitchell Chapple (he always went by Joe) was born July 18, 1867, in La Porte City, Iowa.[2] After his secondary school education, he attended Cornell College of Iowa. In 1904 he received an honorary master's degree from that institution; eleven years later, in 1915, Lincoln Memorial University, Harrogate, Tennessee, conferred on him an honorary doctorate. Why the accolades? Praises were due primarily because of his journalistic abilities—by 1915 he had been involved in that field for over thirty years. In 1883, at age sixteen, he edited a Grand Rapids, North Dakota newspaper, and within a few years he became owner and editor of another paper. Then, for about a decade, he worked as a journalist in Chicago, Washington, and New York. In 1897, at age thirty, Chapple moved to Boston where he assumed duties as editor and publisher of *The Bostonian*. This position proved to be his greatest opportunity, and he made the most of it by remaining in his dual roles for many decades. By 1897 he was presumably known not only for his journalistic abilities but also for his business acumen. He soon demonstrated both of them by increasing the magazine's subscription list and by making it a truly national magazine. With typical promotional flair he emphasized this latter desire by changing the publication's name to *The National Magazine*.

In addition to his "heart" collections, Chapple found time to write several novels, the first of which was *The Minor Chord* (1895) plus books on topics as varied as the Panama Canal, Warren G. Harding, Wendell Willkie, travel, and profiles of American Presidents. A gregarious personality, he also gained a reputation as a Chautauqua lecturer and after-dinner speaker, often basing his comments on his extensive travels and wide contact with celebrities around the world. On the Chautauqua circuit he was especially noted for four talks: "Flashlights of Famous People," "Confessions of an Optimist," "On the Wings of Tomorrow," and "The Great Personality Parade." Just as the Great Depression was getting underway, he launched the radio series "Face to Face with Our Presidents." Later, in 1946, Chapple returned to the airwaves with a short-lived series on NBC, "Personalities Whom I Have Met." This venture proved to be his last foray into the entertainment field because he died at his home in Winthrop, Massachusetts, on April 17, 1950, three months and one day shy of his eighty-third birthday.

Although Chapple himself was, apparently, responsible for the idea behind *Heart Songs*, the selection of material to be included was made by a committee. Possibly this was a relatively large group, but the only three people who now can definitely be identified as responsible for the decisions are Chapple, George W. Chadwick, and Victor Herbert. George Whitefield Chadwick (1854–1931) was a composer, pianist, organist, conductor and teacher, whose compositions included three symphonies and five string quartets, among other works. His greatest work, however, was probably transforming the New England Conservatory from essentially a piano school for training teachers into a full-fledged conservatory in the European sense.[3] Victor August Herbert (1859–1924)—Chapple's other collaborator and the man responsible for two operas, several operettas, and such classics of American popular song as "Ah, Sweet Mystery of Life," "Gypsy Love Song," and "A Kiss in the Dark"—is much better known to modern audiences.

Except for the few hints provided in the book's Foreword, the exact criteria used for making the final selections are unclear. Evidently, one of the most important considerations was that the songs chosen somehow had to represent the "American heart." In Chapple's mind that nebulous term meant something more than it likely would to most people in the late twentieth century. That concept didn't just refer to sentimental songs (although many made the final list of 404 songs) but consisted of at least ten classes of material: "Patriotic and war songs; sea songs; lullabies and child songs; dancing songs, lilts, and jigs; plantation and Negro melodies; sacred songs and hymns; love songs; songs from operas and operettas; popular concert hall songs and ballads; and college, school, and fraternity songs."[4] Apparently, the initial plan was to separate the final choices into these rigid categories, but it soon became apparent that such a scheme wouldn't work. For one thing, it was difficult to separate the songs so easily; most could readily fit into two or more of these categories. For example, "Dixie" could be classified as a patriotic or war song, a dancing song, and a plantation or Negro melody (by which Chapple had in mind mostly pseudo–African-American material mainly from the pens of white songwriters). Chapple readily conceded this problem and opted for the simplest solution: retaining essentially the same general categories and listing several songs under more than one heading.

That there was considerable overlapping between categories is most dramatically demonstrated by the following breakdown listing classifications and the number of songs in each. The first three classes were untitled in the published volume but clearly refer to one of the ten categories listed in the Foreword. Class I (patriotic and war songs)—54 songs; Class II (sea or sea related songs)—47; Class III (lullabies and child songs)—48; Songs that have been popular as Dance Music—48; Negro Melodies and Minstrel Songs—54; Sacred Songs, Revival Hymns—57; Love Songs—80; Songs of the Great Masters in Operas, Operettas, and Oratorios—51; Concerts, Solos and Quartettes—98; College and Fraternal Songs—48. Only 404 songs are contained in the book, so the total of 585 achieved by adding up the number of titles under each category is very graphic evidence that many items appeared under at least two headings. Even so, in a few instances some obvious inclusions are missed. For example, Sanford Fillmore Bennett and Joseph Philbrick Webster's 1868 "Sweet By-and-By," which from its inception has been primarily known as a hymn, is only listed under lullabies and children's songs.[5]

There are some other interesting omissions. Although the book generally contains proper credits, occasionally a lyricist's name is excluded; thus, only Webster is credited with "Sweet By-and-By." Infrequently, as in the case of "Aura Lee," neither the composer's nor the lyricist's name is mentioned. That omission seems especially curious in this instance because in 1909 it was certainly known that George R. Poulton and William Whiteman claimed this song (whose melody was used in 1956 for "Love Me Tender") when it was published in 1861. A few factual errors also appear here, such as the information supplied about the history of "The British Grenadiers." According to *Heart Songs*, this song dates from the sixteenth century, but the earliest known printing was a "half sheet" of about 1750.[6]

Exactly how many people contributed to the body of material from which the final compilation was made is in dispute. The title page proclaims 25,000 people, but Chapple's Foreword has the smaller figure of 20,000. Whichever is correct, it is obvious that a very large group of people played some hand in producing this volume. Those whose song nominations were chosen received letters of acceptance and prizes for their efforts.[7] They also had the satisfaction of knowing that they helped to decide which were the favorite songs of the American people, as least as determined by the judges. While the vast majority of the songs were known in nineteenth century America (most predated 1880), this collection was not just a selection of favorites from that era. In fact, some then relatively recent songs, like Victor Herbert's "Toyland" (1903) and "Because You're You" (1906), were among the finalists. These two numbers also offer proof that the judges were not prevented from choosing their own songs.

*Heart Songs* was not only important in its time but also has value today on several counts; the most obvious is that it contains the words and lyrics to a large number of songs, many of which are difficult to find nowadays. This fact is one of the major reasons why the collection is a popular item in the used book market. However, folklorists, musicologists, historians, and other scholars also find the collection valuable because it tells which songs were judged by a large number of Americans to be the country's most popular ones up through the first few years of the twentieth century. Consequently, the volume provides a mirror reflecting how many Americans felt about their music in 1909.

Evidently, turn-of-the-century audiences were partial to songs that expressed emotions openly and, by late twentieth-century tastes, naively. How else can one explain the following inclusions: four songs by Charlotte Alington Barnard (1830–1869), who published numerous songs of lost love and the "golden days of yore" under the pseudonym of Claribel in the mid-nineteenth century; three songs by Thomas Haynes Bayly (1797–1839), who specialized in sentimental pieces like "Long, Long Ago"; and several selections such as "Darling Nelly Gray" and "Lilly Dale" from the pens of various other songwriters. Perhaps, though, today's readers expect sentiment and naiveté to dominate any collection of favorite popular songs issued almost ninety years ago. What they probably will not expect is the relatively high percentage of songs by Mozart, Schubert, Haydn, Handel, Verdi, Wagner, and Gounod mixed in with numbers by Hanby, Emmett, Claribel, Bland, Thompson, Tucker, and various other popular lyricists and composers. This combination suggests that the rigid distinction between classical and popular music that exists today was less firmly entrenched in the early years of the twentieth century.[8]

It is hardly surprising that the Civil War, a watershed event in America's history and the war costing the most in terms of American lives lost, looms large in these pages. Approximately twenty-five percent of the book's songs were either written during that brief four-year period or were associated with the war in some way. On the other hand, the Revolutionary War and other American wars are sparsely represented. This imbalance is further illustrated by the fact that two of the three songwriters most frequently represented in *Heart Songs* are George F. Root and Stephen C. Foster, both of whom flourished during the Civil War.[9] Indeed, Root's greatest successes came during those years.

Late twentieth-century Americans tend to think of their ancestors as being somewhat provincial, but *Heart Songs* indicates that, in musical tastes at least, this stereotype is inaccurate. Understandably, a majority of the songs included were written by Americans, but a sizeable number were produced by composers and lyricists from other countries. This variety might be expected among the classical numbers because traditionally the operas and symphonies composed by Europeans have been regarded by residents of the United States as superior to similar works produced by their own countrymen. However, as the several numbers here by the English Claribel, Bayly, and Henry Russell plus the Irish Thomas Moore attest, many non-classical items here originated outside America's boundaries.

Interestingly, many of the most popular and successful American songwriters of the nineteenth century are sparsely represented. Will S. Hays (1837–1907), one of the most commercially successful songwriters during the years 1865–1885, produced a large number of hits, including "The Drummer Boy of Shiloh" (1862), "We Parted By the River Side" (1866), "I'll Remember You, Love, in My Prayers" (1869), and "Molly Darling (1871)." Yet, even though some of these songs remain alive in the repertoires of folksingers, they do not appear in *Heart Songs*.[10] Hays is represented only by his 1866 "Nora O'Neal." Even so, he fared better than Charles A. White (1830–1892), his chief rival for the title of most commercially important popular songwriter of the immediate post-Civil War era.[11] White's hits include "The Widow in the Cottage by the Sea Side" (1868), "Come, Birdie, Come" and "Put Me in My Little Bed" (both 1870), and "The Little Church Around the Corner (1871)." These songs had huge sheet music sales (the standard by which hit status was then determined), but neither these nor any other of his several published efforts are found in the Chapple compilation.[12] Hays, White, and some other nineteenth-century American popular songwriters,[13] had several big sellers, but within a few decades they were not considered to have produced more than one song that their fellow countrymen considered a favorite.

It could be argued that Hays, White, and others didn't make the final list because their greatest successes came with minstrel show songs of the late nineteenth century, and such fare is generally missing from *Heart Songs*. Minstrel show songs are liberally represented, but most date from the 1840s–1860s; only one item from minstrelsy's later years (the 1880 Harry Hunter–George D. Fox piece "Over the Garden Wall") is included. It is hard to imagine that songs extremely popular in the 1870s would not have been suggested by several contributors three decades later. Could it be that the judges—two of whom were classically trained musicians—were probably not inclined to look favorably on minstrel songs anyway, simply acted on their prejudices, and excluded them? Perhaps, but if that were the case, why did they include so many songs from minstrelsy's earliest period? After all, they probably weren't inclined to regard such fare as "Lilly Dale" very positively either. It seems best to conclude that the judges tried to be objective and to decide Edwardian America's favorite songs of the past on the basis of submissions.

*Heart Songs* can be fairly characterized in some sense as just a gimmick designed to boost sales of *The National Magazine*. It was, however, much more than that; it was the first large scale, and still the most expansive, attempt to determine America's popular song taste. As such, it is a treasure trove for anyone interested in this country's musical history. For that reason alone, it is good to have this volume generally available once again.

W. K. McNeil
The Ozark Folk Center
Mt. View, Arkansas

1. Just how successful these movies were is uncertain; I have been able to find only two titles that were released, *My Old Sweetheart* and *Annabel Lee*. This scarcity suggests that the series was not very successful, but it is possible that other titles were filmed that have been lost to posterity.

2. It seems that no extensive biography of Chapple has been published. The information given here is taken from *Who Was Who in America 1951–1960* and an unidentified, undated obituary (pasted in the front of a copy of *Heart Songs*) that presumably comes from a Boston newspaper, circa April 18, 1950.

3. See the essay by Steven Ledbetter and Victor Fell Yellin in H. Wiley Hitchcock and Stanley Sadie, *The New Grove Dictionary of American Music* (New York and London: Macmillan Press Limited, 1986), I: 385–386.

4. *Heart Songs: Dear to the American People, And by them Contributed to the Search for Treasured Songs Initiated by the National Magazine* (Boston: The Chapple Publishing Company, 1909), iii.

5. According to Richard Jackson, *Popular Songs of Nineteenth-Century America* (New York: Dover Publications, Inc., 1976), p. 281, the lyrics were written by Bennett (1836–1898) in 1867 in an attempt to cheer up Webster, who was in a gloomy mood. The following year it was published as a hymn with a melody provided by Webster (1819–1875).

6. See James J. Fuld, *The Book of World-Famous Music: Classical, Popular and Folk* (New York: Crown Publishers, Inc., 1973; original edition 1966), pp. 153–154. Fuld notes that there are earlier references to the song, but none predate the eighteenth century.

7. Exactly what the prizes were is unclear; perhaps they were subscriptions to Chapple's magazine.

8. This was certainly true in the early nineteenth century as is made clear in Charles Hamm, *Yesterdays: Popular Music in America* (New York & London: W. W. Norton & Company, 1979), p. 87, among other places.

9. The third person so honored is Sir Arthur Sullivan, the English composer.

10. I myself have collected the last three songs mentioned here from Ozark folksingers on several occasions during the past twenty years. "The Drummer Boy of Shiloh" appears in several published folksong collections including those of Mellinger E. Henry (Southern Appalachians), Frank C. Brown (North Carolina), Lester A. Hubbard (Utah), and Vance Randolph (Ozarks—Missouri). I suspect all of these songs would be better represented in published collections were it not common knowledge among folklorists that they originated in the popular music industry. Hays' material did not just linger on in folksong repertoires; as recently as 1948 Eddy Arnold scored big with "Molly Darling," and his recording of the nineteenth-century hit reached number 10 on the *Billboard* country charts. Arnold was ungentlemanly enough to copyright the piece even though the song was recorded essentially as written by Hays in 1871.

11. See Hamm, p. 265.

12. White also is represented in folksong repertoires, not by any of his bigger hits but by a relatively minor effort of 1870 written in collaboration with one Louis Goullaud. White-Goullaud called this song "A Package of Old Love Letters," but it is generally known in tradition as "Little Rosewood Casket." Versions have

been included in at least nineteen published folksong collections. For a listing o
these see my *Southern Folk Ballads* (Little Rock: August House, 1987), I: 200.

13. One such is Thomas Paine Westendorf (1848–1923), the composer of "I'll Tak‹
You Home Again, Kathleen" and several songs popular with blackface singers iı
minstrel shows and vaudeville.

**THE NATIONAL MAGAZINE**
BOSTON, MASS.
EDITED BY JOE MITCHELL CHAPPLE

Heartily congratulating you upon
having your favorite selection included
in the splendid book of "HEART SONGS," I am
pleased to announce that you have been
awarded a prize for your contribution to
this unrivalled collection of popular
"melodies of today, and the days gone by."

Yours sincerely,

*Jo Mitchell Chapple*

We take pleasure in conferring the
above award.

*G. W. Chadwick*
*Victor Herbert*

For the Committee.

Fac-simile of the letter sent out to those awarded prizes by
the Committee, signed by Mr. George W. Chadwick, Director of the
New England Conservatory of Music, one of the foremost American
musicians and composers, and by Mr. Victor Herbert, the eminent
composer and conductor whose varied compositions so well combine
musical art and popular melody.

# FOREWORD

HEART SONGS is more than a collection of music—it is a book compiled directly by twenty thousand people, who not only sent in their favorite songs, but in accompanying letters told how these songs had been interwoven with the story of their own lives. All have been sent in by men and women who loved them; who cared little for the prizes, but desired to add a truly worthy contribution to the collection of Heart Songs. The personal associations of these melodies add to the familiar words a new thrill of heart interest. Each song recalls to the individual reader some tender, sad, joyous or martial association. It is a book which will be to American musical literature what "Heart Throbs" is to prose and verse.

For four years contributions have poured in from all parts of the republic—from neighboring Canada and Mexico; from distant isles of the sea and almost every continent on the globe—yet the harvest was overwhelmingly American, and although sectional features have added much to the variety of songs and to some extent represent days of strife and dissension, the mass of heart tributes shows how nearly and closely all true American hearts beat in unison, and how the bonds of music are strong and universal.

The original plan was to divide the contributions into ten classes as indicated in the announcements:—Patriotic and war songs; sea songs; lullabies and child songs; dancing songs, lilts and jigs; plantation and negro melodies; sacred songs and hymns; love songs; songs from operas and operettas; popular concert hall songs and ballads; college, school and fraternity songs. It was soon discovered that no balanced classification could be made—the tremendous preponderance of love songs, hymns, college songs, ballads, operatic and patriotic airs, any one of which might have been adjudged correctly to two or more classes, soon convinced the judges that to make the book a true reflection of the contributors' tastes and feelings—a Heart Song book in the true sense—some classes would have to be abridged, and selections made with a view to securing those songs about which cluster personal and heartfelt associations.

In the mails came the yellow, ragged, timeworn music that had been on "mother's" piano when as a young man "father" timidly turned the music and with a glance silently responded to love's message. Old songs and hymns came in, betwixt covers that were familiar thirty, forty and fifty years ago. The old-time singing school was represented, and many a stirring strain that had made the crisp winter air ring, as the refrain was sung on a sleigh ride.

Contributors in the far West sent in songs that have the breezy "go" and dash of the intrepid pioneer. Eastern readers preserved for us songs that have been factors in history-making, and the consensus of opinion on patriotic songs reveals "The Star-Spangled Banner," "Dixie" and "America" as the standard all over the land.

The old-time sea songs, the chanteys and stirring airs, sung at capstan and halyard, were sent in by those whose memories of old days were kindled when a request came for music having in it the tang of salt air, the rush of sharp bows against crested seas, and the vikings of forgotten voyages and old wars. "A Yankee Ship and a Yankee Crew," "Blow, Boys, Blow," "A Life On The Ocean Wave" came in side by side with "Sailing," "Nancy Lee" and many others which suggest the scud of the white foam and the careening deck.

The lullabies include some rare gems—plaintive minor airs of the past century, rich with sacred memories of mothers crooning over old wooden cradles, but modern selections, Emmet's "Lullaby" and the sweet refrain from "Erminie" were not overlooked. "Rock-a-bye, Ba'... ... ...very popular favorite.

Many of the lilts and dancing tunes are full of suggestions of a remote past, and martial events possess a close kinship to love songs because of romantic memories of festal nights when dainty feet kept time to the strains of "Old Dan Tucker," as the couples mustered reluctantly for "the last dance."

Southern contributors brought to light stirring and plaintive melodies that swayed the hearts of millions during the dark days of the Lost Cause, nor did the North forget songs that were sung with heartache and tearful eyes, or cheered march and bivouac. The remarkable interest centering in the old darkey songs—the melodies of the Jubilee singers, breathing of old plantation days, show that the folk songs of America and even our national music of the future must bear the impress of the race that gave us this class of music. This is already indicated in the popularity of "rag time," which has already found its way into well-known symphonies, reflecting the *motif* that rings through such an air as "Swing Low, Sweet Chariot."

Strange to relate, the chief difficulty was in the selection of love songs. While a wide range of selection was offered, the contributors were more insistent on the merit of these particular songs than on any other music sent in, because these melodies had meant so much to them in the days of "love's young dream." The man or woman who had found a thrill in singing "Bonny Eloise" could not understand how "Sweet Genevieve" and more modern songs could mean so much to others. Consequently the judges reduced them all to the common denominator of heart interest and found that the old, old story is ever new, and always bewitching, no matter how the melody may vary. "Annie Laurie" is the one great international favorite ballad of all English-speaking people.

There was remarkable unanimity in the choice of hymns. The universal selection seemed to turn to "mother's favorite," which had meant so much at the turning point of life's highway. The choice of "Lead, Kindly Light" and "Come, Thou Fount," "Rock of Ages," "Nearer, My God, to Thee" and other hymns loved by many celebrated men, proved these songs to be also the favorites of people all over the world.

In operatic selections the familiar arias of Verdi, echoed around the world, were most in favor. The song of Manrico in the tower appeared to touch more hearts than any other aria sung behind American operatic footlights. Popular opera airs were mingled through the other classes.

The long list of concert songs submitted contained many beautiful and rare selections, but the greater number were songs that have been household words for many a day, and some are still largely sold after nearly a half century of publication. These contributions throw an interesting light on national character. The popularity of "Old Folks at Home" and "My Old Kentucky Home" was emphasized, and "Massa's in de Cold, Cold Ground" was a strong universal favorite. The melody and sentiment of the songs of Stephen C. Foster come close to the affections of the American people, and Dan Emmet, Henry C. Work, Root and other composers who flourished between 1840 and 1880 are well represented. "Old Black Joe," "Carry Me Back to Old Virginny" and many other sweetly human songs were sent in by large numbers.

The choice of college songs proved to be a matter of location. There were prime old favorites that have been inherited from the halcyon days of early schools, and are full of patriotic sentiment; many of these are almost classics, being standard tunes with only a variation in the words. "My Bonnie Lies over the Ocean" and "The Quilting Party" appeared equally attractive to various alma maters.

---

Like "Heart Throbs," this book represents the history, the sentiment of the American people of today, as well as of the various European races who, in this new world, have been moulded into a great and powerful nation. "Heart Songs" is a valuable and striking gauge and indicator of the popular taste of the people now comprising the republic of the United States of America. Few "rag time" songs were sent in; operatic selections were not largely in favor. Love ballads, patriotic, sacred and concert melodies were the most popular.

Songs that have entertained thousands from childhood to the grave and have voiced the pleasure and pain, the love and longing, the despair and delight, the sorrow and resignation, and the consolation of the plain people—who found in these an utterance for emotions which they felt but could not express—came in by the thousands. The yellow sheets of music bear evidence of constant use; in times of war and peace, victory and defeat, good and evil fortune, these sweet strains have blended with the coarser thread of human life and offered to the joyful or saddened soul a suggestion of uplift, sympathy and hope.

It is not unlikely that a second volume of "Heart Songs" will be demanded by the American public if the publishers can judge by the orders already received for the first. There is ample material not drawn upon, and still more contributions indicate that the mine has only begun to yield its treasury of heart songs.

Boston, 1909                    *Joe Mitchell Chapple*

# HEART SONGS

## 'Tis All That I Can Say

Tom Hood

Hope Temple

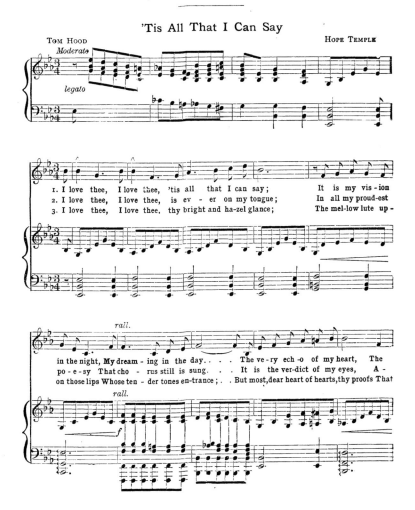

1. I love thee, I love thee, 'tis all that I can say; It is my vis-ion in the night, My dream-ing in the day. . . . The ve-ry ech-o of my heart, The

2. I love thee, I love thee, is ev - er on my tongue; In all my proud-est po-e-sy That cho - rus still is sung. . . It is the ver-dict of my eyes, A -

3. I love thee, I love thee, thy bright and ha-zel glance; The mel-low lute up-on those lips Whose ten - der tones en-trance ; . . But most, dear heart of hearts, thy proofs That

## 'Tis All That I Can Say

bless - ing when I pray, . . I love thee, I love thee, 'tis all that I can say.
midst the gay and young, . . I love thee, I love thee, a thousand maids a-mong.
still these words enhance, . i love thee, I love thee, what - ev - er be thy chance.

## The Dearest Spot on Earth

W. T. WRIGHTON

W. T. WRIGHTON

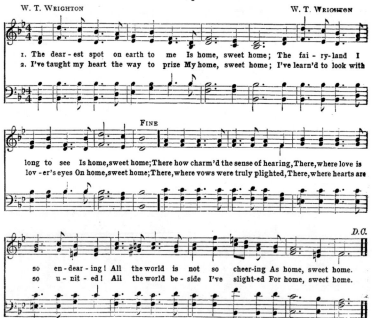

1. The dear - est spot on earth to me Is home, sweet home; The fai - ry-land I
2. I've taught my heart the way to prize My home, sweet home; I've learn'd to look with

long to see Is home, sweet home; There how charm'd the sense of hearing, There, where love is
lov - er's eyes On home, sweet home; There, where vows were truly plighted, There, where hearts are

so en - dear - ing! All the world is not so cheer-ing As home, sweet home.
so u - nit - ed! All the world be - side I've slight-ed For home, sweet home.

# Song of a Thousand Years

HENRY C. WORK

1. Lift up your eyes, de-spond-ing free-men! Fling to the winds your need-less
2. What if the clouds, one lit-tle mo-ment, Hide the blue sky where morn ap-
3. Tell the great world these bless-ed ti-dings! Yes, and be sure the bond-man

fears! He who un-furl'd your beauteous ban-ner, Says it shall wave a thou-sand years!
pears,—When the bright sun, that tints them crimson, Ri-ses to shine a thou-sand years?
hears; Tell the op-pressed of ev-'ry na-tion, Ju-bi-lee lasts a thou-sand years!

CHORUS

"A thou-sand years!" my own Co-lum-bi-ia! 'Tis the glad day so long fore-

told! 'Tis the glad morn whose ear-ly twi-light Wash-ing-ton saw in times of old.

# Auld Lang Syne

ROBERT BURNS

Scotch Folk Song

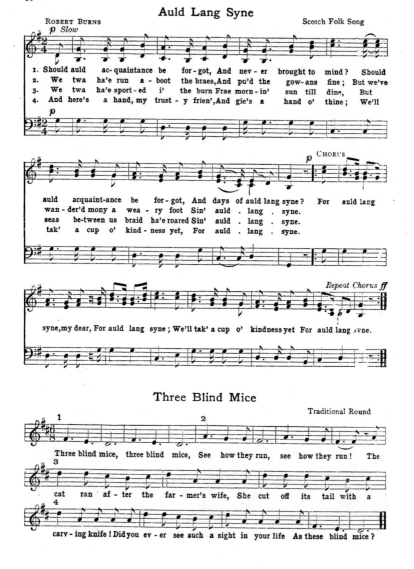

1. Should auld ac-quaintance be for-got, And nev-er brought to mind? Should
2. We twa ha'e run a-boot the braes, And pu'd the gow-ans fine; But we've
3. We twa ha'e sport-ed i' the burn Frae morn-in' sun till dine, But
4. And here's a hand, my trust-y frien', And gie's a hand o' thine; We'll

auld acquaint-ance be for-got, And days of auld lang syne? For auld lang
wan-der'd mony a wea-ry foot Sin' auld lang syne.
seas be-tween us braid ha'e roared Sin' auld lang syne.
tak' a cup o' kind-ness yet, For auld lang syne.

syne, my dear, For auld lang syne; We'll tak' a cup o' kindness yet For auld lang syne.

# Three Blind Mice

Traditional Round

Three blind mice, three blind mice, See how they run, see how they run! The

cat ran af-ter the far-mer's wife, She cut off its tail with a

carv-ing knife! Did you ev-er see such a sight in your life As these blind mice?

## Homeward Bound

W. F. Warren
C. S. Harrington

1. Out on an o - cean all bound - less we ride, We're home-ward bound, home-ward bound; Tossed on the waves of a rough, rest-less tide, We're home-ward bound, home-ward bound; Far from the safe, qui - et har - bor we rode, Seek - ing our Fa - ther's ce - les - tial a - bode; Prom - ise of which on us each He be - stowed: We're home-ward bound, home-ward bound.

2. Wild - ly the storm sweeps us on as it roars, We're home-ward bound, home-ward bound; Look! yon - der lie the bright heav - en - ly shores: We're home-ward bound, home-ward bound; Stead - y O pi - lot! stand firm at the wheel; Stead - y! we soon shall out - weath - er the gale; Oh, how we fly 'neath the loud - creak - ing sail! We're home-ward bound, home-ward bound.

3. In - to the har - bor of heaven now we glide; We're home at last; Soft - ly we drift on its bright sil - ver tide: We're home at last, home at last; Glo - ry to God! all our dan - gers are o'er; We stand se - cure on the glo - ri - fied shore; Glo - ry to God! we will shout ev - er more: We're home at last, home at last.

# Brother, Tell Me of the Battle

THOMAS MANAHAN                                    GEORGE F. ROOT

1. Broth - er, tell me of the bat - tle, How the sol - diers fought and
2. Broth - er, tell me of the bat - tle, For they said your life was
3. Broth - er, tell me of the bat - tle, I can bear to hear it

FINE

fell;   Tell me of the wea-ry march-es, She who loves will lis-ten well.
o'er;   They all told me you had fall - en, That I'd nev - er see you more.
now;    Lay your head up - on my bo - som, Let me soothe your fe-vered brow.

Broth - er, draw thee close be- side me,  Lay your head up - on my
Oh, I've been so sad and lone - ly,  Filled my breast has been with
Tell me, are you bad - ly wound - ed? Did we win the dead - ly

*D.C.*

breast, While you're tell - ing of the bat - tle, Let your fe - vered fore-head rest.
pain, Since they said my dear - est broth - er I should nev - er see a - gain.
fight? Did the vic - t'ry crown our ban - ner? Did you put the foe to flight?

## The Loreley

F. SILCHER

1. O tell me what it mean-eth, This gloom and tear-ful eye? 'Tis mem-'ry that re -
2. A - bove, the maid-en sit - teth, A won-drous form and fair; With jew - els bright she
3. The boat-man on the riv - er Lists to the song, spell - bound; Oh! what shall him de -

tain - eth The tale of years gone by; . The fad - ing light grows dim-mer, The
plait - eth Her shin - ing gold - en hair: With comb of gold pre-pares it, The
liv - er From dan - ger threat'ning round? The wa - ters deep have caught them, Both

Rhine doth calmly flow, . The loft - y hill-tops glim-mer Red with the sun-set glow.
task with song be - guiled; A fit - ful bur - den bears it, That mel - o - dy so wild.
boat and boatman brave; 'Tis Loreley's song hath brought them Beneath the foaming wave.

# Strike the Harp Gently

I. B. Woodbury

*Andante affetuoso*

1. Strike the harp gent-ly, To the mem-'ry of those Who ev-er loved fond-ly, Ere
2. Strike the harp gent-ly, And breathe thy sweet strain For those that loved fond-ly, But
3. Strike the harp gent-ly, Oh! mourn for them not; In the fold that is love-ly, The

call'd to re-pose; Be-neath the green turf, Where the wild flow-ers bloom,
who ne'er a-gain Can meet to ca-ress thee, In all this lone world. The
shep-herd has brought Per-haps a kind fa-ther, And moth-er most dear, A

Scent-ing the earth, And em-broid-'ring the tomb; Oh! strike the harp gent-ly To the
dear ones are hap-py With ser-aphs un-told; Oh! strike the harp gent-ly To the
child or a broth-er Or sis-ter so near; Oh! strike the harp gent-ly To the

mem-'ry of those Who ev-er loved fond-ly, Ere call'd to re-pose.

JENNY LIND
The celebrated Swedish singer whose American appearance was arranged at enormous cost by P. T. Barnum of circus fame. She was born in Stockholm in 1821 and died in 1887. Her popular encore was "Home, Sweet Home"—Heart Songs, p. 374

ADELINA PATTI

The famous operatic singer. She is of Italian extraction, born in Madrid, 1843, and sang in New York at an early age. Her career has been unusually successful. She has sung in all parts of Europe and America, and has been decorated by the Emperor of Russia. She now lives in retirement in Wales, as the wife of Baron Cedarstrom. Her popular encore was "The Last Rose of Summer"—Heart Songs, p. 146.

# Flow Gently, Sweet Afton

ROBERT BURNS

J. E. SPILMAN

1. Flow gen - tly, sweet Af - ton, a-mang thy green braes ;Flow gen - tly, I'll sing thee a
2. How loft - y, sweet Af - ton, thy neigh-bor - ing hills, Far marked with the cours-es of
3. Thy crys -tal stream,Af - ton, how love - ly it glides, And winds by the cot where my

song in thy praise ;My Ma - ry's a - sleep by thy mur-mur - ing stream,Flow gen-tly,sweet
clear-wind-ing rills !There dai - ly I wan-der, as morn ris - es high, My flocks and my
Ma - ry re - sides ! How wan-ton thy wa - ters her snow -y feet lave, As, gath-'ring sweet

Af - ton, dis - turb not her dream. Thou stock-dove whose ech - o re - sounds from the
Ma - ry's sweet cot in my eye. How pleas-ant thy banks and green val - leys be -
flow -'rets, she stems thy clear wave! Flow gen - tly, sweet Af - ton, a - mang thy green

hill, Ye wild whist-ling black-birds in yon thorn - y dell, Thou green-crest - ed
low, Where wild in the wood-lands the prim - ros - es blow ! There oft, as mild
braes, Flow gen - tly, sweet riv - er, the theme of my lays ; My Ma - ry's a -

lap-wing, thy scream-ing for-bear, I charge you, dis - turb not my slum - ber-ing fair.
eve-ning creeps o - ver the lea, The sweet-scent -ed birk shades my Ma - ry and me.
sleep by thy mur- mur - ing stream, Flow gen-tly, sweet Af - ton, dis - turb not her dream.

# Star of the Twilight

L. O. EMERSON

1. Star .. of the twi-light, Beau - ti-ful star, Glad - ly I hail thee,
2. Ea - ger-ly watch-ing, Wait - ing for thee, Looks the lone maid - en

Shi-ning a - far; . Rest from your la - bors, Chil - dren of toil, .. Night clos-es
O'er the dark sea; Soon as thou shi - nest Soft on the air, .. Borne by thy

o'er ye, Rest .. ye a - while; This is thy greet - ing, Sig-nalled a - far;
light breeze, Float - eth her pray'r; Watch o'er him kind - ly, Home from a - far;

Star .. of the twi-light, Beau - ti-ful star; Star of the twi - light,
Light . thou his path - way, Beau - ti - ful star; Star of the twi - light,

Beau - ti - ful star; .. Star .. of the twi-light, Beau-ti-ful star.

# The Battle Cry of Freedom

(RALLYING SONG)

GEORGE F. ROOT

1. Yes, we'll ral - ly round the flag, boys, we'll ral - ly once a - gain,
2. We are spring-ing to the call of our broth -ers gone be - fore,
3. We will wel - come to our num - bers the loy - al true and brave,
4. So we're spring-ing to the call from the East and from the West,

( *Bass with octaves throughout* )

Shout - ing the bat - tle cry of Free - dom, We will ral - ly from the hill - side, we'll
Shout - ing the bat - tle cry of Free - dom, And we'll fill the va -cant ranks with a
Shout - ing the bat - tle cry of Free - dom, And al - tho' they may be poor, not a
Shout - ing the bat - tle cry of Free - dom, And we'll hurl the reb - el crew from the

gath - er from the plain, Shout - ing the bat - tle cry of Free - dom.
mil - lion free - men more, Shout - ing the bat - tle cry of Free - dom.
man shall be a slave, Shout - ing the bat - tle cry of Free - dom.
land we love the best, Shout - ing the bat - tle cry of Free - dom.

CHORUS
*Fortissimo*

The Un - ion for-ev - er, Hur - rah boys, Hur-rah! Down with the trai - tor,

Up with the star; While we ral - ly round the flag, boys,

Ral - ly once a - gain, Shout - ing the bat - tle cry of Free - dom.

## The Dying Volunteer

From the " New Orleans Times "       A. E. A. MUSE

1. Come moth-er, dear moth-er,   oh! come to me now; My soul wings its flight, I would
2. Thou'lt hear, dearest moth-er,   a - las! not from me,   I hunt- d the foe thro' green

see thee once more. A - gain I would feel thy dear hand on my brow One mo - ment on
val - ley and crag, For stamped on my brain were the last words from thee, " Tho' life be the

earth, ere the strug-gle is o'er. Ere life's pulse is stilled, and the cold chill of
for - feit, be true to thy flag!" Those words nerved my arm when I struck the bold

death Creeps o'er my heart I would see thee once more. Fond words of fare - well with my
blow For my country, my flag, For glo - ry, for thee. But now all is o - ver, I've

ver - y last breath I'd whis - per to thee from e - ter - ni - ty's shore.
done with earth's foe, For hea - ven's bright por - tals are op' - ning to me.

# Take Me Home

RAYMOND

Andante affettuoso

1. Take me home to the place where I first saw the light, To the
2. Take me home to the place where the or-ange trees grow, To my
3. Take me home, let me see what is left that I know, Can it

D. C. Take me home to the place where my lit-tle ones sleep, Poor

sweet sun-ny South take me home,
cot in the ev - er - green shade,
be that the old house is gone,
mas-sa lies bur-ied close by,

Where the mocking-bird sung me to
Where the flow-ers on the riv - er's green
The dear friends of my child-hood in -
O'er the grave of the loved ones I

FINE

rest ev - 'ry night, Ah! why was I tempt-ed to roam?
mar - gin may blow Their sweets on the bank where we play'd.
deed must be few, And I must la-ment all a - lone.
long to weep, And a - mong them to rest when I die.

FINE

I    think    with   re-gret    of   the   dear    ones   I   left,    Of    the
The    path    to    our cot - tage they say    has grown green,   And    the
But    yet    I'll   re-turn    to   the place    of   my birth,   Where    my

warm hearts that shelt-er'd me then;      Of the wife    and the dear   ones   of
place    is quite lone - ly a-round;      And   I   know   that the smiles and the
chil - dren have play'd at the door;    Where they pull'd the white blos-soms that

whom    I'm   be-reft,   And   I   sigh    for   the old   place    a - gain.
forms     I   have seen, Now   lie   deep    in   the soft   moss - y   ground.
gar - nish'd the earth, Which will ech - o    their foot - steps   no   more.

D.C.

# To the Evening Star

From WAGNER's "Tannhäuser"

O thou sub-lime sweet eve-ning star, Joy-ful I

greet . . . thee from . . . a-far; With

glow-ing heart, that ne'er . . dis-clos'd, Greet her when

she  in  thy  light . . re-posed,  When  part - ing from  this

vale,  a  vi - sion, she ri - ses  to  an  an - gel's mis - sion,

When  part - ing from  this  vale .  a  vi - sion, she  ri - ses

to  an . .  an - gel's  mis - - - sion. . .

# Sweet Genevieve

GEORGE COOPER                                    HENRY TUCKER

1. O Gen-e-vieve I'd give the world To live a-gain the love-ly past! The rose of youth was dew-im-pearled; But now it with-ers in the blast. I see thy face in ev-'ry dream, My wak-ing tho'ts are full of thee; Thy glance is in the star-ry beam That falls a-long the

2. Fair Gen-e-vieve my ear-ly love, The years but make thee dear-er far! My heart shall nev-er, nev-er rove: Thou art my on-ly guid-ing star. For me the past has no re-gret, What-e'er the years may bring to me; I bless the hour when first we met,— The hour that gave me

By permission WM. A. POND & Co., owners of the copyright

sum - mer sea. O Gen - e - vieve, Sweet Gen - e - vieve, The
love and thee!

days may come, the days may go, But still the hands of

mem - 'ry weave The bliss - ful dreams of long a - go O Gen - e - vieve!

*colla voce*

*CODA ad lib.*

# The Faded Coat of Blue

J. H. McNaughton

1. My brave lad sleeps in his fad-ed coat of blue; In a
2. He cried, "Give me wa-ter and just a lit-tle crumb, And my
3. Long, long years have van-ished, and though he comes no more, Yet my

lone-ly grave un-known lies the heart that beat so true. He sank faint and hun-gry a-
moth-er she will bless you thro' all the years to come; Oh! tell my sweet sis-ter, so
heart will start-ling beat with each foot-fall at my door; I gaze o'er the hill where he

mong the fam-ish'd brave, And they laid him sad and lone-ly with-in his nameless grave.
gen-tle, good and true, That I'll meet her up in heaven, in my fad-ed coat of blue."
waved a last a-dieu, But no gal-lant lad I see, in his fad-ed coat of blue.

No more the bu - gle calls the wea - ry one, Rest, no - ble spir - it,
in thy grave un-known! I'll find you, and know you, a - mong the good and true,
When a robe of white is giv'n for the fad - ed coat of blue.

# We're Tenting To-Night

WALTER KITTREDGE

# The Switzer's Farewell

GEORGE LINLEY

*Andante*

1. A - dieu, dear land, With beau-ty teem - ing, Where first I rov'd a care - less
2. Far from my home I soon must wan - der, In stran - ger land be doom'd to

*legato.*

child; Of thee my heart Will e'er be dream - ing, Thy snow-clad
dwell. O! best be - loved! My heart grows fond - er, While thus I

peaks and moun-tains wild. Dear land! that I cher - ish, Oh! long may'st thou
breathe my last fare - well. Re - ceive this sad to - ken, I leave thee, heart

*rall.*

flour - ish; My mem - 'ry must per - ish, Ere I for - get . . . thee.
bro - ken, Our part - ing is spo - ken, Be - loved one! fare - well.

## Nut Brown Maiden

*Moderato*  (MALE VOICES)

*mf*

1. Nut brown maid-en, Thou hast a bright blue eye for love, Nut brown maid-en, Thou
2. Nut brown maid-en, Thou hast a ru - by lip to kiss, Nut brown maid-en, Thou
3. Nut brown maid-en, Thou hast a slen - der waist to clasp, Nut brown maid-en, Thou
4. Nut brown maid-en, Thou hast such pearl-y, pearl - y teeth, Nut brown maid-en, Thou

FINE   D.C.

hast a bright blue eye ; A bright blue eye is thine, love! The glance in it is mine, love!
hast a ru - by lip ; A ru - by lip is thine, love! The kiss-ing of it's mine, love!
hast a slen-der waist ; A slen-der waist is thine, love! The arm a-round it's mine, love!
hast such pearl-y teeth ; The pearl-y teeth are false, love! They rat-tle when you waltz, love!

## How Gentle God's Commands

P. DODDRIDGE   H. G. NÄGELI

1. How gen - tle God's com - mands! How kind His pre - cepts are!
2. Be - neath His watch - ful eye His saints se - cure - ly dwell:
3. Why should this anx - ious load Press down your wea - ry mind?

Come, cast your bur - dens on the Lord, And trust His con - stant care.
That Hand which bears cre - a - tion up Shall guard His chil - dren well.
Haste to your heav'n-ly Fa - ther's throne, And sweet re - fresh - ment find.

# Kathleen Aroon

Words by Mrs. CRAWFORD

Music by FRANZ ABT

1. Why should we part - ed be, Kath - leen A - roon! When thy fond
2. Give me thy gen - tle hand, Kath - leen A - roon! Come to the
3. Why should we part - ed be, Kath - leen A - roon! When thy fond

heart's with me, Kath - leen A - roon! Come to those gold - en skies,
hap - py land, Kath - leen A - roon! Come o'er the waves with me,
heart's with me, Kath - leen A - roon! Oh! leave these weep - ing skies,

Bright days for us may rise, Oh! dry those tear - ful eyes, Kath-leen A - roon.*
These hands shall toil for thee, This heart will faith- ful be, Kath-leen A - roon.
Where man a mar - tyr dies, Come dry those tear - ful eyes, Kath-leen A - roon.

* Aroon means " secret treasure of my heart."

# The Vacant Chair

Geo. F. Root

1. We shall meet, but we shall miss him, There will be one va - cant
2. At our fire - side, sad and lone - ly, Oft - en will the bo - som
3. True, they tell us wreaths of glo - ry Ev - er - more will deck his
D.C. *We shall meet, but we shall miss him, There will be one va - cant*

chair; We shall lin - ger to ca - ress him, While we breathe our eve - ning pray'r.
swell At re-mem-brance of the sto - ry, How our no - ble Wil - lie fell;
brow, But this soothes the an-guish on - ly Sweep-ing o'er our heart-strings now.
*chair; We shall lin - ger to ca - ress him, While we breathe our eve - ning pray'r.*

When a year a - go we gath-ered, Joy was in his mild blue
How he strove to bear our ban - ner Thro' the thick - est of the
Sleep to - day, O ear - ly fall - en, In thy green and nar - row

eye, But a gold - en cord is sev-ered, And our hopes in ru - in lie.
fight, And up- hold our coun-try's hon - or, In the strength of man-hood's might.
bed, Dir - ges from the pine and cy - press Min - gle with the tears we shed.

# Cradle Song

(Sung by Jenny Lind)

*Andante con espressione*

SWEDISH

1. Light and ro - sy be thy slumbers, Rock'd up-on thy moth-er's breast, . . . .
2. When thy looks her care in - vi - teth, All . the mother turns to thee, . . . . .

She can lull thee with her numbers, To the cradled heav'n of rest. . . . . .
And her in-most life de - light-eth, Drink-ing from thy cup of glee. . . . . .

In her heart is love re - volv-ing, Like the plan- ets round the moon; Hopes and
O'er thee now her spir - it bend-eth ; Child of prom-ise, cher-ish'd well ! With thine

pleas-ures fond-ly solving, Keep-ing ev - 'ry tho't in tune.
own, her be - ing blendeth, Ho- lied by af - fection's spell.

# A Warrior Bold

EDWIN THOMAS

STEPHEN ADAMS

1. In days of old, when knights were bold And barons held their sway, A war-rior bold, with
2. So this brave knight, in ar-mor bright, Went gayly to the fray; He fought the fight, but

spurs of gold, Sang mer-ri-ly his lay, Sang mer-ri-ly his lay: "My love is young and
ere the night, His soul had pass'd a-way, His soul had pass'd a-way. The plighted ring he

fair, My love hath gold-en hair, And eyes so blue, and heart so true, That
wore Was crushed and wet with gore, Yet ere he died, he brave-ly cried, "I've

none with her com - pare.  So  what care I,  tho' death be nigh,  I'll live for love  or
kept  the vow  I  swore.  So  what care I,  tho' death be nigh,  I've fought for love and

*colla voce*

die,  So  what care I,  tho' death be nigh,  I'll live for love  or  die."  death be nigh, I've

fought for love,I've fought for love,I've fought for love,For love,for love I die."

# The Orphan Boys

DUET

From "The Young Choir," 1840

1. Our cot was shel-ter'd in a wood, And near a lake's green mar-gin stood; A
2. When scarce-ly old e-nough to know The mean-ing of a tale of woe, 'Twas
3. But soon for moth-er as we grew, We work'd as much as boys could do; Our

ACCOMPT.

moun-tain bleak be-hind us fr wn'd, Whose top the snow in sum-mer crown'd;
then by moth-er we were told, That fa-ther in . . . his grave was cold!
dai-ly gains to her we bore, But oh! she'll ne'er re-ceive them more:

But pas-tures rich, and warm to boot, Lay smil-ing at the mountain's foot; There
That live-li-hoods were hard to get, And we too young to la-bor yet, And
For long we watched be-side her bed, Then sobb'd to see her lie there dead; And

first we frol-ick'd hand in hand, Hand in hand,
tears with-in her eyes would stand, Eyes would stand,
now we wan-der hand in hand, Hand in hand,

Two in-fant boys of Switz-er-land! Two in-fant boys of Switz-er-land.
For her two boys of Switz-er-land! For her two boys of Switz-er-land.
Two or-phan boys of Switz-er-land! Two or-phan boys of Switz-er-land.

# The Campbells are Coming

Old Scotch Air

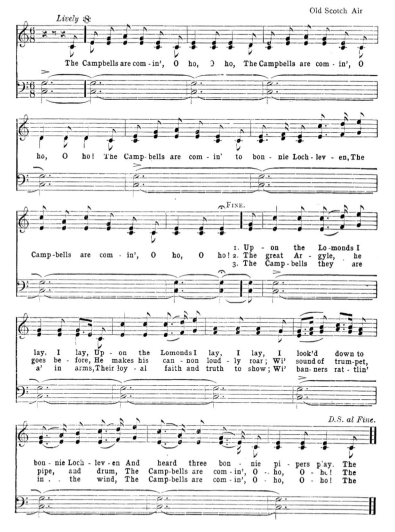

# Buy a Broom

1. From Teutschland I come with my light wares all la-den, To the land where the
2. To brush a - way in-sects that sometimes an-noy you, You'll find it quite
3. Ere win - ter comes on, for sweet home soon de-part-ing, My toils for your

bless-ing of free-dom doth bloom; Then lis - ten, fair la - dy, and young pret-ty
hand - y to use night and day; And what bet - ter ex - er - cise pray can em -
fa - vor a - gain I'll re - sume; And while grat-i - tude's tear in my eye - lid is

maid - en, Oh, buy of the wand'ring Ba-va-rian a broom. Buy a broom,
ploy you,Than to sweep all vex - a-tious in-tru-ders a - way ? Buy a broom,
start-ing,Bless the time that in England I cried,buy a broom. Buy a broom,

Buy a broom, (Buy a broom.) Oh, buy of the wand'ring Ba - va - rian a broom.
Buy a broom, And sweep all vex - a - tious in - tru-ders a - way.
Buy a broom, Bless the time that in England I cried buy a broom.

O mein lie - ber Au - gus - tin, Au - gus - tin, Au - gus - tin, O mein lie - ber

Au - gus - tin, Al - les ist weg: Bock ist weg, Stock ist weg,

Auch ich bin in dem Dreck O mein lie-ber Au - gus - tin, Al - les ist weg.

# O Ye Tears

Franz Abt

1. O ye tears! O ye tears! that have long re-fus'd to flow, Ye are wel - come to my heart, thaw-ing, thaw - ing like the snow; The ice-bound cloud has yield-ed, and the ear - ly snow-drops spring, And the

2. O ye tears! O ye tears! I am thank - ful that ye run, Tho' ye come from cold and dark ye shall glit - ter in the sun: The rain-bow can - not cheer us if the show'rs re - fuse to fall, And the

3. O ye tears! O ye tears! till I felt ye on my cheek, I was self - ish in my sor - row; I was stub - born, I was weak; Ye have giv'n me strength to con - quer, and I stand e - rect and free, And

heal - ing foun-tains gush, and the wil - der-ness shall sing.
eyes that can - not weep are the sad - dest eyes of all.
know that I am hu - man, by the light of sym - pa - thy.

O ye tears!     O ye tears!
O ye tears!     O ye tears?
O ye tears!     O ye tears!

4 O ye tears! O ye tears! ye relieve me of my pain,
The barren rock of pride has been stricken once again;
Like the rock that Moses smote amid Horeb's burning sand,
It yields the flowing water, to make gladness in the land.
         O ye tears! O ye tears!

5 There is light upon my path! there is sunshine in my heart,
And the leaf and fruit of life shall not utterly depart;
Ye restore to me the freshness and the bloom of long ago,
O ye tears! O happy tears! I am thankful that ye flow.
         O ye tears! happy tears!

# Johnny Sands

John Sinclair

1. A man whose name was Johnny Sands Had mar-ried Bet-ty Hague, And
2. "For fear that I should courage lack And try to save my life, Pray

though she brought him gold and lands, She proved a ter-ri-ble plague; For
tie my hands be-hind my back;" "I will" re-plied his wife. She

oh! she was a scold-ing wife, Full of ca-price and whim, He said, that he was
tied them fast as you may think, And when se-cure-ly done, "Now stand" she says "up-

tired of life, And she was tired of him, And she was tired of him, And she was tired of
on the brink And I'll prepare to run, And I'll pre-pare to run, And I'll prepare to

him. Says he "Then I will drown myself—The riv-er runs be-low," Says
run." All down the hill his lov-ing bride Now ran with all her force To

she, "Pray do, you sil-ly elf, I wished it long a-go." Says he "Up-on the
push him in;—he stepped a-side, And she fell in of course. Now splash-ing, dashing

brink I'll stand, Do you run down the hill, And push me in with all your might," Says
like a fish, "Oh save me, John-ny Sands." "I can't, my dear, tho' much I wish, For

she "My love, I will," Says she "My love, I will," Says she "My love, I will."
you have tied my hands, For you have tied my hands, For you have tied my hands."

44

# The British Grenadiers

16th Century

*Allegro con spirito*

1. Some talk of Al - ex - an - der, And some of Her - cu - les, Of
2. When-e'er we are com - mand - ed To storm the pal - i - sades, Our
3. Then let us fill a bump - er, And drink a health to those Who

Hec - tor and Ly - san - der, And such great names as these;
lead - ers march with fu - sees, And we with hand - gre - nades;
car - ry caps and pouch - es, And wear the loup - ed clothes:

But of all the world's brave he - roes There's none that can com -
We throw them from the gla - cis A - bout the en - e - mies'
May they and their com - mand - ers Live hap - py all their

pare   With a  tow row row row row   row, To the Brit-ish  Gren - a - dier.
ears,  Sing   tow row row row row   row, The  Brit-ish  Gren - a - diers.
years, With a  tow row row row row   row, For the Brit-ish  Gren - a - diers.

## Free America *

### Tune —" BRITISH GRENADIERS "

1 That seat of science, Athens,
   And earth's proud mistress, Rome ;
  Where now are all their glories ?
   We scarce can find a tomb.
  Then guard your rights, Americans,
   Nor stoop to lawless sway,
  Oppose, oppose, oppose, oppose
   For North America.

2 We led fair Franklin hither,
   And, lo ! the desert smiled ;
  A paradise of pleasure
   Was opened to the world !
  Your harvest, bold Americans,
   No power shall snatch away !
  Huzza, huzza, huzza, huzza
   For free America.

3 Torn from a world of tyrants,
   Beneath this western sky,
  We formed a new dominion,
   A land of liberty.
  The world shall own we're masters here ;
   Then hasten on the day :
  Huzza, huzza, huzza, huzza
   For free America.

4 Proud Albion bowed to Cæsar,
   And numerous lords before ;
  To Picts, to Danes, to Normans,
   And many masters more ;

But we can boast, Americans,
 We've never fallen a prey ;
Huzza, huzza, huzza, huzza
 For free America.

5 God bless this maiden climate,
   And through its vast domain
  May hosts of heroes cluster,
   Who scorn to wear a chain :
  And blast the venal sycophant
   That dares our rights betray ;
  Huzza, huzza, huzza, huzza
   For free America.

6 Lift up your heads, ye heroes,
   And swear with proud disdain
  The wretch that would ensnare you
   Shall lay his snares in vain ;
  Should Europe empty all her force,
   We'll meet her in array,
  And fight and shout, and shout and fight
   For free America.

7 Some future day shall crown us
   The masters of the main.
  Our fleets shall speak in thunder
   To England, France and Spain ;
  And the nations o'er the oceans spread
   Shall tremble and obey
  The sons, the sons, the sons, the sons
   Of brave America.

* By voice, sword and pen, Joseph Warren contributed to the cause of Independence. In 1772 and 1775, he
delivered orations on the Boston Massacre. During the delivery of the second oration, the British soldiery lined
the pulpit stairs, but nevertheless it was pronounced in defiance of their threats. Not long, it is thought, before
his lamented death, he wrote the above ballad.

# The Land o' the Leal

Lady NAIRNE

*Adagio*

1. I'm wear - in' a-wa', Jean, Like snaw-wreaths in thaw, Jean, I'm wear-in' a-wa' To the
2. Ye aye were leal and true, Jean, Your task's ended noo, Jean, And I'll wel-come you To the
3. Then dry that tearfu' e'e, Jean, My soul langs to be free, Jean, And an-gels wait on me To the

land o' the leal. There's nae sor - row there, Jean, There's neither cauld nor care, Jean, The
land o' the leal. Our bonnie bairn's there, Jean, She was baith gude and fair, Jean, And
land o' the leal. Now fare ye weel, my ain Jean, This warld's care is vain, Jean, We'll

day is aye fair In the land o' the leal.
we grudged her sair To the land o' the leal.
meet and aye be fain In the land o' the leal.

# The Mariner

1. Soft blew the air, and smooth flow'd the tide, And blue the heav'n's in its mirror smiled; The
2. Eve yields to night, the breeze of wintry gales, In one vast head the seas and shores repose, He
3. Oh! what avails the seaman's toiling care? The straining cords are burst, the mast are riv'n, Sad

white sail trembling and ex-panding wide, The bus-y sail-or at the an-chor toil'd. The
turns his ach-ing eyes, his spir-its fail, The chill tear falls, sad to the deck he goes, The
sounds of ter-ror groan a-long the air, Then from a-far, the bark on rock was driv'n; Fierce

last dread moment comes, the sail-or youth Hides the big drop and smiles a-mid his pain;
storm of midnight swell, the sails are furled, Deep sounds the lead, but sounds a-las in vain,
o'er the wreck, the whelming wa-ters passed, The help-less crew sunk in the roar-ing main.

Soothes his sad bride and vows e-ter-nal truth, "Fare-well, fare-well, fare-
Then o'er the waves, the wretch-ed bark is hurled, "Fare-well, fare-well, fare-
Hen-ry's faint ac-cents trem-bled in the blast, "Fare-well, fare-well, fare-

*ad lib.*

well," he crys, "we soon shall meet again."
well," he crys, "we ne'er shall meet again." *mf*
well, my love, we ne'er shall meet again."

## Come Where My Love Lies Dreaming

S. C. FOSTER

way, . . . Dream - ing the hap-py hours a - way. . . . . . .

way, . . . Dream - ing the hap-py hours a - way. . . . . .

way, . . . Dream - ing the hap-py hours a - way. . . . . .

Soft is her slumber, Tho'ts, bright and free,   Dance thro' her dreams like gushing melo-dy,

Light is her young heart, Light may it be,   Come, where my love lies dream - ing.

# Then You'll Remember Me

WEBB

M. W. BALFE

1. When oth-er lips and oth-er hearts Their tales of love shall
   cold-ness or de-ceit shall slight The beau-ty now they

tell, In lan-guage whose ex-cess im-parts The pow'r they feel so
prize, And deem it but a fad-ed light Which beams with-in your

well, There may per-haps in such a scene Some rec-ol-lec-tion be Of
eyes; When hol-low hearts shall wear a mask,'Twill break your own to see, In

days that have as hap-py been, And you'll re-mem-ber
such a mo-ment I but ask That you'll re-mem-ber

me, . . . . and you'll re-member,you'll re - mem - ber me.    2. When
me, . . . that you'll re-member,you'll re - mem - ber ( *Omit.* . . . . . .) me.

## Clime Beneath Whose Genial Sun

Old Scotch Folksong

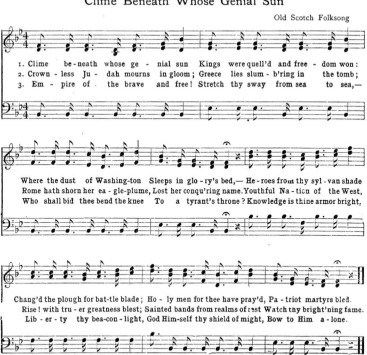

1. Clime be-neath whose ge - nial sun  Kings were quell'd and free - dom won:
2. Crown - less Ju - dah mourns in gloom; Greece lies slum - b'ring in the tomb;
3. Em - pire of the brave and free! Stretch thy sway from sea to sea,—

Where the dust of Washing-ton  Sleeps in glo - ry's bed,— He - roes from thy syl - van shade
Rome hath shorn her ea - gle-plume, Lost her conqu'ring name. Youthful Na - tion of the West,
Who shall bid thee bend the knee  To a tyrant's throne? Knowledge is thine armor bright,

Chang'd the plough for bat-tle blade ; Ho - ly men for thee have pray'd, Pa - triot martyrs bled.
Rise! with tru - er greatness blest; Sainted bands from realms of rest Watch thy bright'ning fame.
Lib - er - ty thy bea - con-light, God Him-self thy shield of might, Bow to Him a - lone.

# Captain Jinks

Arranged by CHARLES E. PRATT

1. I'm Cap-tain Jinks, of the Horse Ma-rines; I feed my horse on corn and beans, And
2. I joined my corps when twen-ty-one, Of course I thought it cap-i-tal fun; When the
3. The first time I went out to drill, The bu-gle sound-ing made me ill; Of the

sport young la-dies in their teens, Tho' a cap-tain in the
en-e-my came, of course I run, For I'm not cut out for the
bat-tle-field I'd had my fill, For I'm not cut out for the

ar-my. I teach young la-dies how to dance, How to dance,
ar-my. When I left home, Ma-ma, she cried, Ma-ma, she cried, Ma-
ar-my. The of-fi-cers, they all did shout, They all did shout, They

How to dance, I teach young la-dies how to dance, For I'm the pet of the ar-my.
ma she cried, When I left home, Ma-ma she cried, He's not cut out for the ar-my.
all did shout, The of-fi-cers they all did shout, Why! kick him out of the ar-my.

Captain Jinks  55

Cap - tain Jinks of the Horse Ma-rines; I feed my horse on corn and beans, And oft - en live be - yond my means, Tho' a cap - tain in the ar - my.

## Chinese Baby-Song

Snail, snail, come out and be fed, Put out your horns, and then your head, And your Pa - pa and your Ma - ma Will give you boiled mut - ton.

*Repeated ad infinitum.*

# Call Me Pet Names

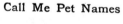

Mrs. Osgood

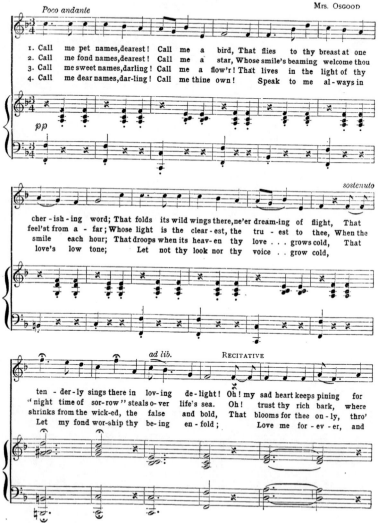

*Poco andante*

1. Call me pet names, dearest! Call me a bird, That flies to thy breast at one
2. Call me fond names, dearest! Call me a star, Whose smile's beaming welcome thou
3. Call me sweet names, darling! Call me a flow'r! That lives in the light of thy
4. Call me dear names, dar-ling! Call me thine own! Speak to me al-ways in

*sostenuto*

cher-ish-ing word; That folds its wild wings there, ne'er dream-ing of flight, That
feel'st from a - far; Whose light is the clear-est, the tru-est to thee, When the
smile each hour; That droops when its heav-en thy love . . . grows cold, That
love's low tone; Let not thy look nor thy voice . . grow cold,

*ad lib.* Recitative

ten - der-ly sings there in lov-ing de-light! Oh! my sad heart keeps pining for
"night time of sor-row" steals o-ver life's sea. Oh! trust thy rich bark, where
shrinks from the wick-ed, the false and bold, That blooms for thee on-ly, thro'
Let my fond wor-ship thy be-ing en-fold; Love me for-ev-er, and

one    fond     word !   Call   me  pet  names, dear-est ! Call  me    a  bird !
its   warm  rays are,    Call   me  pet  names, dar-ling ! Call  me    thy star !
sun - light  and show'r. Call   me  pet  names, dar-ling ! Call  me    a  flow'r !
love - light  a - lone !  Call   me  pet  names, dar-ling ! Call  me    thine own !

## See at Your Feet

M. W. BALFE
From "Bohemian Girl"

1. See  at your feet  a  suppliant one, Whose place should be . . your  heart;  Be-hold the on-ly
2. Oh ! do not spurn the on - ly friend  On whom  she  could  de - pend ;   I  was the on-ly

liv - ing thing  To which she had to  cling.  And  saved her life, watch'd o'er her years,

With all the fondness faith endears, And her affec-tion  won.  Rend not such ties  a-part.

58

## "Vive La Compagnie"

As sung by the Maryland Cadets

1. Let Bac-chus to Ve-nus li - ba-tions pour fast, Vi - ve la com - pa - gnie, And
2. Let ev -'ry old bach -e - lor fill up his glass, Vi - ve la com - pa - gnie, And
3. Let ev -'ry old mar-ried man drink to his wife, Vi - ve la com - pa - gnie, The

let us make use of our time to the last, Vi - ve la com - pa - gnie... Oh!
drink to the health of his fav - o - rite lass, Vi - ve la com - pa - gnie... Oh!
friend of his bos - om and com - fort of life, Vi - ve la com - pa - gnie... Oh!

CHORUS

Vi - ve la, vi - ve la, vi - ve l'a-mour, vi - ve la, vi - ve la, vi - ve l'a-mour,

Vi - ve la, vi - ve la, vi - ve l'a-mour, vi - ve la, vi - ve la, vi - ve l'a-mour,

Ped.      Ped.      Ped.      Ped.

Vi - ve l'a-mour, vi - ve l'a-mour, vi - ve la com - pa - gnie.

Vi - ve l'a-mour, vi - ve l'a-mour, vi - ve la com - pa - gnie.

4 Come fill up your glasses — I'll give you a toast,
Vive la compagnie.
Here's a health to our friend — our kind, worthy host,
Vive la compagnie. Cho.

5 Since all, with good humor, I've toasted so free,
Vive la compagnie.
I hope it will please you to drink now with me,
Vive la compagnie. Cho

## How Can I Leave Thee

*Moderato*                                   Thuringian Folksong

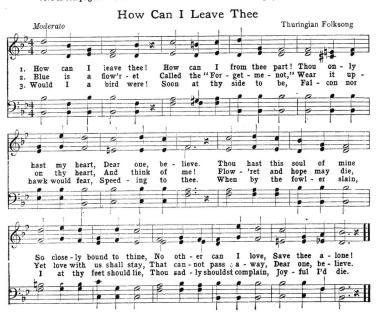

1. How can I leave thee! How can I from thee part! Thou on - ly hast my heart, Dear one, be - lieve. Thou hast this soul of mine So close - ly bound to thine, No oth - er can I love, Save thee a - lone!

2. Blue is a flow'r - et Called the "For - get - me - not," Wear it up - on thy heart, And think of me! Flow - 'ret and hope may die, Yet love with us shall stay, That can - not pass a - way, Dear one, be - lieve.

3. Would I a bird were! Soon at thy side to be, Fal - con nor hawk would fear, Speed - ing to thee. When by the fowl - er slain, I at thy feet should lie, Thou sad - ly shouldst complain, Joy - ful I'd die.

# The Bonnie Blue Flag

HARRY MACARTHY

1. We are a band of broth-ers, and na - tive to the soil, . . And
2. As long as the old Un-ion was faith - ful to her trust; . . Like

Fight - ing for the prop - er - ty we gain'd by hon - est toil; . . And
friends and like broth - ers, kind were we and just; . . But

when our rights were threaten'd, the cry rose near and far, . . . Hur-
now, when North-ern treach-ery at-tempts our rights to mar, . . . We

rah for the Bon - nie Blue Flag, that bears a Sin - gle Star.
hoist on high the Bon - nie Blue Flag, that bears a Sin - gle Star.

CHORUS

1-6. Hur - rah! Hur - rah! for South - ern Rights, Hur - rah!
7. Hur - rah! Hur - rah! for South - ern Rights, Hur - rah!

Hur - rah! for the Bon - nie Blue Flag, that bears a Sin - gle Star.
Hur - rah! for the Bon - nie Blue Flag has gain'd th' E - lev - enth Star.

3 First, gallant South Carolina nobly made the stand;
 Then came Alabama, who took her by the hand;
 Next, quickly Mississippi, Georgia and Florida,
 All rais'd on high the Bonnie Blue Flag that bears a Single Star.   Cho.

4 Ye men of valor, gather round the Banner of the Right,
 Texas and fair Louisiana join us in the fight;
 Davis, our loved President, and Stephens, statesman rare,
 Now rally round the Bonnie Blue Flag that bears a Single Star.   Cho.

5 And here's to brave Virginia! the Old Dominion State
 With the young Confederacy at length has linked her fate;
 Impell'd by her example, now other states prepare
 To hoist on high the Bonnie Blue Fag that bears a Single Star.   Cho.

6 Then here's to our Confederacy, strong we are and brave,
 Like patriots of old, we'll fight our heritage to save;
 And rather than submit to shame, to die we would prefer,
 So cheer for the Bonnie Blue Flag that bears a Single Star.   Cho.

7 Then cheer, boys, cheer, raise the joyous shout,
 For Arkansas and North Carolina now have both gone out;
 And let another rousing cheer for Tennessee be given —
 The Single Star of the Bonnie Blue Flag has grown to be Eleven.   Cho.

# Kiss Me Quick, and Go

F. Buckley

*Allegretto ma moderato*

1. The oth - er night, while I was sparking Sweet Tar-li - na Spray, The more we whis-per'd
2. Soon af - ter that I gave my love A moonlight prom-e - nade, At last we fetch'd up
3. One Sun-day night we sat to - geth- er, Sigh-ing, side by side, Just like two win - ter

our love talk - ing, The more we had to say: . . The old folks and the
to the door, Just where the old folks stay'd; The clock struck twelve, her
leaves of cab - bage, In the sun - shine fried. . My heart with love was

lit - tle folks, We tho't were fast in bed, We heard a foot-step on the stairs,
heart struck too, And peep-ing o - ver head, We saw a night-cap raise the blind,
nigh to split, To ask her for to wed, Said I, "Shall I go for the priest,

*rall.*

And what d'ye think she said? O! "Kiss me quick, and go! my hon-ey,

*a tempo*

Kiss me quick and go ! . . To cheat surprise, and prying eyes, Why, kiss me quick and go ! "

**CHORUS**

" Kiss me quick ! and go ! my hon - ey, Kiss me quick and go ! . . To cheat sur-prise, and

*Sing one octave only*

pry-ing eyes, Why, kiss me quick, and go ! "

# A Thousand Leagues Away

W. C. Bennett

J. Barnby

Allegro con spirito

1. The wind is blow-ing fresh, Kate, The boat rocks there for me; One kiss and I'm a-
2. I half could be a landsman, While those dear eyes I see, To hear the gale rave
3. One kiss; the tide ebbs fast, love; I must not lag-gard be Up-on the voy-age

way, Kate, For two long years to sea; For two long years to
by with-out, While you sat snug with me; But I must hear the
which, I hope, Will give my Kate to me. Pray for us, Kate; such

think of you, Dream of you night and day, To long for you a-
storm howl by, The salt breeze whist-ling play Its weird sea-tune a-
pray'rs as yours God bids the winds o-bey, By for-tune heard, your

cross the sea, . . A thou-sand leagues a - way,    A thou - sand leagues a -
mong the shrouds, A thou-sand leagues a - way,    A thou - sand leagues a -
lov - ing word Will speed us far a - way,    A thou - sand leagues a -

way, dear Kate, A thousand leagues a-way, While round the pole we toss and roll, . . A
way, dear Kate, A thousand leagues a-way, While south we go, blow high, blow low, . . A
way, my Kate, A thousand leagues a-way, God will be-friend the lad you send . . A

thou-sand leagues a - way.

# The Girl I Left Behind Me

Author Unknown

Old Irish Air

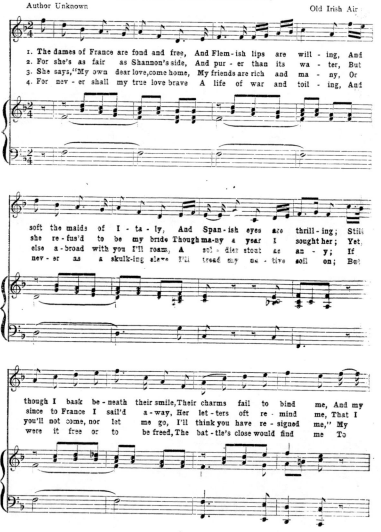

1. The dames of France are fond and free, And Flem-ish lips are will - ing, And soft the maids of I - ta - ly, And Span-ish eyes are thrill - ing; Still though I bask be-neath their smile, Their charms fail to bind me, And my
2. For she's as fair as Shannon's side, And pur - er than its wa - ter, But she re-fus'd to be my bride Though ma-ny a year I sought her; Yet, since to France I sail'd a - way, Her let - ters oft re - mind me, That I
3. She says, "My own dear love, come home, My friends are rich and ma - ny, Or else a - broad with you I'll roam, A sol - dier stout as an - y; If you'll not come, nor let me go, I'll think you have re - signed me," My
4. For nev - er shall my true love brave A life of war and toil - ing, And nev - er as a skulk-ing slave I'll tread my na - tive soil on; But were it free or to be freed, The bat - tle's close would find me To

heart falls back to E - rin's Isle, To the girl I left be - hind me.
prom - is'd nev - er to gain - say The girl I left be - hind me.
heart nigh broke when I an-swered "No" To the girl I left be - hind me.
Ire - land bound, nor mes-sage need From the girl I left be - hind me.

## A Song of the Sea

Written from memory, by Mrs. W. A. FISHER

Probably 100 years old

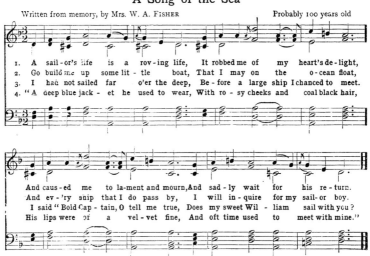

1. A sail - or's life is a rov - ing life, It robbed me of my heart's de - light,
2. Go build me up some lit - tle boat, That I may on the o - cean float,
3. I had not sailed far o'er the deep, Be - fore a large ship I chanced to meet.
4. "A deep blue jack - et he used to wear, With ro - sy cheeks and coal black hair,

And caus - ed me to la-ment and mourn, And sad - ly wait for his re - turn.
And ev - 'ry ship that I do pass by, I will in - quire for my sail - or boy.
I said "Bold Cap - tain, O tell me true, Does my sweet Wil - liam sail with you?
His lips were of a vel - vet fine, And oft time used to meet with mine."

5 "Oh no, fair maid, it sails not here,
    He's drowned in the deep, I fear,
Near that lone island, which you passed by,
    You've chanced to lose your sailor boy."

6 She wrung her hands, she tore her hair,
    Like some fair maid in deep despair,
Her boat against the rocks she run,
    Crying, "Alas, I am undone.

7 "Now, I'll go home and write a song,
    I'll write it true, I'll write it long,
On every line I'll shed a tear,
    On every verse, 'Fare you well, my dear.'"

8 Go dig my grave both wide and deep,
    Place a marble stone at my head and feet,
And, on my breast, a turtle dove,
    To show this world, I died for love.

## Beautiful Star in Heaven so Bright

S. M. Sayles

*Allegretto con anima*

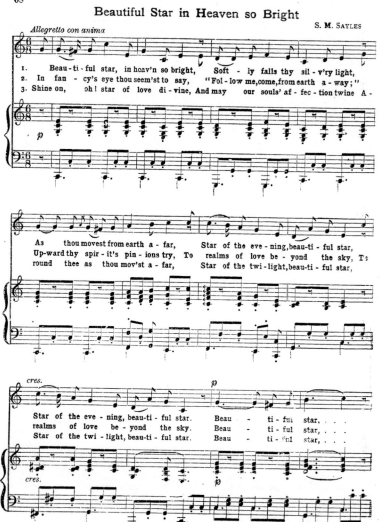

1. Beau-ti-ful star, in heav'n so bright, Soft - ly falls thy sil-v'ry light,
2. In fan - cy's eye thou seem'st to say, "Fol-low me, come, from earth a - way;"
3. Shine on, oh! star of love di - vine, And may our souls' af - fec - tion twine A-

As thou movest from earth a - far, Star of the eve - ning, beau-ti - ful star,
Up-ward thy spir - it's pin - ions try, To realms of love be - yond the sky, To
round thee as thou mov'st a - far, Star of the twi - light, beau-ti - ful star,

Star of the eve - ning, beau-ti - ful star. Beau - ti - ful star, . . .
realms of love be - yond the sky. Beau - ti - ful star, . . .
Star of the twi - light, beau-ti - ful star. Beau - ti - ful star, . . .

Beau - ti-ful star, . . Star . . of the eve - ning, Beautiful, beauti-ful star.

## Arise, My Soul

CHARLES WESLEY                                    LEWIS EDSON

1. A - rise, my soul, a - rise; Shake off thy guilt - y fears; The bleed-ing Sac - ri -
2. He ev - er lives a - bove, For me to in - ter - cede; His all - re - deem-ing
3. Five bleeding wounds He bears, Re-ceived on Cal - va - ry; They pour ef - fect - ual
4. My God is rec - on - ciled; His pardoning voice I hear: He owns me for His

fice In my be - half ap - pears: Be - fore the throne my Sure - ty stands, Be -
love, His pre - cious blood, to plead; His blood a - toned for all our race, His
prayers, They strong-ly plead for me: "For - give him, Oh, for - give," they cry, "For -
child; I can no lon - ger fear: With con - fi - dence I now draw nigh, With

fore the throne my Sure - ty stands, My name is writ - ten on His hands.
blood a - toned for all our race, And sprin-kles now the throne of grace.
give him, Oh, for - give," they cry, "Nor let that ran-somed sin - ner die."
con - fi - dence I now draw nigh, And, "Fa - ther, Ab - ba, Fa - ther," cry.

# Angels Ever Bright and Fair

HÄNDEL

ev - er bright and fair, take, oh, take me to your care,

take, oh, take me to your care.

Speed to your own courts my flight, clad in robes of vir - gin

white, clad in robes of vir - gin white, clad in robes of vir - gin white, take me,

# A Yankee Ship, and a Yankee Crew

C. M. King

1. A yan - kee ship and a yan - kee crew, Tal - ly hi ho, you know; O'er the
2. A yan - kee ship and a yan - kee crew, Tal - ly hi ho, you know; With
3. A yan - kee ship and a yan - kee crew, Tal - ly hi ho, you know; The
4. A yan - kee ship and a yan - kee crew, Tal - ly hi ho, you know;

bright blue waves like a sea - bird flew, Sing hey a - loft and a - low. . Her
hearts on board both gal-lant and true; The same a - loft, and a - low. . The
boats all clear, the wreck we now view, "All hands" a - loft and a - low. . A
Free-dom de - fends the land where it grew, We're free a - loft and a - low. . Bearing

wings are spread to the fai - ry breeze The spray sparkling as thrown from her
black - en'd sky, and the whist - ling wind, Fore - tell the ap - proach of the
ship's his throne, the sea his world, He ne'er sheers from a ship - mate dis -
down is a foe in re - gal pride, De - fi - ance at each mast -

# Oh! Willie, We Have Miss'd You

S. C. FOSTER

*Allegretto moderato*

1. Oh! Wil-lie, is it you, dear, Safe, safe at home? They did not tell me true, dear, They
2. We've long'd to see you nightly, But this night of all; The fire was blaz-ing bright-ly, And
3. The days were sad without you, The nights long and drear; My dreams have been about you, Oh!

said you would not come. I heard you at the gate, And it made my heart re-joice,
lights were in the hall; The lit-tle ones were up Till 'twas ten o'-clock and past,
wel-come, Wil-lie dear! Last night I wept and watch'd By the moonlight's cheerless ray,

*cres. un poco*

*rall.*     *a tempo*

For I knew that wel-come foot-step, And that dear, fa-mil-iar voice, Mak-ing
Then their eyes be-gan to twin-kle, And they're gone to sleep at last; But they
Till I thought I heard your foot-step, Then I wip'd my tears a-way; But my

mu - sic on my ear, In the lone - ly mid - night gloom: Oh!
lis - ten'd for your voice, Till they thought you'd nev - er come: Oh!
heart grew sad a - gain, When I found you had not come: Oh!

Willie, we have miss'd you; Welcome, welcome home!

English Chanty

1. Come, ship - mates and broth - ers, Ho yo! Cheer - ly, men,
2. The wind it blows hard, Ho yo! Cheer - ly, men, Each
3. Come, loose ev - 'ry sail, Ho yo! Cheer - ly, men, We'll
4. Our hearts they are light, Ho yo! Cheer - ly, men, Each

Haul all to - geth - er, Ho yo! Cheer - ly, men, Help one an - oth - er,
tar knows his card, Ho yo! Cheer - ly, men, We'll soon man the yards,
soon face the gale, Ho yo! Cheer - ly, men, Stout hearts which ne'er fail,
eye it seems bright, Ho yo! Cheer - ly, men, We bid you good - night,

Ho yo! Cheer - ly, men, O hau - ley, ho yo, Cheer - ly, men!

# De Boatmen's Dance

Dan D. Smith

High row, de boat-men, row, float-in' down de rib-ber, de O-hi-o. 1. De
2. Do
3. I

boat-men dance, de boat-men sing, De boat-men up to eb-ry ting, An
oys-ter boat should keep to de shore, De fish-in smack should ven-ture more. Do
went on board de od-der day To see what de boat-men had to say; An

when de boat-men gets on shore, He spends his cash an works for more, Den
schoon-er sails be-fore de wind, De steam-boat leaves a streak be-hind. O
dar I let my pas-sion loose, An dey cram me in de cal-la-boose. O

dance de boat-men dance, O dance de boat-men dance, O dance all night till

broad day - light An go home wid de gals in de morn - ing.

4 I've come dis time, I'll come no more,
Let me loose, I'll go ashore;
For dey whole hoss, an dey a bully crew
Wid a hoosier mate an a captain too.
O dance, etc.

5 When you go to de boatmen's ball,
Dance wid my wife, or don't dance at all;
Sky blue jacket an tarpaulin hat,
Look out, my boys, for de nine-tail cat.
O dance, etc.

6 De boatman is a thrifty man,
Dar's none can do as de boatman can;
I nebber see a putty gal in my life
But dat she was a boatman's wife.
O dance, etc.

7 When de boatman blows his horn,
Look out, old man, your hog is gone;
He cotch my sheep, he cotch my shoat,
Den put em in a bag an toat em to de boat.
O dance, etc.

## Just as I Am

CHARLOTTE ELLIOTT

WM. B. BRADBURY

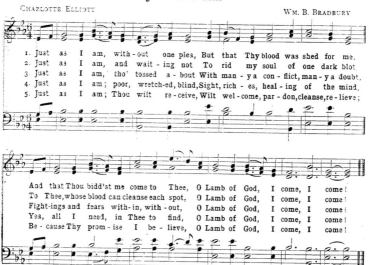

1. Just as I am, with - out one plea, But that Thy blood was shed for me,
2. Just as I am, and wait - ing not To rid my soul of one dark blot,
3. Just as I am, tho' tossed a - bout With man - y a con - flict, man - y a doubt,
4. Just as I am, poor, wretch - ed, blind, Sight, rich - es, heal - ing of the mind,
5. Just as I am; Thou wilt re - ceive, Wilt wel - come, par - don, cleanse, re - lieve;

And that Thou bidd'st me come to Thee, O Lamb of God, I come, I come!
To Thee, whose blood can cleanse each spot, O Lamb of God, I come, I come!
Fight-ings and fears with-in, with - out, O Lamb of God, I come, I come!
Yea, all I need, in Thee to find, O Lamb of God, I come, I come!
Be - cause Thy prom - ise I be - lieve, O Lamb of God, I come, I come!

# Larboard Watch

DUET

T. WILLIAMS

1. At drear - y mid - night's cheer - less hour, De - sert - ed e'en by
2. With anx - ious care he eyes each wave, That swell - ing, threat-ens

Cyn-thia's beams, When tempests beat and tor-rents pour, And twinkling stars no lon - ger gleam;
to o'er-whelm, And his storm-beat-en bark to save, Di-rects with skill the faith-ful helm.

The wea - ried sai - lor, spent with toil, Clings firm-ly to the weather shrouds And
With joy he drinks the cheering grog, 'Mid storms that bellow loud and hoarse, With

still the lengthen'd hour to guile, And still the lengthen'd hour to guile,
joy he heaves the reel - ing log, With joy he heaves the reel - ing log,

Sings as he views the gath - 'ring clouds,  Sings as he views  the
And marks the lee - way and the course,  And marks the lee - way

gath - ring clouds,  "Lar - board Watch, A - hoy!  Lar - board Watch, A - hoy!"
and the course,  "Lar - board Watch, A - hoy!  Lar - board Watch, A - hoy!"

But who can speak the joy he feels While o'er the foam his ves - sel

reels, And his tir'd eye - lids slumb'ring fall, He rous - es at the welcome call Of

## Larboard Watch

*adagio ad lib.*

"Lar - board Watch, A- hoy! Lar-board Watch, Lar - board Watch, Larboard Watch, A- h oy!"

## Bonnie Dundee

WALTER SCOTT

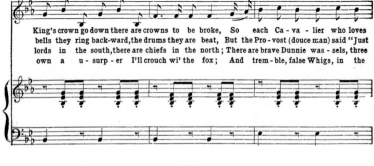

1. To the Lords of Con - ven - tion 'twas Cla - ver - house spoke, "Ere the
2. Dun - dee he is mount - ed, he rides up the street, The
3. There are hills be - yond Pent - land, and lands be - yond Forth, If there's
4. Then a - wa' to the hills, to the lea, to the rocks, Ere I

King's crown go down there are crowns to be broke, So each Ca - va - lier who loves
bells they ring back-ward, the drums they are beat, But the Pro - vost (douce man) said "Just
lords in the south, there are chiefs in the north; There are brave Dunnie was - sels, three
own a u - surp - er I'll crouch wi' the fox; And trem - ble, false Whigs, in the

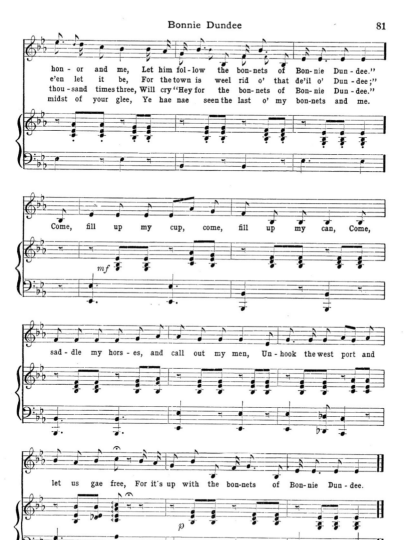

hon - or and me, Let him fol - low the bon-nets of Bon- nie Dun - dee."
e'en let it be, For the town is weel rid o' that de'il o' Dun - dee;"
thou - sand times three, Will cry "Hey for the bon- nets of Bon- nie Dun - dee."
midst of your glee, Ye hae nae seen the last o' my bon-nets and me.

Come, fill up my cup, come, fill up my can, Come,

sad - dle my hors - es, and call out my men, Un - hook the west port and

let us gae free, For it's up with the bon-nets of Bon- nie Dun - dee.

# Hard Times Come Again No More

S. C. FOSTER

1. Let us pause in life's pleas-ures, and count its ma-ny tears, While we
2. While we seek mirth and beau-ty, and mu-sic light and gay, There are
3. 'Tis a sigh that is waft-ed a-cross the trou-bled wave, 'Tis a

all sup sor-row with the poor; . . There's a song that will lin-ger for
frail forms faint-ing at the door: . . Tho' their voi-ces are si-lent, their
wail that is heard up-on the shore; . . 'Tis a dirge that is mur-mur'd a-

ev-er in our ears, "Oh! Hard times, come a-gain no more." . . .
plead-ing looks will say, "Oh! Hard times, come a-gain no more." . . .
round the low-ly grave, "Oh! Hard times, come a-gain no more." . . .

First, SOLO; then, CHORUS

'Tis the song, the sigh of the wea - ry, Hard times, hard times, come a - gain no more; Ma - ny days you have lin - ger'd a - round my cab - in door, Oh! Hard times, come a - gain no more. . . .

# Douglas! Tender and True

Author Unknown

Lady JOHN SCOTT

*Soave*

1. Could ye come back to me, Doug-las! Doug-las!
2. Nev-er a scorn-ful word should pain you,
3. I was not half wor-thy of you, Doug-las!
4. Oh! to call back the days that are not;
5 Stretch out your hand to me, Doug-las! Doug-las!

*rall.*      *p*

In the old like-ness that I knew, I would be so faith-ful, so lov-ing, Douglas!
I'd smile as sweet as an-gels do; Sweet as your smile on me shone ev-er,
Not half wor-thy the like of you; Now all men be-sides are to me like shadows,
Mine eyes were blinded, your words are few; Do you know the truth now up in Heaven?
Drop forgiveness from Heav'n like dew, As I lay my heart on your dead heart, Douglas!

Doug - las! Doug - las! ten-der and true.

*cres.*      *dim.*

# When the Swallows

FRANZ ABT

1. When the swal - lows home - ward fly, When the ro - - ses scat - tered
2. When the white swan south - ward roves, To seek at noon the or - ange
3. Hush, my heart! why thus com - plain? Thou must, too, thy woes con -

lie, When from nei - ther hill nor dale Chants the sil - v'ry night - in - gale;
groves, When the red tints of the west Prove the sun has gone to rest;
tain. Tho' on earth no more we rove, Fond - ly breath-ing words of love.

In these words my bleed-ing heart Would to thee its grief im - part,
In these words my bleed-ing heart Would to thee its grief im - part,
Thou, my heart, must find re - lief, Yield - ing to these words be - lief:

"When I . . . thus thy im - age lose, Can I, ah, can I
"When I . . . thus thy im - age lose, Can I, ah, can I
"I shall see thy form a - gain, Though to - day . . .

e'er know re - pose, Can I, ah, can I e'er know re - pose?"
e'er know re - pose, Can I, ah, can I e'er know re - pose?"
we part in pain, Though to - day we part in pain."

# I've Left the Snow-Clad Hills

G. LINLEY

*Allegretto ma non troppo*

1. I've left the snow-clad hills, Where my fa - ther's hut doth stand, . My
2. Be - side those snow-clad hills, Where my fa - ther's hut doth stand, . Dwells

own, my dear Dal - kar - lia, For a stran - ger land. I'm
one, to whom I'm plight - ed To be - stow my hand. But

but a poor, young girl, In my sim - ple, peas - ant guise; . Un -
not with - out a heart, Would I pledge with word or vow, . . And

skill'd in all the arts and wiles That world - lings prize; . I
I've no heart to give him, For he has it now. That

*Piu mosso*

trill my moun-tain lay, Ev - 'ry-where I chance to roam; Oh!
youth he is so no - ble, That youth he is so brave, Oh!

*rall.*

sweet the song to me, For it takes me back to home. No
soon - er than de - sert him I'd lie me in my grave. No

*col voce.*

*A tempo*     *rall.*

place can ev - er be, to me, Like that dear home. My
won - der, I am pi - ning then, For home a - gain. My

*rall.*

own, sweet home! My own· be - lov - ed home!

*ritard.*

*f*

# Upidee

1. The shades of night were fall-ing fast, Tral la la, Tral la la, As
2. His brow was sad, his eye be-neath, Tral la la, Tral la la, Flashed
3. "O stay," the maid-en said,"and rest," Tral la la, Tral la la, "Thy

through an Al - pine vil - lage passed, Tral la la la la! A
like a faul - chion from his sheaf, Tral la la la la! And
wea - ry head up - on this breast," Tral la la la la! A

*ritard.*

youth, who bore, 'mid snow and ice A ban - ner with the strange de - vice,
like a sil - ver clar - ion rung The ac - cents of that un - known tongue,
tear stood in his bright blue eye, But still he an-swered with a sigh,

*ritard.*

*f* Chorus

U - pi - dee - i, dee - i, da, U - pi - dee, U - pi - da, U - pi - dee - i, dee - i, da,

U - pi-dee-i-da !    * r-r-r-r-r-r-r-r-r-r-r-r-r-r-r-r-r   r-r-r-r-r-r-r-r-ryah!yah!yah!yah !

FINE

4 At break of day as heavenward
   Tral la la, Tral la la !
The pious monks of Saint Bernard,
   Tral la la la la !
  Uttered the oft repeated prayer,
  A voice cried through the startled air,
        Chorus.

5 A trav'ler, by the faithful hound,
   Tral la la, Tral la la !
Half buried in the snow was found,
   Tral la la la la !
  Still grasping in his hand of ice,
  That banner with the strange device,
        Chorus.

\* Imitating a watchman's rattle.

## Jerusalem the Golden

St. Bernard, a.d., 1150.  Neale, Tr.            Alexander Ewing.

1. Je - ru - sa - lem the gold - en! With milk and hon - ey blest, Be - neath thy con-tem -
2. They stand, those halls of Zi - on, All ju - bi - la - nt with song, And bright with many an
3. And they who with their Lead - er Have con-quer'd in the fight, For - ev - er and for -
4. Oh, sweet and bless - ed coun - try, The home of God's e - lect! Oh, sweet and bless-ed

pla - tion Sink heart and voice op - press'd. I know not,—oh, I know not,
an - gel, And all the mar - tyr throng. There is the throne of Da - vid,
ev - er Are clad in robes of white. Oh, land that see'st no sor - row !
coun - try, That ea - ger hearts ex - pect! Je - sus, in mer - cy bring us

What joys a - wait me there, What ra-dian - cy of glo - ry, What bliss be - yond com-pare.
And there from toil re - leased, The shout of them that tri - umph, The song of them that feast.
Oh, state that fear'st no strife ! Oh, roy - al land of flow - ers ! Oh, realm and home of life !
To that dear land of rest ; Who art, with God the Fa - ther, And Spir-it ev - er blest.

# Break, Break, Break

Alfred Tennyson

Wm. R. Dempster

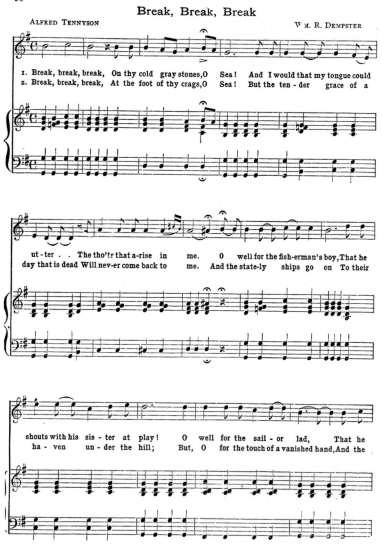

1. Break, break, break, On thy cold gray stones, O Sea! And I would that my tongue could
2. Break, break, break, At the foot of thy crags, O Sea! But the ten - der grace of a

ut - ter . . The tho'ts that a-rise in me. O well for the fish-erman's boy, That he
day that is dead Will nev-er come back to me. And the state-ly ships go on To their

shouts with his sis - ter at play! O well for the sail - or lad, That he
ha - ven un - der the hill; But, O for the touch of a vanished hand, And the

sings in his boat on the bay! Break, break, break, On thy cold gray stones, O Sea!
sound of a voice that is still! Break, break, break, At the foot of thy crags, O Sea!

## Oft in the Stilly Night

THOMAS MOORE

*Andantino*

1. Oft in the still-y night, Ere slum-ber's chain has bound me.
2. When I re-mem-ber all The friends, so link'd to - geth - er,
D.C.—*Thus, in the still-y night, Ere slum-ber's chain has bound me,*

Fond mem - 'ry brings the light Of oth - er days a - round me.
I've seen a - round me fall. Like leaves in win - try weath - er,
*Sad mem - 'ry brings the light Of oth - er days a - round me.*

The smiles, the tears Of boy-hood's years, The words of love then spo - ken. The
I feel like one Who treads a - lone Some ban - quet hall de - sert - ed, Whose

eyes that shone, Now dimm'd and gone, The cheer - ful hearts now bro - ken!
lights are fled, Whose gar - lands dead, And all but he de - part - ed.

## Dream Faces

W. M. Hutchinson

1. The shad - ows lie a - cross the dim old room, The fire - light
2. Once more I see a - cross the dis-tant years A face, long

glows and fades in - to the gloom, While mem - 'ry sails to
gone with all its smiles and tears, Once more I press a

child - hood's distant shore, And dreams, and dreams of days that are no more.
ten - der, lov-ing hand, And with my dar - ling 'neath the old oak stand.

Sweet dreamland fa - ces, pass-ing to and fro, . . Bring back to

mem - 'ry days of long a - go, . . . Mur - mur - ing gent - ly

thro' a mist of pain, "Hope on, dear loved one, we shall meet a - gain!" Once

gain!"3. But all I loved are gone, And I a - lone in life, To wait, and wait, and

wait,  Till Death shall end the strife; Un - til once more I   join    The

hearts   that   loved   me   best,    Where the wick - ed cease from

troub - ling,   And the wea - ry are   at   rest! . . . . .

gain,   We shall meet, shall meet a - gain!" . . . . . . . .

## Bridal Chorus, from Lohengrin

RICHARD WAGNER

Guid-ed by us, thrice hap-py pair, En-ter this door-way,'tis love that in-vites;

All that is brave, all that is fair, Love now tri-umph-ant for-ev-er u-nites.

Cham-pion of vir-tue, bold-ly ad-vance, Flow'r of all beau-ty, gen-tly ad-vance;

Now the loud mirth of rev-'ling is end-ed, Night, bring-ing peace and bliss, has de-

scend-ed. Fann'd by the breath of hap-pi-ness, rest, Clos'd to the world, by love on-ly blest!

umph-ant for ev-er u-nites, for-ev-er u-nites.

# Oh! Don't You Remember Sweet Alice

### Or Ben Bolt

1. Oh! don't you re-mem-ber sweet Al-ice, Ben Bolt, Sweet Al-ice with hair so
2. Oh! don't you re-mem-ber the wood, Ben Bolt, Near the green sun-ny slope of the
3. Oh! don't you re-mem-ber the school, Ben Bolt, And the mas-ter so kind and so

brown, . . She wept with de-light when you gave her a smile, And
hill, . . . When oft we have sung 'neath its wide spread - ing shade, And kept
true, . . . And the lit-tle nook by the clear run-ning brook, Where we

trem-bled with fear at your frown; . . In the old church-yard, in the val-ley, Ben Bolt,
time to the click of the mill; . . The mill has gone to de-cay, Ben Bolt,
gath-ered the flow'rs as they grew; . . On the Mas-ter's grave grows the grass, Ben Bolt,

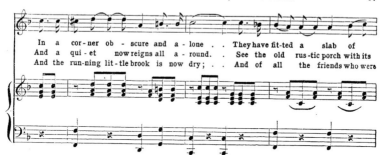

In a cor - ner ob - scure and a - lone . . They have fit-ted a slab of
And a qui - et now reigns all a - round. . See the old rus -tic porch with its
And the run-ning lit - tle brook is now dry ; . . And of all the friends who were

gran - ite so grey, And sweet Al - ice lies un - der the stone. . . They have
ro - ses so sweet, Lies scat - ter'd and fall'n to the ground. . . See the
school - mates then, There re - main, Ben, but you and I . . . . And of

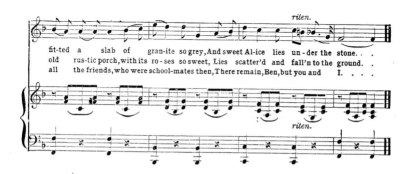

fit - ted a slab of gran-ite so grey, And sweet Al-ice lies un - der the stone. . .
old rus-tic porch, with its ro - ses so sweet, Lies scatter'd and fall'n to the ground. .
all the friends, who were school-mates then, There remain, Ben, but you and I . . .

# Fading, Still Fading

Portuguese Melody

*Andantino mf*

1. Fad - ing, still fad - ing, the last . . . beam is shin - ing,
2. Fa - ther in heav - en, Oh! hear . . . when we call, . . .

Fa - ther in heav - en, the day . . is de - clin - ing;
Hear for Christ's sake, who is Sav - iour of all, . . . .

Safe - ty and in - no - cence fly with the light, Temp -
Fee - ble and faint - ing we trust in Thy might, In

ta - tion and dan - ger walk forth with the night; From the
doubt - ing and dark - ness Thy love be our light; Let us

fall of the shade till the morn - ing bells chime,
sleep on Thy breast while the night ta - per burns, And

Shield me from dan - ger and save me from crime.
wake in Thy arms when the morn - ing re - turns.

QUARTET

Fa - ther, have mer - cy, Fa - ther, have mer - cy,

Fa - ther, have mer - cy, thro' Je - sus Christ our Lord.

# Katey's Letter

Lady DUFFERIN

1. Och girls dear, did you ev-er hear, I wrote my love a let-ter, And al-
2. My heart was full, but when I wrote I dar'd not put the half in, The
3. I wrote it, and I fold-ed it, and put a seal up-on it, 'Twas a
4. Now girls, would you be-lieve it, that post-man so con-sait-ed, No

tho' he can-not read, sure I tho't 'twas all the bet-ter, For
neigh-bors know I love him, and they're might-y fond of chaff-ing, So I
seal al-most as big, as the crown of my best bon-net, For I
an-swer will he bring me, so long as I have wait-ed, But

why should he be puz-zled with hard spell-ing in the mat-ter, When the
dar'd not write his name out-side, for fear they would be laugh-ing, So I
would not have the Post-mas-ter make his re-marks up-on it, As I
may-be there mayn't be one, for the ra-son that I stat-ed, That my

mane - ing was so plain that I love him faith - ful-ly,
wrote,"From lit - tle Kate to one whom she loves faith - ful-ly,"
said in - side the let-ter, that I lov'd him faith - ful-ly,
love can neith - er read nor write but he loves me faith - ful-ly,

love him faithful - ly, And he knows it, oh! he knows it, with-out one word from me.
love him faithful - ly, And he knows it, oh! he knows it, with-out one word from me.
love him faithful - ly, And he knows it, oh! he knows it, with-out one word from me.
loves me faithful - ly, And I know where'er my love is, that he is true to me.

## Baby Bunting

Bye, O Ba - by Bunt - ing, Dad - dy's gone a hunt - ing, To

get a lit - tle rab - bit-skin To wrap his Ba - by Bunt - ing in.

# Long Ago

FRANK MUSGRAVE

1. "Long, long a - go, . . long, long a - go," Do not these words re -
2. "Long, long a - go," when ma - ny a sound A - woke to mirth that
3. "Long, long a - go," the hopes we nurs'd — In sol - i - tude — of
4. "Long, long a - go," who breathes there here, O'er whom the past hath

call past years, And scarce - ly know-ing who they flow,
sad - dens now, And ma - ny a spark-ling eye went round,
earth - ly fame Were bright as bub-bles as that burst,
no such pow'r? Young heart if now thy sky is clear,

Bring to the eyes un - bid - den tears; Do you not
That weeps be - neath a dark - en'd brow; When with our
A glit - t'ring drop, an emp - ty name: Oh, but to
Be - ware, be - ware the fu - ture hour: Per - chance the

feel   as   back   they   come, . .   Those   dim sweet
whole   young   hap - py   hearts, . .   We   lov'd and
be . .   one   hour   a - gain . .   (What - ev - er
tones   that   ech - - o   now, . .   In   af - ter

dreams   of   old - en   days, . .   A yearn - ing   to   your
laugh'd   a - way   the   time, . .   Nor thought how   quick - ly
that   sweet hour   might   cost!) . .   Free   from   mem - 'ry's
years   thou'lt hear   a - gain ; . .   And gaz - ing   on   each

child - hood's   home,   Peo - pled with tones of   love and   praise.
all   de - parts,   So   cher - ish'd   in   life's ear - ly   prime.
tor - turing   pain,   With   those we   loved, with those we   lost.
fa - ded   brow,   Wilt sigh - ing   say,   I   heard that   strain.

# Long Ago

Long, long a - go, Long, long a - go, In the young soul's ear - ly flow,

Long, long a-go, Long, long a-go, In the young soul's ear - ly flow,

Long, long a-go, Long, long a-go, In the young soul's ear - ly flow,

Long, long a- go, Long, long a-go, In the young soul's ear - ly flow,

*Allegretto moderato*

We sang the songs of home and love, Round the fire - side's laugh-ing glow.

Long long a-go, Long, long a-go, Round the fire - side's laughing glow.

Long, long a-go, Long, long a-go, Round the fire - side's laughing glow.

Long, long a-go, Long, long a-go, Round the fire - side's laughing glow.

# Drink to Me Only with Thine Eyes

Ben Jonson

W. A. Mozart

1. Drink to me on - ly with thine eyes, and I will pledge with mine, . .
2. I sent thee late a ro - sy wreath, not so much hon - 'ring thee, . .

Or leave a kiss with - in the cup, and I'll not ask for wine; . . . The
As giv - ing it a hope that there it could not with - ered be; . . . But

thirst that from the soul doth rise, doth ask a drink di - vine, . .
thou there - on didst on - ly breathe, and send'st it back to me, . . .

But might I of Jove's nec - tar sip, I would not change for thine, . . for thine.
Since when it grows and smells, I swear, not of it - self, but thee, . . but thee.

# Tempest of the Heart

From VERDI'S "Il Trovatore"

1. Her bright eyes whose ra-diant gleam-ing Pales the stars in yon fair
2. Airs that wan-der, mur-m'ring round us, Waft the prayer that I, so

*1. Il ba-len del suo sor-ri-so d'u-na stel-la vin-ce il*

heav-en, With her smile in beauty beam-ing, Round me throw their witching spell, new ardor
lonely, Breathe for those blest ties that bound us, While her love, oh! rare sweet dream, is mine, mine

*rag-gio; il ful-gor del suo bel vi-so no-vo in-fon-de, no-vo infonde a me co-*

giv-en! Ah! this pas-sion pure with-in me burn-ing, More than
on-ly! Ah! this pas-sion pure with-in me burn-ing, More than

*rag-gio. Ah! l'a-mor, l'a-mo-re ond' ar-do le fa-*

words shall plead a lov-er's part; .... Her bright glan-ces on me ...

*vel-li in mi-o fa-vor. ..... sper-da il so-le d'un suo ...*

turn-ing, Calm the tem-pest, Calm the tem-pest, in my heart.

*sguar-do la tem-pes-ta, la tem-pes-ta del mio cor.*

# Bonny Eloise

### The Belle of the Mohawk Vale

A song taken up by Military Bands North and South in 1861

C. W. Elliott

J. R. Thomas

1. O, sweet is the Vale where the Mohawk gent - ly glides On its
2. O, sweet are the scenes of my boy-hood's sun - ny years, That be -
3. O, sweet are the mo - ments when dream - ing I roam, Thro' my

clear wind - ing way to the sea, And dear - er than all sto - ried
span - gle the gay val - ley o'er, And dear are the friends seen thro'
loved haunts now mos - sy and grey, And dear - er than all is my

streams on earth be - sides, In this bright roll - ing riv - er to me;
mem - o - ries' fond tears That have lived in the blest days of yore;
child-hood's hal-low'd home, That is crumb - ling now slow - ly a - way;

*First*, Solo ; *then* Chorus

But sweet-er dear - er, yes, dear-er far than these Who charm where others all

fail Is blue-eyed, bon-ny, bon-ny E - lo - ise, The Belle of the Mohawk Vale.

## Soft, Soft Music is Stealing

*Andante*                                    German Melody

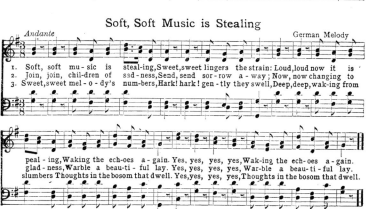

1. Soft, soft mu - sic is steal-ing, Sweet, sweet lingers the strain: Loud, loud now it is
2. Join, join, chil-dren of sad - ness, Send, send sor - row a - way ; Now, now changing to
3. Sweet, sweet mel - o - dy's num-bers, Hark! hark! gen - tly they swell, Deep, deep, wak-ing from

peal - ing, Waking the ech-oes a - gain. Yes, yes, yes, yes, Wak-ing the ech-oes a - gain.
glad - ness, Warble a beau-ti - ful lay. Yes, yes, yes, yes, War-ble a beau-ti - ful lay.
slumbers Thoughts in the bosom that dwell. Yes, yes, yes, yes, Thoughts in the bosom that dwell.

# Hoop de Dooden Do

A. NISH

1. Some hun-dred years a-go or so, . . Good ole Mas - sa set me free,
2. I walk'd a-long a mile or two, Wid-out a boot, wid-out a shoe;
3. I did - n't go so ber - ry far, Be-fore I seen de rail-road car,
4. I went to pick a ba-by up, And look to see if it was hurt, Soon

Den de mis - sus she did cry; "Hoop de doo - den do!" . I
Den my feet did hurt me so,— "Hoop de doo - den do!" . I
Jump - ing ober a turn - pike bar; "Hoop de doo - den do!" . I
it be - gan a squeal - ing out; "Hoop de doo - den do!" . An -

clap't my trunk up - on my back, And start - ed for de rail - way track, And
stood my trunk down on de ground, Just for to take a look a - round, De
heard de noise and see de sight, Den run a - way wid all my might:
oth - er fel - low broke his leg, He now goes on a wood - en peg; Don't

ALICE NIELSEN

The charming American lyric soprano. She was
born in Nashville, Tennessee, 1876, studied music
in San Francisco, and made her first public appear-
ance in California. She was a popular member of
the Bostonians, and has played in both light and
grand opera. Her popular encore is "Bonnie
Eloise"—Heart Songs, p. 108.

MARY GARDEN

An American singer of world-wide renown. She was born in Chicago, and received
her musical education in Paris. She was for some time with the Opera Comique,
Paris, and has since toured in Europe and America. Her popular encore is "The
Blue Bells of Scotland"—Heart Songs, p. 387.

soon   I heard   the whis-tle   hol - ler;   "Hoop   de   doo - den   do!  . .
whis - tle scream'd wid all  his   might   "Hoop   de   doo - den   do!  . .
(All   de  cars   went  off  de   track)   "Hoop   de   doo - den   do!  . .
ask   for   an - y   more  I   beg—   "Hoop   de   doo - den   do!  . .

## Holy, Holy, Holy

R. HEBER                                                                J. B. DYKES

1. Ho - ly,   ho - ly,   ho - ly!   Lord God Al - might - y!   Ear - ly  in  the
2. Ho - ly,   ho - ly,   ho - ly!   all the saints a - dore Thee, Cast - ing down their
3. Ho - ly,   ho - ly,   ho - ly! though the dark-ness hide Thee, Though the eye of
4. Ho - ly,   ho - ly,   ho - ly!   Lord God Al - might - y!   All thy works shall

morn - ing  our  song shall  rise   to  Thee.   Ho - ly,   ho - ly,   ho - ly,
gold - en crowns a - round the glass - y   sea;   Cher - u - bim and Ser - a - phim
sin - ful man Thy  glo - ry  may not  see,   On - ly  Thou  art  ho - ly!
praise Thy name in earth, and sky, and sea.   Ho - ly,   ho - ly,   ho - ly!

mer - ci - ful and might - y,  God  in three per - sons, bless - ed Trin - i - ty!
fall - ing down be - fore Thee, Which wert, and  art,  and  ev - er - more shalt be.
there is none be - side Thee Per - fect in  pow - er, in love, and pu - ri - ty.
mer - ci - ful and might - y,  God  in three per - sons, bless - ed Trin - i - ty!

# The Heart of a Sailor

Stephen Adams

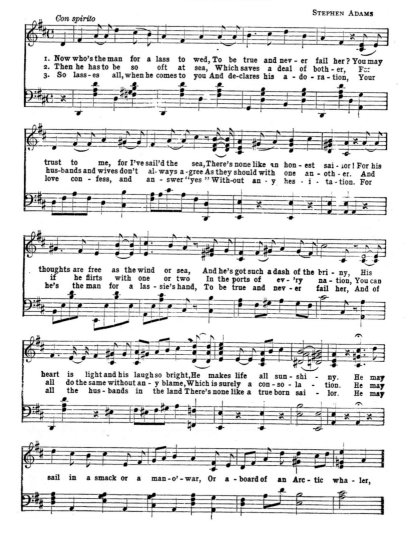

*Con spirito*

1. Now who's the man for a lass to wed, To be true and nev-er fail her? You may
2. Then he has to be so oft at sea, Which saves a deal of both-er, For
3. So lass-es all, when he comes to you And de-clares his a-do-ra-tion, Your

trust to me, for I've sail'd the sea, There's none like an hon-est sai-lor! For his
hus-bands and wives don't al-ways a-gree As they should with one an-oth-er. And
love con-fess, and an-swer "yes" With-out an-y hes-i-ta-tion. For

thoughts are free as the wind or sea, And he's got such a dash of the bri-ny, His
if he flirts with one or two In the ports of ev-'ry na-tion, You can
he's the man for a las-sie's hand, To be true and nev-er fail her, And of

heart is light and his laugh so bright, He makes life all sun-shi-ny. He may
all do the same without an-y blame, Which is surely a con-so-la-tion. He may
all the hus-bands in the land There's none like a true born sai-lor. He may

sail in a smack or a man-o'-war, Or a-board of an Arc-tic wha-ler,

But it's all the same, If Jack's his name, And he's

got the heart of a sai - lor.   got the heart of a sai - lor.

## Comin' Thro' the Rye

ROBERT BURNS
*Lively*

1. If a bod-y meet a bod-y Com-in' thro' the rye,   If a bod-y
2. If a bod-y meet a bod-y Com-in' frae the town,   If a bod-y
3. Amang the train there is a swain I dear-ly love my-sel'; But what's his name, or

kiss a bod-y, Need a bod-y cry?   Ev-'ry las-sie has her lad-die,
greet a bod-y, Need a bod-y frown?   Ev-'ry las-sie has her lad-die,
where's his hame, I din-na choose to tell.   Ev-'ry las-sie has her lad-die,

Nane, they say, ha'e I;   Yet a' the lads they smile on me, When com-in' thro' the rye.

# Some Day

HUGH CONWAY                                    MILTON WELLINGS

1. I know not when the day shall be, I know not where our eyes may
2. I know not are you far or near, Or are you dead, or do you

meet, What wel-come you may give to me, Or will your words be sad or
live; I know not who the blame should bear, Or who should plead, or who for-

sweet; It may not be till years have passed, . Till eyes are dim and tress-es
give. But when we meet some day, some day, . . Eyes clear-er grown the truth may

gray, . . The world is wide—but, love, at last, Our hands, our hearts, must meet some day.
see, . . And ev-'ry cloud shall roll a-way, That dark-ens love, 'twixt you and me.

*L'istesso tempo*

Some day, some day, Some day I shall meet you, Love, I know not when or how,

Love, I know not when or how, On - ly this, on - ly this, this, that once you loved me,

**1** *ad lib.*

On - ly this, I love you now, I love you now, I love you now.

*colla voce*

*a tempo* *rit.*

D.C.

**2** *ad lib.* *rit.*

On - ly this, I love you now, I love you now, I love you now.

*colla voce* *rit.*

# Darling Nelly Gray

B. R. HANBY

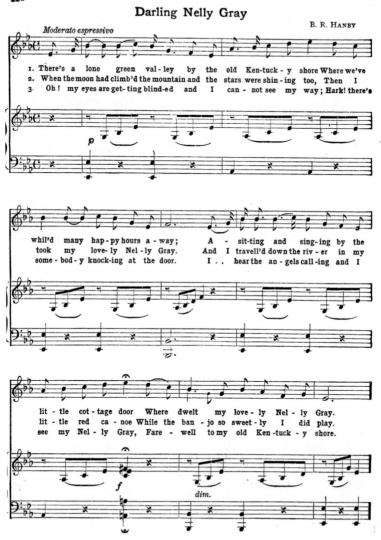

1. There's a lone green val-ley by the old Ken-tuck-y shore Where we've
2. When the moon had climb'd the mountain and the stars were shin-ing too, Then I
3. Oh! my eyes are get-ting blind-ed and I can-not see my way; Hark! there's

whil'd many hap-py hours a-way;     A - sit-ting and sing-ing by the
took my love-ly Nel-ly Gray.     And I travell'd down the riv-er in my
some-bod-y knock-ing at the door.     I .. hear the an-gels call-ing and I

lit - tle cot - tage door     Where dwelt my love - ly Nel - ly Gray.
lit - tle red ca - noe     While the ban - jo so sweet-ly I did play.
see my Nel - ly Gray,     Fare - well to my old Ken -tuck - y shore.

Oh! my poor Nel-ly Gray, they have tak-en you a-way, And I'll
nev-er see my dar-ling an-y more; I am sit-ting by the riv-er and I'm
weep-ing all the day, For you're gone from the old Ken-tuck-y shore.

# Beautiful Dreamer

### Serenade

STEPHEN C. FOSTER
( His last song)

*Moderato*

1. Beau-ti-ful dream-er, wake un-to me, Starlight and dewdrops are waiting for
2. Beau-ti-ful dream-er, out on the sea Mermaids are chanting the wild lore-

thee; . . . . . Sounds of the rude world heard in the day,
lie; . . . . . O-ver the stream-let va-pors are borne,

Lull'd by the moonlight, have all pass'd a - way! . . . . Beau-ti-ful dream-er,
Wait-ing to fade at the bright coming morn. . . . . Beau-ti-ful dream-er,

queen of my song, List while I woo thee with soft mel-o-dy;
beam on my heart, E'en as the morn on the streamlet and sea;

Gone are the cares of life's bu-sy throng, Beau-ti-ful dreamer, a-wake un-to
Then will all clouds of sor-row de-part, Beau-ti-ful dreamer, a-wake un-to

me! . . . . . . Beau-ti-ful dream-er, a-wake un-to me.

*ad lib.*

## Our Baby
### French Folksong

1. Cheeks of rose, Ti-ny toes, Has our lit-tle ba-by;
2. Mouth so fair, Skin so clear, Just as soft as may be;
3. Thee I love, Sweet-est dove, Dar-ling lit-tle ba-by!
4. Crow and play All the day, Hap-py lit-tle ba-by!

Eyes of blue, Fin-gers too, Cun-ning all as may be.
Bon-ny eyes, Look-ing wise, Such a pre-cious ba-by.
While I live, Thee I'll give Kiss-es warm as may be.
May your life, Free from strife, Pure as 'tis to-day be.

# The Old Folks at Home

S. C. Foster

Still   long-ing for de old   plan - ta - tion, And   for   de old folks at   home. .
Oh!    take me  to  my kind  old   mud - der, Dere   let   me live  and  .  die. . .
When  will  I  hear de ban - jo  tum- ming Down  in  my good  old  .  home. .

*First,* SOLO ; *then* CHORUS

All   de world am   sad   and wea - ry,  Eb' - ry- where  I   roam,

Oh !  dark- ies, how my heart grows wea - ry,  Far  from the old folks at home.

# Old Shady

B. R. HANBY

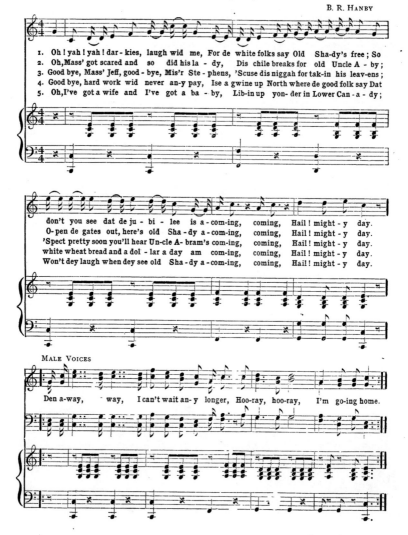

1. Oh! yah! yah! dar-kies, laugh wid me, For de white folks say Old Sha-dy's free; So
2. Oh, Mass' got scared and so did his la - dy, Dis chile breaks for old Uncle A - by;
3. Good bye, Mass' Jeff, good - bye, Mis'r Ste - phens, 'Scuse dis niggah for tak-in his leav-ens;
4. Good bye, hard work wid never an-y pay, Ise a gwine up North where de good folk say Dat
5. Oh, I've got a wife and I've got a ba - by, Lib-in up yon- der in Lower Can - a - dy;

don't you see dat de ju - bi - lee is a-com-ing, coming, Hail! might - y day.
O-pen de gates out, here's old Sha - dy a-com-ing, coming, Hail! might - y day.
'Spect pretty soon you'll hear Un-cle A- bram's com-ing, coming, Hail! might - y day.
white wheat bread and a dol - lar a day am com-ing, coming, Hail! might - y day.
Won't dey laugh when dey see old Sha-dy a-com-ing, coming, Hail! might - y day.

MALE VOICES

Den a-way, way, I can't wait an-y longer, Hoo-ray, hoo-ray, I'm go-ing home.

# Körner's Battle Prayer

KÖRNER                                                   HIMMEL

1. Fa - ther! I bend to Thee, Life, it was Thy gift,
2. Fa - ther! I trust in Thee, When midst the bat - tle's strife,
3. All I give back to Thee! When at Thy call, I my

Thou now canst shield it, From Thee it came, And to Thee I yield it! In
Death did sur-round me, E'en at the can-non's mouth Death has not found me.
life then shall yield, When in the cold tomb My fate shall be seal'd,

life or death, For-sake not me. Fa - ther, I bend to Thee.
Fa-ther,'twas Thy will! I trust in Thee. Fa - ther, still guide Thou me.
Fa - ther, my soul take un - to Thee! Fa - ther, for-sake not me.

# Darby and Joan

F. E. WEATHERLY

J. L. MOLLOY

1. Dar - by dear, we are old and gray, Fif - ty years since our wed-ding-day,
2. Dar - by dear, but my heart was wild When we bur - ied our ba - by child,
3. Hand in hand when our life was May, Hand in hand when our hair is gray,

Shad - ow and sun for ev - 'ry one As the years roll on:
Un - til you whis - pered "Heav'n knows best!" And my heart found rest;
Shad - ow and sun for ev - 'ry one As the years roll on;

Dar - by dear, when the world went wry, Hard and sor - row-ful then was I.
Dar - by dear, 'twas your lov - ing hand Show'd me the way to the bet - ter land;
Hand in hand when the long night-tide Gen - tly cov - ers us side by side:

Ah! lad, how you cheer'd me then. "Things will be bet - ter, sweet wife, a - gain!"
Ah! lad, as you kissed each tear, Life grew bet - ter and heav'n more near:
Ah! lad, though we know not when, Love will be with us for - ev - er then:

Al - ways the same, Dar - by my own, Al - ways the same to your

old wife Joan, Al - ways the same to your old wife Joan.

## Make Me No Gaudy Chaplet

From Donizetti's " Lucrezia Borgia"

Make me no gau - dy chap - let, Weave it of sim - ple flow - ers;

Seek them in low-ly val - lies, Af-ter the gen-tle show - ers. Bring me the dark red

ro - ses, Gay in the sun-shine glow - ing, Bring me the pale moss

rose - bud, Be-neath the fresh leaves growing. Bring not the proud-eyed

MARCELLA SEMBRICH

An Austrian opera singer who particularly endeared herself to American audiences. She was born in Lemberg, Galacia, 1858, and made her first appearance in grand opera at Athens. Her first American appearance was in 1883, and she has since made several American tours. Her popular encore is "Comin' Thro' the Rye"—Heart Songs, p. 113.

EMMA ABBOTT

The noted American opera singer. She was born in Chicago in 1849 and first sang
in public at the age of nine. Clara Louise Kellogg was her friend and patron, and
helped her prepare for her formal debut, made in London, 1878. She died in 1891.
Her popular encore was "Then You'll Remember Me"—Heart Songs, p. 52

blos - som,   Dar - ling of East - ern daugh - ters,   Bring me the snow - y  li - ly,

Floating on si - lent wa - ters.   Gems of the low - ly val - ley, Buds which the leaves are

shad  ing ;   Li - lies of peace - ful wa - ters,   Emblems be mine un - fad - ing.

Li - lies of peace - ful wa - ters,   Emblems be mine, be mine.

# Last Night

HALFDAN KJERULF

1. Last night the night-in-gale woke me, Last night when all was still, It
2. I think of you in the day - time, I dream of you by night, I
3. O think not I can for-get you; I could not, tho' I would! I

sang in the gold - en moon - light, From out .. the wood - land hill. I
- wake, and would you were here, love, And tears . are blinding my sight. I
see you in all a - round me, The stream, the night, the wood, The

o-pen'd my win - dow so gent - ly; I look'd on the dream-ing dew, .. And
hear a low breath in the lime - tree, The wind is float-ing thro', . And
flow'rs that slum - ber so gent - ly, The stars a - bove the blue, .. Oh!

oh! the bird, my dar-ling, Was sing-ing, sing-ing of you, of you.
oh! the night, my dar-ling, Is sigh-ing, sigh-ing for you, for you.
heav'n its - self, my dar-ling, Is pray-ing, pray-ing for you, for you.

*colla voce* $p$

## Lightly Row

Spanish Melody

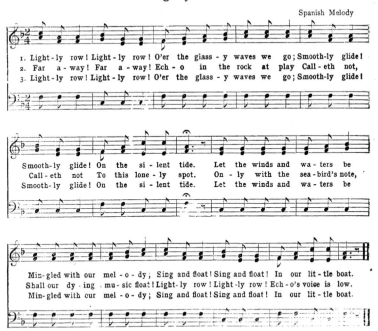

1. Light-ly row! Light-ly row! O'er the glass - y waves we go; Smooth-ly glide!
2. Far a-way! Far a-way! Ech - o in the rock at play Call-eth not,
3. Light-ly row! Light-ly row! O'er the glass - y waves we go; Smooth-ly glide!

Smooth-ly glide! On the si - lent tide. Let the winds and wa-ters be
Call-eth not To this lone - ly spot. On - ly with the sea-bird's note,
Smooth-ly glide! On the si - lent tide. Let the winds and wa-ters be

Min-gled with our mel - o - dy; Sing and float! Sing and float! In our lit - tle boat.
Shall our dy - ing mu - sic float! Light-ly row! Light-ly row! Ech - o's voice is low.
Min-gled with our mel - o - dy; Sing and float! Sing and float! In our lit - tle boat.

# Far Away

Miss M. Lindsay

Mrs. J. W. Bliss

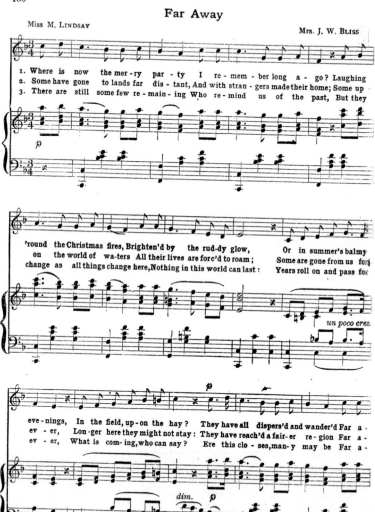

1. Where is now the mer-ry par-ty I re-mem-ber long a-go? Laughing
2. Some have gone to lands far dis-tant, And with stran-gers made their home; Some up
3. There are still some few re-main-ing Who re-mind us of the past, But they

'round the Christmas fires, Brighten'd by the rud-dy glow,
on the world of wa-ters All their lives are forc'd to roam;
change as all things change here, Nothing in this world can last:

Or in summer's balmy
Some are gone from us for
Years roll on and pass for

*un poco cres.*

eve-nings, In the field, up-on the hay? They have all dispers'd and wander'd Far a-
ev-er, Lon-ger here they might not stay: They have reach'd a fair-er re-gion Far a-
ev-er, What is com-ing, who can say? Ere this clo-ses, man-y may be Far a-

*dim.  p*

way, Far a-way; They have all dis-pers'd and wander'd Far a - way, Far a-way.
way, Far a-way; They have reach'd a fair-er re-gion, Far a - way, Far a-way.
way, Far a-way; Ere this clo-ses, man-y may be Far a - way, Far a-way.

## Come, All Ye Faithful

J. READING

1. O come, all ye faith-ful, Joy-ful and tri-um-phant, O come ye, O come ye to
2. Sing al-le-lu-ia, All ye choirs of an-gels; O sing, all ye blissful ones of
3. Yea, Lord, we greet Thee, Born this happy morn-ing; Je-sus, to Thee be the
*Ad - es - te, fi - de - les, Læ - ti tri-um-phan-tes, Ve - ni - te, ve - ni - te in*

Beth - le-hem. Come and be-hold Him, Mon-arch of An-gels! O come,let us a-
Heav'n a-bove. Glo - ry to God In the highest, glo-ry! O come,let us a-
glo - ry giv'n. Word of the Fa-ther,Now in flesh ap-pear-ing, O come,let us a-
*Beth - le hem; Na - tum vi - de - te Regem an-ge - lo - rum! Ve-ni-te, a-do-*

dore Him, O come,let us a-dore Him, O come,let us a-dore Him, Christ the Lord.
*re - mus, Ve-ni - te, a - do-re-mus, Ve-ni - te, a-do-re-mus Do - mi-num.*

132

# Christians, Awake

An old English Christmas Carol

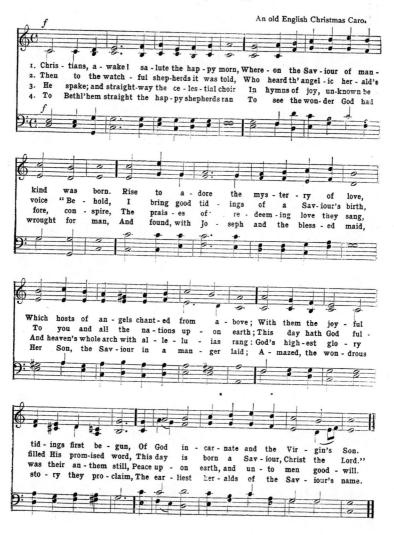

1. Chris - tians, a - wake! sa - lute the hap - py morn, Where - on the Sav - iour of man -
2. Then to the watch - ful shep-herds it was told, Who heard th' angel - ic her - ald's
3. He spake; and straight-way the ce - les - tial choir In hymns of joy, un-known be -
4. To Bethl'hem straight the hap - py shepherds ran To see the won- der God had

kind was born. Rise to a - dore the mys - ter - ry of love,
voice "Be - hold, I bring good tid - ings of a Sav-iour's birth,
fore, con - spire, The prais - es of · re - deem-ing love they sang,
wrought for man, And found, with Jo - seph and the bless - ed maid,

Which hosts of an - gels chant-ed from a - bove; With them the joy - ful
To you and all the na - tions up - on earth; This day hath God ful -
And heaven's whole arch with al - le - lu - ias rang: God's high-est glo - ry
Her Son, the Sav - iour in a man - ger laid; A - mazed, the won - drous

tid - ings first be - gun, Of God in - car - nate and the Vir - gin's Son.
filled His prom-ised word, This day is born a Sav - iour, Christ the Lord."
was their an - them still, Peace up - on earth, and un - to men good - will.
sto - ry they pro - claim, The ear - liest her - alds of the Sav - iour's name.

5 Let us like these good shepherds, then employ
Our grateful voices to proclaim the joy ;
Trace we the Babe, who hath retrieved our loss,
From His poor manger to His bitter cross ;
Treading His steps, assisted by His grace,
Till man's first heavenly state again takes place.

6 Then may we hope, the angelic thrones among,
To sing, redeemed, a glad triumphal song ;
He, that was born upon this joyful day,
Around us all His glory shall display :
Saved by His love, incessant we shall sing
Of angels and of angel-men the King.

## Hush, My Babe

ISAAC WATTS

J. J. ROUSSEAU

1. Hush, my babe, lie still and slum-ber, Ho-ly an-gels guard thy bed,
2. Soft and ea-sy is thy cra-dle, Coarse and hard thy Sav-iour lay:
3. Hush, my child, I did not chide thee,Though my song may seem so hard;

Heav'n-ly bless-ings with-out num-ber, Gent-ly fall-ing on thy head.
When His birth-place was a sta-ble, And his soft-est bed was hay.
'Tis thy moth-er sits be-side thee, And her arms shall be thy guard.

How much bet-ter thou'rt at-tend-ed Than the Son of God could be,
Oh, to tell the won-drous sto-ry, How his foes a-bused their King ;
May'st thou learn to know and fear Him, Love and serve Him all thy days ;

When from heav-en He de-scend-ed, And be-came a child like thee !
How they killed the Lord of glo-ry, Makes me an-gry while I sing.
Then to dwell for-ev-er near Him, Tell His love and sing His praise.

# Roy's Wife of Aldivalloch

# Maggie By My Side

S. C. FOSTER

1. The land of my home is flit - ting, Flit-ting from my view,   A
2. The wind howl - ing o'er the bil - low From the dis - tant lea,   The
3. Storms can ap - pal me nev - er, While her brow is clear,

gale in the sails is sit - ting, Toils the mer - ry crew.   Here let my home be,
storm rag-ing round my pil - low Brings no care to me.   Roll on, ye dark waves,
Fair weather lin - gers ev - er Where her smiles ap - pear.   When sorrow's break-ers

On the wa - ters wide, I roam with a proud heart, Maggie's by my side; My
O'er the trou-bled tide, I heed not your an - ger, Maggie's by my side; My
Round my heart shall hide, Still may I find her, Sit-ting by my side; My

own love, Maggie dear, Sit-ting by my side.    Maggie dear, my own love, Sitting by my side.

## Jordan Am a Hard Road to Trabbel

*Animato con spirito*                                   T. F. BRIGGS

1. I   ri - bed in - to New York,   to   pass de time a - way,   I
2. Den I   look   to de Norf,   and I   look   to de East,   And I
3.   Clem   in de hay-loft,    try'n to get a - sleep,
4. I   went an' made a ban-jo,   so   well I kept it strung,   An'

trabbel'd ober de Russ pav'ent ac - cord-in'.     Dar gawne to hab it fin-ish'd when de
hol - ler for de ox - cart to come on,     Wid four   grey   hor - ses   a
Mas - sa John   went out to maul um,     He hit him on de head   wid a
rang'd   all my mu - sic now ac - cord-in',     I play'd up a tune   call'd

*Repeat this burden in Chorus. forte*

Cit - y  Hall  bell  Sounds o - ber on  de  or - der  side of  Jor - dan.  I
driv - en on  de lead,  To take us  to  de  or - der  side of  Jor - dan.  I
bar  of  soft  soap,  An' it sound-ed  on  de  or - der  side of  Jor - dan.  I
"go it while you're young,"An' dey sing it  on  de  or - der  side of  Jor - dan.  I

took off  my coat,and roll up  my sleeve,  Jor - dan am  a hard road to  trabbel.  I

*Repeat from this sign in Chorus*

took off  my coat,and  roll up  my sleeve,  Jor-dan am  a hard road  to  trab-bel,  I  be - lieve.

138

# Killarney

M. W. BALFE'S Last Song

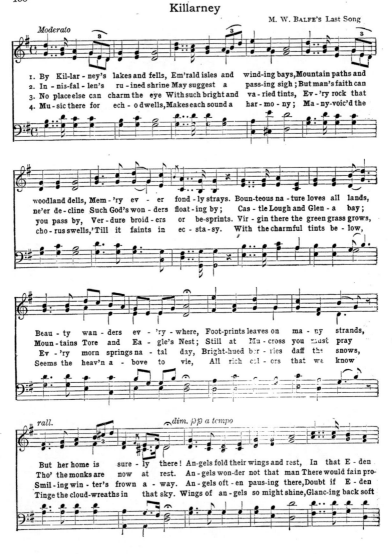

1. By Kil-lar - ney's lakes and fells, Em'rald isles and wind-ing bays, Mountain paths and
2. In - nis-fal - len's ru - ined shrine May suggest a pass-ing sigh ; But man's faith can
3. No place else can charm the eye With such bright and va - ried tints, Ev - 'ry rock that
4. Mu - sic there for ech - o dwells, Makes each sound a har - mo - ny ; Ma - ny-voic'd the

woodland dells, Mem - 'ry ev - er fond - ly strays. Boun-teous na - ture loves all lands,
ne'er de - cline Such God's won - ders float-ing by ; Cas - tle Lough and Glen - a bay;
you pass by, Ver - dure broid - ers or be-sprints. Vir - gin there the green grass grows,
cho - rus swells,'Till it faints in ec - sta - sy. With the charmful tints be - low,

Beau - ty wan - ders ev - 'ry - where, Foot-prints leaves on ma - ny strands,
Moun - tains Tore and Ea - gle's Nest; Still at Mu - cross you must pray
Ev - 'ry morn springs na - tal day, Bright-hued ber - ries daff the snows,
Seems the heav'n a - bove to vie, All rich col - ors that we know

But her home is sure - ly there! An-gels fold their wings and rest, In that E - den
Tho' the monks are now at rest. An-gels won-der not that man There would fain pro-
Smil-ing win - ter's frown a - way. An-gels oft - en paus-ing there,Doubt if E - den
Tinge the cloud-wreaths in that sky. Wings of an - gels so might shine,Glanc-ing back soft

Killarney

*cres.* *f*

of   the West, Beau-ty's home, Kil - lar - ney, Ev - er fair Kil - lar - ney.
long  life's span, Beau-ty's home, Kil - lar - ney, Ev - er fair Kil - lar - ney.
were more fair, Beau-ty's home, Kil - lar - ney, Ev - er fair Kil - lar - ney.
light di - vine, Beau-ty's home, Kil - lar - ney, Ev - er fair Kil - lar - ney.

## Song of the Fowler

From MOZART's " Magic Flute "

1. A  fow - ler bold in me you see, A man of mirth and min-strel - sy; My
2. I  am a fow - ler bold and free, A man of mirth and min-strel - sy; My

name is ev - er in de - mand, With old and young thro'-out the land. I
name is ev - er in de - mand, With old and young thro'-out the land. A -

set my traps, the birds flock round, I whis - tle and they know the sound, For
far from men who delve with spades, Ho! mine's the rar - est of all trades! For

wealth my lot I'd not re - sign, For ev - 'ry bird that flies is mine.
e'en the sweep of moun-tain blast But brings my birds all fly - ing fast.

# O Dear! What Can the Matter Be?

1. O dear! what can the mat - ter be? Dear, dear! what can the mat - ter be?
2. O dear! what can the mat - ter be? Dear, dear! what can the mat - ter be?

O dear! what can the mat - ter be? John - ny's so long at the fair!
O dear! what can the mat - ter be? John - ny's so long at the fair!

He prom - ised to bring me a fair - ing to please me, And then for a
He prom - ised to bring me a bas - ket of po - sies, A gar - land of

kiss, Oh! he vowed he would tease me; He prom - ised to bring me a
lil - ies, a gar - land of ro - ses; A lit - tle straw hat to set

bunch of blue rib - bons To tie up my bon - nie brown hair.
off the blue rib - bons That tie up my bon - nie brown hair.

# Landlord, Fill the Flowing Bowl

1. Come, land-lord, fill the flow-ing bowl, Un - til it doth run o - ver, Come,
2. The man that drinks good whis - ky punch, And goes to bed right mel - low, The
3. The man who drinks cold wa - ter pure, And goes to bed quite so - ber, The
4. But he who drinks just what he likes, And get - teth "half seas o - ver," But
5. The pret - ty girl that gets a kiss, And goes and tells her moth - er, The

land - lord, fill the flow - ing bowl, Un - til it doth run o - ver,
man that drinks good whis - ky punch, And goes to bed right mel - low,
man who drinks cold wa - ter pure, And goes to bed quite so - ber,
he who drinks just what he likes, And get - teth "half seas o - ver,"
pret - ty girl that gets a kiss, And goes and tells her moth - er,

CHORUS

For to-night we'll mer - ry, mer - ry be, For to-night we'll mer - ry, mer - ry be,
Lives as he ought to live, Lives as he ought to live,
Falls as the leaves do fall, Falls as the leaves do fall,
Will live un - til he dies, Will live un - til he dies,
Does a ver - y fool - ish thing, Does a ver - y fool - ish thing,

For to - night we'll mer - ry, mer - ry be, To - mor - row we'll be so - ber.
Lives as he ought to live, And dies a jol - ly fel - low.
Falls as the leaves do fall, So rare - ly in Oc - to - ber.
Will live un - til he dies, per - haps, And then lie down in clo - ver.
Does a ver - y fool - ish thing, And don't de - serve an - oth - er.

## The Danube River

*Tempo di mazurka

HAMILTON AIDE

1. Do you re - call that night in June, Up -
2. Our boat kept meas - ure with its oars, The

on the Dan-ube riv - er? We list-en'd to a Länd - ler tune, We
mu - sic rose in snatches From peas-ants danc - ing on the shore, With

*a little slower*

watch'd the moonbeams quiv-er. I oft since then have watch'd the moon, But
boist' - rous songs and catch -es. I know not why that Länd-ler rang Through

*original time*

nev-er, love, oh, nev - er, nev - er Can I for-get that
all my soul, but nev - er, nev - er Can I for-get the

* To be played in moderate time but with great variation according to the sentiment of the words.

# Sing, Smile, Slumber

### (Canti, Ridi, Dormi)

CHARLES GOUNOD

1. When at twi - light so soft - ly thy voice breaks in - to song,
2. When the smile on thy lip chas - es doubt far from my breast,
3. In the si - lence of night when mine eye vig - il doth keep,
1. Quand tu chan - tes ber - cé - e Le soir en - tre mes bras,

Can'st thou tell . . the sweet mem - 'ries of old that round me throng,
All my gloom . is dis - pelled and for - ev - er in light I rest,
And thy lips . . mur - mur soft - ly of love, e'en in thy sleep,
En - tends tu . . ma pen - sé - e Qui te ré - pond tout bas.

All the dear hap - py days then return to me, hallowed by thee. . . Ah ! . . . then
In thy sweet smile confiding, 'tis in - nocence on - ly I see. . . . Ah ! . . . then
Ah ! the sight of thy beau - ty my soul with rapture doth fill. . . . Ah ! . . . then
Ton doux chant me rap - pel - le les plus beaux de mes jours; . . Ah ! . . . Chan-

*cres.*  *p*

sing, ah ! sing for - ev - er, then sing, ah ! sing to me, Then sing, ah ! sing for -
smile, ah ! smile for - ev - er, then smile, ah ! smile on me, Then smile, ah ! smile for -
slum - ber on, my fair one, ah ! slumber, slum - ber still, Then slum - ber, fair one,
tez, chan - tez, ma bel - le, chan - tez, chan - tez tou - jours, chan - tez, chan - tez, ma

*cres.*

ev - er, sing still to  me.   Ah!  sing  for - ev-er, still  sing  to  me.
ev - er, smile still on  me.   Ah!  smile  for - ev-er, still  smile  on  me.
slum-ber, slum-ber  still,   Then  (*Omit*). . . . . . . . . . . .
*bel-le, chan -tez  tou - jours,   chan - tez,   ma   bel-le,  chan - tez   tou - jours.*

slumber, my   fair one, ah!   slum - ber,   slum - ber   still.

## Good-night

### Male Voices

1. Good - night,  la - dies!   good - night,  la - dies!   Good - night,
2. Fare - well,  la - dies!   fare - well,  la - dies!   Fare - well,
3. Sweet dreams,  la - dies!   sweet dreams,  la - dies!   Sweet dreams,

la - dies!  We're going  to  leave  you  now.   Mer - ri - ly  we  roll a - long,

roll a - long,  roll a - long,  Mer - ri - ly  we  roll  a - long,  O'er  the  dark  blue  sea.

# The Last Rose of Summer

English Air

1. 'Tis the last Rose of Sum-mer left bloom-ing a-lone, All her
2. I'll not leave thee, thou lone one, to pine on the stem; Since the
3. So soon may I fol-low, when friend-ships de-cay, And from

love-ly com-pan-ions are fa—ded and gone. No flow'r of her kin-dred, no
love-ly are sleep-ing, go sleep thou with them; Thus kind-ly I scat-ter thy
love's shin-ing cir-cle, the gems drop a-way! When true hearts lie withered, and

*ad lib.*

rose-bud is nigh . . . To re-flect back her blush-es, or give . . sigh for sigh.
leaves o'er the bed, . . Where thy mates of the gar-den lie scent - less and dead.
fond ones are flown, . O! who would in - hab - it this bleak world a - lone?

# No, Never, No

Written from memory by EDNA DEAN PROCTOR

Old Ballad

1. They sat by the fire-side, his fair daugh-ters three, They talked of their
2. "I'll give him this vest all of sat-in so fine;" "And I'll be his
3. "O did ye not hear it?" the sis-ters de-clare,"There's sure-ly a
4. "It is but the tem-pest that ra-ges so strong; The gale will it-
5. Pre-pare ye, fair maid-ens, pre-pare ye to weep! Your fa-ther lies

fa-ther who sail'd on the sea: "Oh! when he comes back, we will all love him
car-ver when he sits to dine;" "And I'll climb his knee and such kiss-es be-
spir-it that talks in the air; And wheth-er we speak eith-er loud-ly or
self waft our fa-ther a-long; Go look at the vane and see how the winds
cold in the dark-roll-ing deep; Look not at the vane nor ask how the winds

so, . . . He nev-er a-gain to the salt sea shall go. No! nev-er, no!"
stow . . He nev-er a-gain to the salt sea shall go. No! nev-er, no!"
low, . . It an-swers in accents all mournful and slow, 'No! nev-er, no!'"
blow:. . He'll bring us gay things for he promised us so." "No! nev-er, no!"
blow, . . His ghost in the storm whispers mournful and slow: "No! nev-er, no!"

## Jingle, Bells

*Allegro mf*

1. Dash - ing thro' the snow, In a one - horse o - pen sleigh;
2. A day or two a - go I thought I'd take a ride, And
3. Now the ground is white; Go it while you're young;

O'er the fields we go, Laughing all the way; Bells on bob-tail ring
soon Miss Fan - nie Bright Was seat-ed by my side. The horse was lean and lank; Mis-
Take the girls to-night, And sing this sleighing song. Just get a bob-tail'd bay, Two-

Mak-ing spir - its bright; What fun it is to ride and sing A sleighing song to-night!
for-tune seem'd his lot; He got in-to a drift-ed bank, And we, we got up-sot.
for - ty for his speed; Then hitch him to an o-pen sleigh, And crack! you'll take the lead.

CHORUS * *f*

Jin-gle, bells! Jin-gle, bells! Jin-gle all the way! Oh! what fun it is to ride In a

*f*

\* Accompanied by jingling glasses.

one-horse o - pen sleigh! Jin-gle, bells! jin-gle, bells! Jin-gle all the way!

Oh! what fun it is to ride In a one-horse o - pen sleigh!

## Gaily the Troubadour

THOMAS HAYNES BAYLEY

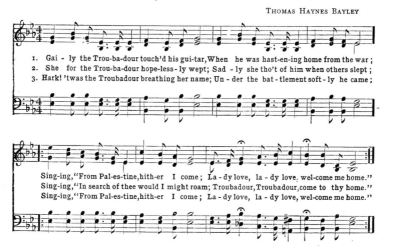

1. Gai - ly the Trou-ba-dour touch'd his gui-tar, When he was hast-en-ing home from the war;
2. She for the Trou-ba-dour hope-less-ly wept; Sad - ly she tho't of him when others slept;
3. Hark! 'twas the Troubadour breathing her name; Un - der the bat - tlement soft - ly he came;

Sing-ing, "From Pal-es-tine, hith-er I come; La - dy love, la - dy love, wel-come me home."
Sing-ing, "In search of thee would I might roam; Troubadour, Troubadour, come to thy home."
Sing-ing, "From Pal-es-tine, hith-er I come; La - dy love, la - dy love, wel-come me home."

# Birds in the Night

Lionel H. Lewin

Arthur S. Sullivan

1. Birds in the night that soft - ly call,
2. Life may be sad for us that wake,

Winds in the night that strange - ly sigh, Come to me, help me,
Sleep, lit - tle bird, and dream not why. Soon is the sleep but

one and all, And murmur, mur-mur, mur-mur, mur-mur ba - by's
God can break, When an - gels whis-per, whis-per, an - gels whis - per

lul - la - by, Lul - la - by, Lul - la - by, . . . . Lul - la -

lul - la  lul - la  lul - la  lul - la - by,  Lul - la - by  ba - by,

While the hours run,  Fair may the day be,  When night is done,

Lul - la - by  ba - by,  While the hours run, Lul - la - by,  Lul - la - by,  Lul - la -

by, . . . .  Lul - la - by,  Lul - la - by. . . . . . . . .

# Kingdom Coming

Words and music by HENRY C. WORK

1. Say, dar-keys, hab you seen de mas-sa, Wid de muff-stash on his face, Go long de road some time dis morn-in', Like he gwine to leab de place? He seen a smoke, way up de rib-ber, Whar de Link-um gum-boats lay; He

2. He six foot one way, two foot tud-der, An' he weigh tree hun-dred pound. His coat so big, he couldn't pay de tail-or, An' it won't go half way round. He drill so much dey call him Cap-'an, An' he get so dref-ful tann'd, I

3. De dar-keys feel so lone-some lib-ing In de log-house on de lawn, Dey move dar tings to mas-sa's par-lor For to keep it while he's gone. Dar's wine an' ci-der in de kit-chen, An' de dar-keys dey'll hab some; I

4. De o-ber-seer he made us trou-ble, An' he dribe us round a spell; We lock him up in de smoke-house cel-lar, Wid de key trown in de well. De whip is lost, de han'-cuff bro-ken, But de mas-sa'll hab his pay. He's

took    his    hat,    an'    lef    ber-ry    sud-den, An'   I   spec he's   run ´   a-way!
spec    he    try    an'    fool    dem    Yan-kees For  to  tink he's  con - tra-band.
spose  dey'll  all    be    con - fis - ca-ted When de Lin - kum  so - jers come.
ole e-nough, big e-nough, ought to know   bet-ter Dan to went an'  run    a-way.

CHORUS

De   mas - sa   run?   ha,   ha!   De   dar - key   stay?   ho,   ho!   It

mus'  be   now   de   king-dom  com-in',  An'  de  year   ob   Ju - bi - lo!

# The Blue Juniata

Mrs. M. D. SULLIVAN

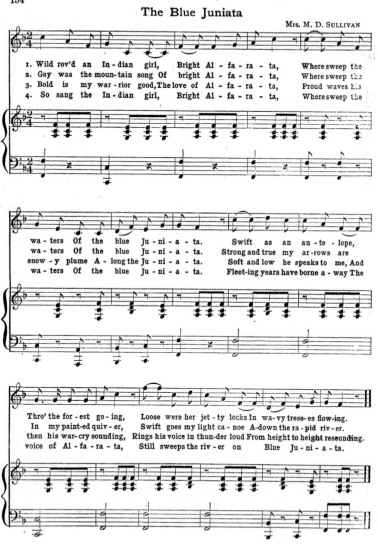

1. Wild rov'd an In - dian girl, Bright Al - fa - ra - ta, Where sweep the
2. Gay was the moun - tain song Of bright Al - fa - ra - ta, Where sweep the
3. Bold is my war - rior good, The love of Al - fa - ra - ta, Proud waves his
4. So sang the In - dian girl, Bright Al - fa - ra - ta, Where sweep the

wa - ters Of the blue Ju - ni - a - ta. Swift as an an - te - lope,
wa - ters Of the blue Ju - ni - a - ta. Strong and true my ar - rows are
snow - y plume A - long the Ju - ni - a - ta. Soft and low he speaks to me, And
wa - ters Of the blue Ju - ni - a - ta. Fleet - ing years have borne a - way The

Thro' the for - est go - ing, Loose were her jet - ty locks In wa - vy tress - es flow - ing.
In my paint - ed quiv - er, Swift goes my light ca - noe A - down the ra - pid riv - er.
then his war - cry sounding, Rings his voice in thun - der loud From height to height resounding.
voice of Al - fa - ra - ta, Still sweeps the riv - er on Blue Ju - ni - a - ta.

# Dutch National Song

Composer Unknown

*Andante*

1. Let him in whom old Dutch blood flows, Un-taint-ed, free and strong; Whose
2. We broth-ers, true un-to a man, Will sing the old song yet; A-

heart for Prince and coun-try glows, Now join us in our song; Let him with us lift
way with him who ev-er can His Prince or land for-get; A hu-man heart glow'd

up his voice, And sing in pa-triot band, The song at which all
in him ne'er, We turn from him our hand, Who cal-lous hears the

hearts re-joice, For Prince and Fa-ther-land, For Prince and Fa-ther-land!
song and pray'r, For Prince and Fa-ther-land, For Prince and Fa-ther-land!

# My Old Dog Tray

S. C. Foster

*Andantino con moto*

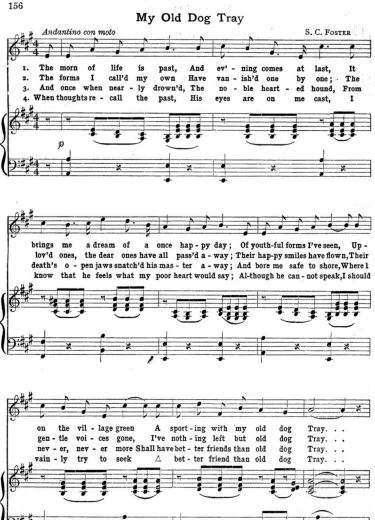

1. The morn of life is past, And ev' - ning comes at last, It
2. The forms I call'd my own Have van - ish'd one by one; The
3. And once when near - ly drown'd, The no - ble heart - ed hound, From
4. When thoughts re - call the past, His eyes are on me cast, I

*p*

brings me a dream of a once hap-py day; Of youth-ful forms I've seen, Up -
lov'd ones, the dear ones have all pass'd a - way; Their hap-py smiles have flown, Their
death's o - pen jaws snatch'd his mas - ter a - way; And bore me safe to shore, Where I
know that he feels what my poor heart would say; Al-though he can-not speak, I should

on the vil - lage green A sport - ing with my old dog Tray. . .
gen - tle voi - ces gone, I've noth - ing left but old dog Tray. . .
nev - er, nev - er more Shall have bet - ter friends than old dog Tray. . .
vain - ly try to seek A bet - ter friend than old dog Tray. . .

Old dog Tray's ev - er faith - ful, Grief can-not drive him a-way, . . He's

gentle, he is kind, I shall never,nev-er find  A bet-ter friend than old dog  Tray. . .

## America

National Hymn

1. My coun-try! 'tis  of thee,Sweet land of lib - er - ty! Of thee I  sing; Land where my
2. My na - tive coun-try! thee, Land of  the no - ble free,Thy name I  love;  I love thy
3. Our Fá-ther's God! to thee, Au-thor of lib - er - ty! To thee we sing; Long may our

fa- thers died,Land of  the pil-grim's pride,From ev -'ry moun-tain side Let  free-dom ring.
rocks  and rills,Thy woods and templed hills,My  heart with rap-ture thrills,Like that a - bove.
land  be bright,With freedom's ho-ly light,Pro- tect  us  by Thy might,Great God,our King.

# Dearest Mae

FRANCIS LYNCH

L. H. V. CROSBY

1. Now dar - kies, list - en to me, a sto - ry I'll re -
2. My Mas - sa gib me a ho - li - day, he said he'd gib me
3. Be - neath de sha - dy old oak - tree, we sat for ma - ny

late, It hap-pen'd in de val - ley of de old Car - li - na State; A-
more, I tank him ber - ry kind - ly, and I push'd my boat from shore; As
hours, As hap - py as de buz - zard bird dat flies a - mong de flow'rs; Oh!

way down in de mead - ows 'twas dere I mow'd de hay, And I
down the rib - ber I glide a - long, wid a heart so light and free, To de
dere's de de - pot where's dear-est Mae, she al - ways looks so sweet, Her

al - ways work de hard - er when I tink ob dear - est Mae. . .
cot - tage ob my dear - est Mae, I lub'd so much to see. . . .
eyes dey spar - kle like de stars, and her lips as red as beet. . .

*p First* SOLO; *then* CHORUS

Oh! dear - est Mae, you're lub - ly as de day, Your eyes so bright dey

shine at night, When de moon am gwan a - way.

# Goodbye, Sweetheart, Goodbye

J. L. HATTON

1. The bright stars fade, the morn is break-ing, The dew-drops pearl each bud and leaf, And I from thee my leave am tak-ing, With bliss too brief, with bliss, . . . with bliss . . . too brief. How sinks my heart with fond a-larms, The tear is hid-ing in mine eye, For time doth tear me

2. The sun is up, the lark is soar-ing, Loud swells the song of chan-ti-cleer, The lev-'ret bounds o'er earth's soft flow'ring, Yet I am here, yet I, . . . yet I . . . am here. For since night's gems from heav'n do fade, And morn to flo-ral lips doth hie, I could not leave thee

*con calore*

from thine arms, Good-bye, sweetheart, good-bye, Good - bye, sweetheart, good-
though I said Good-bye, sweetheart, good-bye, Good - bye, sweetheart, good-

bye, For time doth tear me from thine arms, Good-bye, sweetheart, good-bye.
bye, I could not leave thee though I said Good-bye, sweetheart, good-bye.

*colla voce*

## Heaven is My Home

T. R. TAYLOR A. S. SULLIVAN

1. I'm but a stran-ger here, Heav'n is my home; Earth is a des-ert drear, Heav'n is my home.
2. What tho' the tempest rage, Heav'n is my home; Short is my pil-grimage, Heav'n is my home.
3. There at my Saviour's side, Heav'n is my home; I shall be glo-ri-fied, Heav'n is my home.

Dan - ger and sorrow stand Round me on ev'ry hand, Heav'n is my father-land, Heav'n is my home.
Time's cold and wintry blast Soon will be o-ver-past, I shall reach home at last, Heav'n is my home.
There are the good and blest, Those I lov'd most and best, There, too, I soon shall rest, Heav'n is my home.

# My Old Kentucky Home

S. C. FOSTER

**Rather slow**

1. { The sun shines bright in the old Ken-tuck-y home, 'Tis sum-mer, the dark-ies are gay:
{ The young folks roll on the lit-tle cab-in floor, All mer-ry, all hap-py and bright;

2. { They hunt no more for the pos-sum and the coon, On the mead-ow, the hill and the shore;
{ The day goes by like a shad-ow o'er the heart, With sor-row where all was de-light;

3. { The head must bow and the back will have to bend, Wher-ev-er the dark-ey may go;
{ A few more days for to tote the wea-ry load— No mat-ter, 'twill nev-er be light;

The corn-top's ripe and the meadow's in the bloom, While the birds make music all the day.
By'm-by hard times comes a-knock-ing at the door, Then my (*Omit . . . . . . . . .*)
They sing no more by the glim-mer of the moon, On the bench by the old cab-in door.
The time has come when the dark-ies have to part, Then my (*Omit . . . . . . . . .*)
A few more days, and the trou-ble all will end, In the field where the sugar-canes grow;
A few more days till we tot-ter on the road, Then my (*Omit . . . . . . . . .*)

old Ken-tuck-y home, good-night! Weep no more, my la-dy, O weep no more to-day!

CHORUS

We will sing one song for the old Kentucky home, For the old Kentucky home, far a-way.

# Marching Along

WILLIAM B. BRADBURY

*March movement*

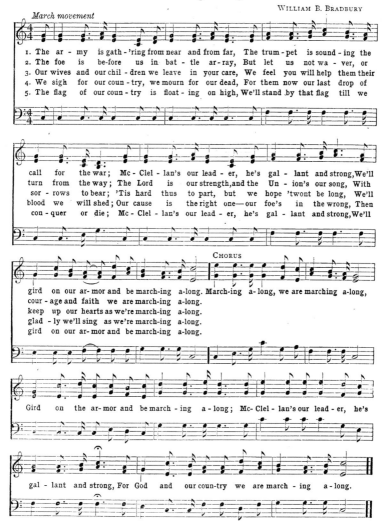

1. The ar - my is gath - 'ring from near and from far, The trum - pet is sound - ing the
2. The foe is be - fore us in bat - tle ar - ray, But let us not wa - ver, or
3. Our wives and our chil - dren we leave in your care, We feel you will help them their
4. We sigh for our coun - try, we mourn for our dead, For them now our last drop of
5. The flag of our coun - try is float - ing on high, We'll stand by that flag till we

call for the war; Mc - Clel - lan's our lead - er, he's gal - lant and strong, We'll
turn from the way; The Lord is our strength, and the Un - ion's our song, With
sor - rows to bear; 'Tis hard thus to part, but we hope 'twont be long, We'll
blood we will shed; Our cause is the right one—our foe's in the wrong, Then
con - quer or die; Mc - Clel - lan's our lead - er, he's gal - lant and strong, We'll

CHORUS

gird on our ar - mor and be march - ing a-long. March-ing a-long, we are marching a-long,
cour - age and faith we are march - ing a-long.
keep up our hearts as we're march - ing a-long.
glad - ly we'll sing as we're march - ing a-long.
gird on our ar - mor and be march - ing a-long.

Gird on the ar - mor and be march - ing a - long; Mc - Clel - lan's our lead - er, he's

gal - lant and strong, For God and our coun - try we are march - ing a - long.

# Carry Me Back to Old Virginny

JAMES BLAND

Moderato

1. Car-ry me back to old Vir-ginny, There's where the cotton and the corn and tatoes grow,
2. Car-ry me back to old Vir-ginny, There let me live till I wither and de-cay,

There's where the birds war-ble sweet in the spring-time, There's where the old dar-key's
Long by the old Dis-mal Swamp have I wan-dered, There's where this old dar-key's

heart am long'd to go, There's where I la-bored so hard for old Mas-sa,
life will pass a-way. Mas-sa and Mis-sis have long gone be-fore me,

Day af-ter day in the field of yel-low corn, No place on earth do I
Soon we will meet on that bright and gold-en shore, There we'll be hap-py and

Used by arrangement with the OLIVER DITSON COMPANY, owners of the copyright.

love more sin-cere-ly Than old Vir-gin-ny, the state where I was born.
free from all sor-row, There's where we'll meet and we'll nev-er part no more.

CHORUS
SOPRANO AND ALTO

Car-ry me back to old Vir-gin-ny, There's where the cot-ton and the

TENOR AND BASS

corn and ta-toes grow, There's where the birds war-ble

sweet in the spring-time, There's where this old dar-key's heart has long'd to go.

# Dixie

Adapted by COLLIN COE

DAN EMMET

1. I wish I was in de land ob cot-ton, Old times dar am not for-got-ten, Look a-
2. Old Mis-sus mar-ry "Will de Wea-ber," Willium was a gay de-ceab-er; Look a-
3. His face was sharp as a butcher's clea-ber, But dat did not seem to greab 'er; Look a-

way! Look a-way! Look away! Dixie Land. In Dix-ie Land whar I was born in,
way! Look a-way! Look away! Dixie Land. But when he put his arm a-round 'er, He
way! Look a-way! Look away! Dixie Land. Old Mis-sus acted de fool-ish part, And

Ear-ly on one frost-y mornin', Look a-way! Look a-way! Look a-way! Dixie Land.
smiled as fierce as a for-ty-pounder, Look a-way! Look a-way! Look a-way! Dixie Land.
died for a man dat broke her heart, Look a-way! Look a-way! Look a-way! Dixie Land.

Den I wish I was in Dix-ie, Hoo-ray! Hoo-ray! In Dix-ie Land I'll take my stand, To lib and die in Dix-ie, A-way, A-way, A-way down south in Dix-ie, A-way, A-way, A-way down south in Dix-ie.

4 Now here's a health to the next old Missus,
  An all de gals dat want to kiss us;
      Look away! etc.
  But if you want to drive 'way sorrow,
  Come and hear dis song to-morrow,
      Look away! etc.
      Cho.  Den I wish I was in Dixie, etc.

5 Dar's buckwheat cakes an' Ingun' batter,
  Makes you fat or a little fatter;
      Look away! etc.
  Den hoe it down and scratch your grabble,
  To Dixie's land I'm bound to trabble,
      Look away! etc.
      Cho.  Den I wish I was in Dixie, etc.

# Italian National Hymn.

*Canto.*

1. All for-ward! All for-ward! All for-ward to bat-tle! The trumpets are
2. All for-ward! All for-ward! Al. for-ward for Freedom! I_ ter-ri-ble
3. All for-ward! All for-ward! All forward to conquer! Where free hearts are

cry-ing, All for-ward! All for-ward! Our own flag is fly-ing. When lib-er-ty
splen-dor She comes to the loy-al who die to de-fend her; Her stars and her
beat-ing, Death to the cow-ard who dreams of re-treat-ing! Lib-er-ty

calls us we lin-ger no lon-ger; Reb-els, come on! tho' a thou-sand to one!
stripes o'er the wild wave of bat-tle Shall float in the heavens to wel-come us on. All
calls us from mountain and val-ley; Wav-ing her ban-ner, she leads to the fight.

Lib-er-ty! Lib-er-ty! death-less and glo-rious, Un-der thy ban-ner thy
for-ward! to glo-ry, though life-blood is pouring, Where bright swords are flashing, and
For-ward! all for-ward! the trum-pets are cry-ing; The drum beats to arms, our old

sons are vic-to-rious, Free souls are val-iant, and strong arms are stronger.
can-ons are roar-ing, Wel-come to death in the bul-let's quick rat-tle,
flag, it is fly-ing; Stout hearts and strong hands a-round it shall ral-ly,

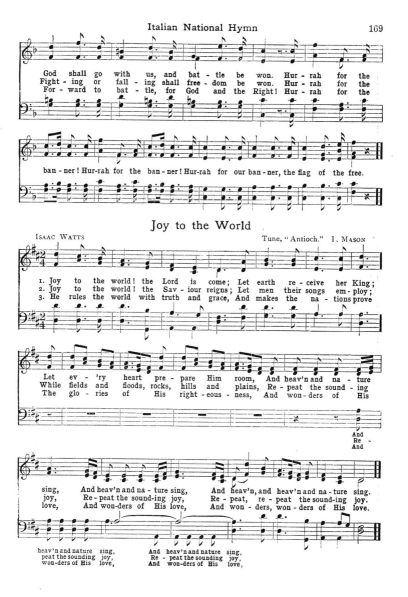

God shall go with us, and bat - tle be won. Hur - rah for the
Fight - ing or fall - ing shall free - dom be won. Hur - rah for the
For - ward to bat - tle, for God and the Right! Hur - rah for the

ban - ner! Hur-rah for the ban - ner! Hur-rah for our ban - ner, the flag of the free.

## Joy to the World

Isaac Watts

Tune, "Antioch." L. Mason

1. Joy to the world! the Lord is come; Let earth re - ceive her King;
2. Joy to the world! the Sav - iour reigns; Let men their songs em - ploy;
3. He rules the world with truth and grace, And makes the na - tions prove

Let ev - 'ry heart pre - pare Him room, And heav'n and na - ture
While fields and floods, rocks, hills and plains, Re - peat the sound - ing
The glo - ries of His right - eous - ness, And won - ders of His

And
Re -
And

sing, And heav'n and na - ture sing, And heav'n, and heav'n and na - ture sing.
joy, Re - peat the sound-ing joy, Re - peat, re - peat the sound-ing joy.
love, And won - ders of His love, And won - ders, won - ders of His love.

heav'n and nature sing, And heav'n and nature sing,
peat the sounding joy, Re - peat the sounding joy,
won-ders of His love, And won-ders of His love,

# I'm a Pilgrim

M. S. B. SHINDLER.

Italian Melody

*Allegretto con amour*

1. I'm a pil-grim, and I'm a stran-ger, I can tar-ry, I can tar-ry but a night;
2. There the sun-beams are ev-er shin-ing, I am long-ing, I am long-ing for the sight;
3. Of that coun-try to which I'm go-ing, My Re-deem-er, my Re-deem-er is the light;

I'm a pil-grim, and I'm a stran-ger, I can
There the sun-beams are ev-er shin-ing, I am
Of that coun-try to which I'm go-ing, My Re-

tar-ry, I can tar-ry but a night; Do not de-tain me, for I am
long-ing, I am long-ing for the sight! With-in a coun-try, unknown and
deem-er, my Re-deem-er is the light; There no sor-row, nor an-y

go - ing    To where the stream-lets    are ev - er   flow - ing.   I'm  a
drear - y,   I have been wandering,      for-lorn and   wea - ry.    I'm  a
sigh - ing,  Nor an - y  sin there,      nor an - y    dy - ing.     I'm  a

pil - grim, and I'm a  stran-ger,   I can tar-ry, I can tar-ry but a night.

## Cradle Song

C. M. von Weber

*Moderato*

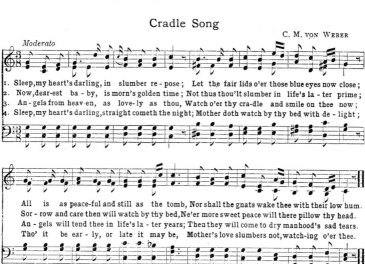

1. Sleep, my heart's darling, in  slumber re - pose;   Let the fair lids o'er those blue eyes now close;
2. Now, dear-est ba - by,  is morn's golden time;  Not thus thou'lt slumber in  life's la - ter prime;
3. An - gels from heav-en, as  love-ly as  thou,  Watch o'er thy cra-dle  and smile on thee now;
4. Sleep, my heart's darling, straight cometh the night; Mother doth watch by thy bed with de - light;

All  is  as peace-ful and still as  the  tomb, Nor shall the gnats wake thee with their low hum.
Sor - row and care then will watch by thy bed, Ne'er more sweet peace will there pillow thy head.
An - gels will tend thee in life's la - ter years; Then they will come to dry manhood's sad tears.
Tho'  it  be ear-ly, or  late it may be, Mother's love slumbers not, watch-ing o'er thee.

## Oh! Susanna

*Allegretto*

1. I came from A - la - ba - ma, Wid my ban - jo on my knee, I'm
2. I jumped a - board de tel - e - graph, And trab - bled down de riber, De
3. I had a dream de od - der night When eb - 'ry ting was still, I
4. I soon will be in New Or - leans, And den I'll look all round, And

gwyne to Loui - si - a - na, My true love for to see; It
lec - tric fiu - id mag - ni - fied, And killed five hun - dred nigger. De
thought I saw Su - san - na A - - com - ing down de hill; The
when I find Su - san - na, I will fall up - on de ground. And

rained all night the day I left, The weath - er it was dry, The
bull - gine bust, de horse run off, I real - y thought I'd die; I
buck-wheat cake was in her mouth, The tear was in her eye; Says
if I do not find her, Dis dar - kie'l sure - ly die, And

sun so hot I froze to death, Su - san- na, don't you cry.
shut my eyes to hold my breath, Su - san- na, don't you cry.
I, "I'm com - ing from de south, Su - san- na, don't you cry."
when I'm dead and bur - i - ed, Su - san- na, don't you cry.

CHORUS.

Oh! Su - san - na, Oh don't you cry for me, I've

come from A - la - ba - ma Wid my ban - jo on my knee.

# Old Dan Tucker

**Allegro**

1. I come to town de ud - der night, I hear de noise an saw de fight, De watch - man was a run - nin roun, Cry - in "Old . . . Dan . . Tuck - er's come to . . . town," So
2. Old Dan he went down to de mill, To get some meal to put in the swill; The mil - ler he swore by the point of his knife He nev - er . . . seed such a man in his life! So
3. Ole Dan and I we did fall out And what you tink it was a - bout? He tread on my corn; I kick him on the shin And dat's . the . . way dis row be - gin! So
4. Ole Dan be - gun in ear - ly life To play de ban - jo and de fife; He play de nig - gers all to sleep An den . . in - to his bunk he creep. So
5. And now Ole Dan is a gone suck-er And neb - ber can go home to sup - per; Ole Dan he has had his last ride And de Ban - jo's bur - ied by his side. So

get out de way, Ole Dan Tuck - er, get out de way, Ole Dan Tuck - er

get out de way, Ole Dan Tuck - er, You're too late to come to sup - per.

## Adieu! 'Tis Love's Last Greeting

SCHUBERT

1. A - dieu! 'tis love's last greet - ing, The part - ing hour is come! And fast thy soul is
2. A - dieu! go thou be - fore me, To join the ser - aph throng! A se - cret sense comes

fleet - ing, To seek its star - ry home! Yet dare I mourn when Heaven Has bid thy soul be
o'er me, I tar - ry here not long! A - dieu! there comes a morrow, To ev - 'ry day of

free; A life of bliss has giv - en For - ev - er - more to thee! Yet ev - er - more to thee!
pain! On earth we part in sor - row, To meet in bliss a - gain! A - meet in bliss a - gain!

# The Kerry Dance

J. L. MOLLOY

And the Ker - ry pi - per's tun - ing Made us long with wild de - light:
Ah! the mer - ry - heart - ed laugh - ter Ring - ing through the hap - py glen!
And the Ker - ry pi - per's tun - ing Made us long with wild de - light:

*rit.*

Oh, to think of it, Oh, to dream of it, fills my heart with tears!

*piu lento*

3. Time goes on, and the hap - py years are dead, And one by one the mer - ry hearts are

fled; Si - lent now is the wild and lone - ly glen, Where the bright  laugh will

D.C.

ech - o    ne'er a-gain, On - ly dreaming of days gone by, in my heart I hear,

D.C.

## Castanets are Sounding

Spanish "La Cachuca"

*Allegretto*

1. Come, O come! Cas-ta - nets are gai - ly sound-ing; Light feet to their notes are
2. Day is past: Stars now bright-ly beam a - bove us, Hearts are near that fond - ly

bound-ing;   Mer - ry dance and joy-ous song Glad-den now that hap - py throng.
love us;   Sweet gui - tar and man - do - lin Give new pleas-ure to the scene.

Nev - er, nev - er yet did mu - sic's meas - ure Bear such thrill-ing notes of
Come, then come! nev-er yet did mu - sic's meas - ure Bear such thrill-ing notes of

pleasure; Hearts and eyes are filled with glee, And gay - est of the gay we'll be.

# Bonnie

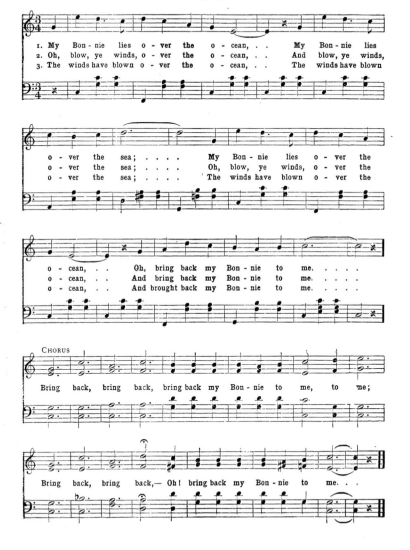

1. My Bon - nie lies o - ver the o - cean, . . My Bon - nie lies
2. Oh, blow, ye winds, o - ver the o - cean, . . And blow, ye winds,
3. The winds have blown o - ver the o - cean, . . The winds have blown

o - ver the sea; . . . . My Bon - nie lies o - ver the
o - ver the sea; . . . . Oh, blow, ye winds, o - ver the
o - ver the sea; . . . . The winds have blown o - ver the

o - cean, . . Oh, bring back my Bon - nie to me. . . . .
o - cean, . . And bring back my Bon - nie to me. . . . .
o - cean, . . And brought back my Bon - nie to me. . . . .

CHORUS

Bring back, bring back, bring back my Bon - nie to me, to me;

Bring back, bring back,— Oh! bring back my Bon - nie to me. . .

## See-Saw Waltz Song

A. G. Crowe

See - saw, see - saw, now we're up or down, See-saw, see - saw, Now we're

off to Lon-don Town. See - saw, see - saw, Boys and girls come out and play, See - saw,

see - saw, On this our hol - i - day. 1. There's Pol-ly and John-ny and Kit-ty and
2. Then come, boys and girls, and all join hands a -

Jane, All run-ning to get on the See-saw a - gain, But Bob-by and Sai-ly al -
round, And mer - ri - ly skip with de - light o'er the ground, Such frol - ic-some games ne'er be -

read-y are there, And swinging the See-saw up high in the air. Ha! ha, ha, ha, ha,
fore have been seen, As we'll have to - day on the old village green. Ha! ha, ha, ha, ha,

See-Saw Waltz Song

ha, ha, ha, ha, What fun! Ha! ha, ha, ha, ha, ha, ha, ha, ha, What fun!

## Angelic Songs are Swelling

Rev. F. W. Faber

J. M. Armstrong, arr.

1. Hark! hark! my soul, an - gel - ic songs are swell - ing O'er earth's green fields and
2. On - ward we go, for still we hear them sing - ing, "Come, wea - ry souls, for
3. Far, far a - way, like bells at eve - ning peal - ing, The voice of Je - sus
4. Rest comes at length; tho' life be long and drear - y, The day must dawn, and
5. An - gels, sing on! your faith-ful watch - es keep - ing; Sing us sweet frag - ments

o-cean's wave beat shore. How sweet the truth those bless-ed strains are tell - ing
Je - sus bids you come!" And, through the dark, its ech - oes sweet-ly ring - ing,
sounds o'er land and sea; And la - den souls by thousands meek-ly steal - ing,
darksome night be past; All jour - neys end in wel-come to the wea - ry,
of the songs a - bove; Till morn-ing's joy shall end the night of weep - ing,

*dim.*                                   Chorus

Of that new life when sin shall be no more. An - gels of Je - sus,
The mu - sic of the gos - pel leads us home
Kind Shep-herd, turn their wea - ry steps to thee.
And heav'n, the heart's true home, will come at last.
And life's long shad - ows break in cloud - less sky.

*rall.*

An - gels of light, Sing - ing to wel - come the pil - grims of the night.

# Good-Night, Farewell

F. KÜCKEN

1. Good-night, fare-well, my own true heart, A thou-sand times good-night; . . . . Each thought of thee bids grief de-part, And ren-ders joy more bright: Tho' far, thy im-age

2. I see thy heart re-flect-ed by A star with-in the stream; . . . It shines forth from thy clear blue eye, And sheds o'er me its beams: And though no more than

dark - 'ning clouds I see, Thy love . . guides me a - far.
heart will e'er en - trance, And ren - der ev - er blest.

Fare - well, . . . . . my own true heart, A .

thou - sand times fare - well! Good - night, fare - well, my

own true heart. . . . .

## Ah! So Pure

From Flotow's "Martha"

# Ah! So Pure

gloom. Woe! she fled, Quick-ly sped All my joy in fleet-ing gleams; As I

wake, Hopes for-sake, Rob-bing me of god - like dreams, of god - like dreams. . .

*pp*

Ah! so pure, Ah! so bright Burst her beau-ty on my sight, Oh! so mild, so di-

*ad lib.* *piu animato*

vine, She beguil'd this heart of mine. Mar - tha, Martha! Thou has ta-ken ev - 'ry

*colla voce.*

Lauriger Horatius

*Pitch in B♭ when possible*   Male Voices

1. Lau - ri - ger  Ho - ra - ti - us,  Quam dix - is - ti  ve - rum!  Fu - git Eu - ro
2. Cre - scit u - va mol - li - ter  Et  pu - el - la  cre - scit,  Sed  po - e - ta
3. Quid  ju - vat  æ - ter - ni - tas  No - mi - nis,  a - ma - re  Ni - si  ter - ræ

ci - ti - us,  Tem - pus e - dax  re - rum!  U - bi sunt  O poc - u - la,
tur - pi - ter  Si - ti - ens  ca - ne - scit.
fi - li - as  Li - cet, et  po - ta - re!

CHORUS

Dul - ci - o - ra  mel - le,  Rix - æ, pax et  os - cu - la,  Ru - ben - tis  pu - el - læ.

# The Enchanted Isle

From Verdi's "Hernani"

*Allegro con brio*

1. The morn is fair, our hearts are light, And mu - sic sings her sweet-est lay; The
2. The air is calm, the sky is clear, That bends a - bove that is - land fair; And

lake is sleep - ing calm and bright, Come, let us a - way; We'll ply the
si - ren mu - sic there we hear, Our hearts to en - snare. The flow'rs may

oar, and o - ver the sea Our boat will bear us hap - py and free, And seek a -
bloom, but soon de - cay; The songs be sweet, yet seem to say, "Be - ware the

far the flower - y isle To rest our oar where ro - ses smile; And seek a -
false, de - lu - sive smile That lights up life's en - chant - ed isle; Be - ware the

far the flower - y isle To rest our oar where ro - ses smile; And seek a -
false, de - lu - sive smile That lights up life's en - chant - ed isle; Be - ware the

far the flower - y isle To rest our oar where ro - ses smile.
false, de - lu - sive smile That lights up life's en - chant - ed isle."

## Jamie's on the Stormy Sea

BERNARD COVERT

1. Ere the twi - light bat was flit - ting, In the sun - set, at her knit - ting,
2. Warm - ly shone the sun - set glowing; Sweet - ly breath'd the young flow'rs blowing;
3. Cur - few bells re - mote - ly ring - ing Min - gled with that sweet voice sing - ing,
4. How could I but list, and lin - ger, To the song, and near the sing - er,

Sang a lone - ly maid - en, sit - ting Un - der - neath her thres - hold tree;
Earth with beau - ty o - ver - flow - ing, Seemed the home of love to be.
And the last red ray seemed cling - ing, Lin - ger - ing - ly to tower and tree;
Sweet - ly woo - ing Heav'n to bring her Ja - mie from the storm - y sea;

And, ere day - light died be - fore us, And the ves - per stars shone o'er us,
As those an - gel tones as - cend - ing, With the scene and sea - son blend - ing,
Near - er as I came, and near - er, Fin - er rose the notes and clear - er!
And while yet her lips did name me, Forth I sprang, my heart o'er - came me;

Fit - ful rose her ten - der cho - rus, "Ja-mie's on the storm - y sea."
Ev - er had the same low end - ing, "Ja-mie's on the storm - y sea."
Oh! 'twas Heaven it - self to hear her, "Ja-mie's on the storm - y sea!"
"Grieve no more, love, I am Ja - mie, Home re - turned to love and thee."

# The Heart Bowed Down

M. W. BALFE

1. The heart bowed down by weight of woe, To
2. The mind, will, in its worst de-spair, Still

weak - est hopes will cling; To thought and im - pulse
pon - der o'er the past, On mo - ments of de -

while they flow, That can no com - fort bring, that can, that
light, that were Too beau - ti - ful .... to last, too beau - ti -

can no com - fort bring, With those ex - ci - ting
ful, too beau-ti- ful to last. To long de - part - ed

LUISA TETRAZZINI

The great Spanish coloratura soprano. She is an Italian by birth. Her first
operatic success was in San Francisco, followed by triumphs in London and Euro-
pean countries. The flute-like qualities of her voice are the marvel of audiences.
Her popular encore is "Bonnie Dundee"—Heart Songs, p. 80.

JESSIE BARTLETT DAVIS

An American contralto who was most successful as Alan-a-Dale in "Robin Hood."
(This photograph shows her in the role.) She was born in Morris, Illinois, the
daughter of well-known musicians. Her professional debut was in 1880, in "Pina-
fore." She died in 1905. Her popular encore was "Robin Adair"—Heart Songs,
p. 288.

scenes will blend,     O'er   pleas - ure's   path - way thrown;     But
years ex-tend         Its    vis - ions     with - them flown,      For

mem - 'ry   is   the   on - ly friend   That   grief   can   call . . .   its

own;       That   grief   can   call   its   own; . .   That

grief   can   call   its   own.       2. The       own.

# Three Fishers Went Sailing

C. KINGSLEY

J. HULLAH

*Andantino*

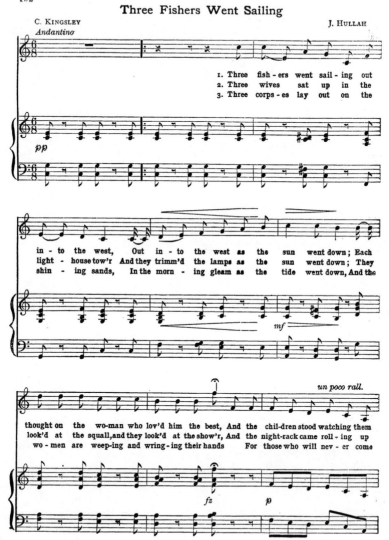

1. Three fish - ers went sail - ing out
2. Three wives sat up in the
3. Three corps - es lay out on the

in - to the west, Out in - to the west as the sun went down; Each
light - house tow'r And they trimm'd the lamps as the sun went down; They
shin - ing sands, In the morn - ing gleam as the tide went down, And the

thought on the wo-man who lov'd him the best, And the chil-dren stood watching them
look'd at the squall, and they look'd at the show'r, And the night-rack came roll - ing up
wo-men are weep-ing and wring-ing their hands For those who will nev - er come

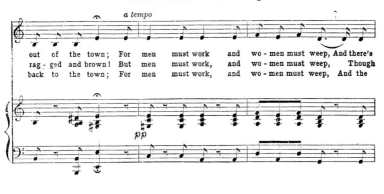

out of the town; For men must work and wo - men must weep, And there's
rag - ged and brown! But men must work, and wo - men must weep, Though
back to the town; For men must work, and wo - men must weep, And the

lit - tle to ea. ... and man - y to keep; Tho' the har - bor bar .. be
storms be sud-den, and wa - ters deep, And the har - bor bar .. be
soon - er it's o - ver, the soon-er to sleep, And good - bye to the bar and its

moan - - - - - - ing. ing.

# The Tar's Farewell

STEPHEN ADAMS

*Moderato con energia*

1. When forced to bid fare-well to Loo, Pull a-way, my boys, pull a-way, I did not know what I should do, pull a-way, pull a-way, I left her weep-ing on the quay, She said she would be true to me, As we sailed a-way to the south-ern sea, Pull a-way, my boys, pull a-

2. But then, if false should prove my fair, Pull a-way, my boys, pull a-way, I'd burn this lit-tle lock of hair, pull a-way, pull a-way, If she be false and I be free, I'll sail a-gain to the south-ern sea, Where there are plen-ty as good as she, Pull a-way, my boys, pull a-

way,      pull a-way, pull away, pull a - way. . . . . . .      For the   wind must

blow, and the ship must go,   And lov - ing souls must part,      But the ship will

tack and the Tar come back,   To the first love of   his heart,      For the wind must

blow, and the ship must go,   And lov - ing souls must part,      And the ship will

# The Tar's Farewell

tach and the Tar come back, To the first love of his heart, To the first love of his heart. . . To the first love of his heart. . .

# Rocked in the Cradle of the Deep

Mrs. EMMA WILLARD

JOSEPH PHILIP KNIGHT

1. Rocked in the cra-dle of the deep, . . . I lay me down . . . in peace to sleep ; Se-cure I rest up-on the wave, . . For thou, O! Lord, hast pow'r to
2. And such the trust that still were mine . . . Tho' storm-y winds . . . swept o'er the brine, Or tho' the tempest's fiery breath . Rous'd me from sleep to wreck and

save.
death!
I know Thou wilt not slight my call,
In o-cean's cave still safe with Thee,
For Thou dost mark the sparrow's
The germ of im-mortal - i -

fall!
ty;
And calm    and peaceful is my sleep, . . . . .    Rock'd in the cradle of the
And calm    and peaceful is my sleep, . . . . .    Rock'd in the cradle of the

deep,    And calm    and peace-ful is my sleep, . . .

Rock'd in the cra-dle of the deep.    Rock'd in the cra-dle of the deep.

# I Would That My Love

From the German of H. Heine

Felix Mendelssohn

*Allegretto con moto*

1. I would that my love could si - lent - ly flow in a sin - gle word; I'd
2. To thee on their wings, my fair-est, that soul-felt word they would bear, Should's

give it the mer - ry breez - es, They'd waft it a-way in sport, I'd
hear it at ev - 'ry mo - ment, And hear it ev - 'ry-where, Should's

give it the mer - ry breez - es, They'd waft it a-way in sport, a-way in
hear it at ev - 'ry mo - ment, And hear it ev - 'ry-where, and ev - 'ry

sport, a-way in sport, they'd waft it a-way in sport. 3. At night, when thine eye-lids
where, and ev - 'ry - where, and hear it ev - 'ry-where.

slum - ber have closed thine bright heav'nly beams, Still there, my love, it will haunt thee,

e'en in thy deepest dreams, Still there, my love, it will haunt thee, e'en in . . thy deepest

dreams, e'en in thy deep-est, thy deepest dreams, E'en in . . thy deepest, deep - est dreams.

## Sleep, Beloved, Sleep

W. Taubert

*Andantino con moto*

1. Sleep, be - lov - ed, sleep; Round thee watch we keep; List how the rain doth fall,
2. Close thy wea - ry eye; Wind doth rus - tle by; Hare doth lift a list - 'ning ear,
3. Sleep, till morn a - rise In yon az - ure skies; Watch-dog now hath ceased to bark:

How the neighbor's dog doth call: He hath bit - ten some one stray-ing, That's the cause of
As the hun-ter's foot draws near; Coat of green is hun - ter wear-ing But the hare is
Beg - gar hides where all is dark; Lit - tle dove her young is tend-ing Where no hun -ter's

all this bay - ing, Round thee care - ful watch we keep. Sleep, be lov - ed, sleep.
lit - tle car - ing; Hun - ter can - not come him nigh. Close thy wea - ry eye.
foot is wend-ing; Hare is hid in ver - dure deep. Sleep, my dar - ling, sleep.

# Bunker Hill

*Sung at the Dedication of Bunker Hill Monument, June 17, 1843*

JAMES B. TAYLOR

HENRY L. TUCKERMAN

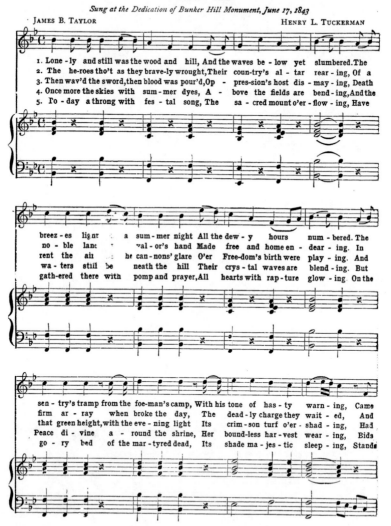

1. Lone - ly and still was the wood and hill, And the waves be - low yet slumbered. The
2. The he - roes tho't as they brave - ly wrought, Their coun - try's al - tar rear - ing, Of a
3. Then wav'd the sword, then blood was pour'd, Op - pres - sion's host dis - may - ing, Death
4. Once more the skies with sum - mer dyes, A - bove the fields are bend - ing, And the
5. To - day a throng with fes - tal song, The sa - cred mount o'er - flow - ing, Have

breez - es light a sum - mer night All the dew - y hours num - bered. The
no - ble land val - or's hand Made free and home en - dear - ing. In
rent the air he can - nons' glare O'er Free - dom's birth were play - ing. And
wa - ters still be neath the hill Their crys - tal waves are blend - ing. But
gath - ered there with pomp and prayer, All hearts with rap - ture glow - ing. On the

sen - try's tramp from the foe - man's camp, With his tone of has - ty warn - ing, Came
firm ar - ray when broke the day, The dead - ly charge they wait - ed, And
that green height, with the eve - ning light Its crim - son turf o'er - shad - ing, Had
Peace di - vine a - round the shrine, Her bound - less har - vest wear - ing, Bids
go - ry bed of the mar - tyred dead, Its shade ma - jes - tic sleep - ing, Stands

low    and    clear    to the yeo-man's ear    As he watch'd the ear - ly    dawn - ing.
side    by    side    in    si - lent pride    With skill    their prow - ess    mat - ed.
ho - ly    grown    as    Free-dom's throne    Like her star - ry    crown un -    fad - ing.
us    pro - claim    to    a death-less fame,    Our    fa - thers' match-less    dar - ing.
Free - dom's pile    in    glo - ry's smile,    E - ter - nal    vig - il    keep - ing.

## Missionary Hymn

Bishop HEBER                                        L. MASON

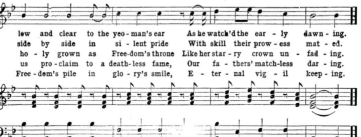

1. From Greenland's i - cy moun-tains, From In - dia's cor - al strand, Where Af - ric's sun - ny
2. What tho' the spi - cy breez - es Blow soft o'er Cey-lon's isle ; Though ev - 'ry pros-pect
3. Waft, waft, ye winds, his sto - ry, And you, ye wa - ters, roll, Till, like a sea of

foun - tains Roll down their gold - en    sand,—From    ma-ny an an-cient riv - er, From
pleas - es    And on - ly man is    vile ;    In    vain with lav - ish kind - ness The
glo - ry,    It spreads from pole to    pole ;    Till    o'er our ran-somed na - ture The

ma-ny a palm - y    plain, They call    us    to    de - liv - er    Their land from er - ror's chain.
gifts of    God are strown ; The hea - then, in his blind-ness, Bows down to wood and stone !
Lamb for    sin - ners slain, Re - deem - er, King, Cre - a - tor, In bliss re-turns to reign !

# Rory O'Moore

S. LOVER

1. Young Ro - ry O - Moore court-ed Kath-leen Bawn, He was bold as a hawk and she
2. "In - deed then," says Kathleen, "don't think of the like, For I half gave a prom-ise to
3. "Arrah, Kathleen, my dar - lint, you've teas'd me enough, And I've thrash'd for your sake Dinny

soft as the dawn, He wish'd in his heart pret - ty Kath-leen to please, And he
Sooth - er - ing Mike; The ground that I walk on, he loves, I'll be bound;" "Faith" say
Grimes and Jim Duff, And I've made my - self drink-ing your health quite a baste, So I

thought the best way to do that was to tease. "Now Ro - ry, be ai - sy," sweet
Ro - ry, "I'd rath - er love you than the ground." "Now Ro - ry, I'll cry, if you
think af - ter that, I may talk to the Priest." Then Ro - ry, the rogue, stole his

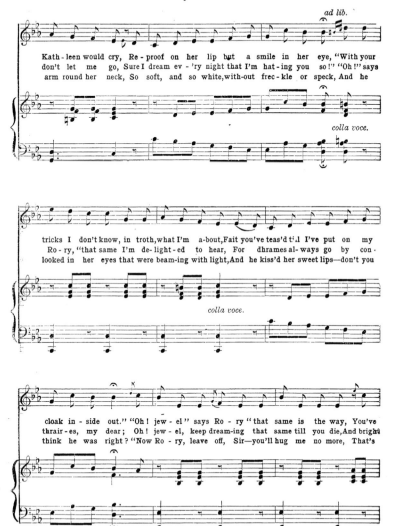

# Rory O'Moore

thrat-ed my heart for this ma - ny a day, And 'tis plaz'd that I am, and why
morn-ing will give dir - ty night the black lie, And 'tis plaz'd that I am, and why
eight times to - day that you've kissed me be-fore;" "Then here goes an - oth - er" says

not to be sure, For 'tis all for good luck" says bold Ro - ry O'- Moore.
not to be sure? Since 'tis all for good luck" says bold Ro - ry O'- Moore.
he "to make sure, For there's luck in odd num-bers," says Ro - ry O'- Moore.

# Sweet Hour of Prayer

W. W. WALFORD

W. B. BRADBURY

1. Sweet hour of prayer! sweet hour of prayer! That calls me from a world of care,
And bids me, at my Fa-ther's throne, Make all my wants and ( *Omit* .) wish-es known.
2. Sweet hour of prayer! sweet hour of prayer! Thy wings shall my pe- ti - tion bear
To Him whose truth and faith- ful- ness En- gage the wait-ing ( *Omit* .) soul to bless:

D.C. *And oft es - caped the tempt-er's snare, By thy re-turn, sweet* (Omit . .) *hour of prayer.*
D.C. *I'll cast on Him my ev - 'ry care, And wait for thee, sweet* (Omit . .) *hour of prayer.*

In sea - sons of dis-tress and grief, My soul has oft - en found re - lief,
And, since He bids me seek His face, Be - lieve His word, and trust His grace,

# Danish National Hymn

*Marziale*

JOHANNES ERALD

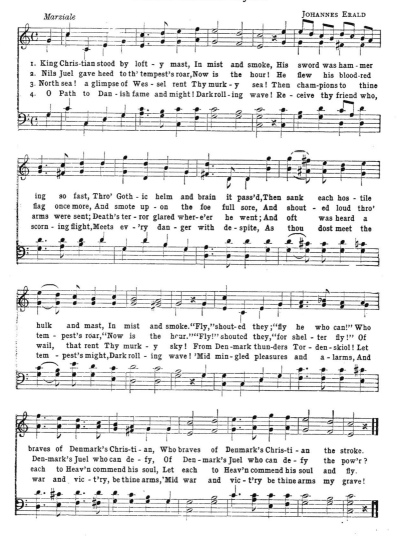

1. King Chris-tian stood by loft - y mast, In mist and smoke, His sword was ham - mer
2. Nils Juel gave heed to th' tempest's roar, Now is the hour! He flew his blood-red
3. North sea! a glimpse of Wes - sel rent Thy murk - y sea! Then cham-pions to thine
4. O Path to Dan - ish fame and might! Dark roll-ing wave! Re - ceive thy friend who,

ing so fast, Thro' Goth - ic helm and brain it pass'd, Then sank each hos - tile
flag once more, And smote up - on the foe full sore, And shout - ed loud thro'
arms were sent; Death's ter - ror glared wher-e'er he went; And oft was heard a
scorn - ing flight, Meets ev - 'ry dan - ger with de - spite, As thou dost meet the

hulk and mast, In mist and smoke. "Fly," shout-ed they; "fly he who can!" Who
tem - pest's roar, "Now is the hour." "Fly!" shouted they, "for shel - ter fly!" Of
wail, that rent Thy murk - y sky! From Den-mark thun-ders Tor - den-skiol! Let
tem - pest's might, Dark roll - ing wave! 'Mid min - gled pleasures and a - larms, And

braves of Denmark's Chris-ti - an, Who braves of Denmark's Chris-ti - an the stroke.
Den-mark's Juel who can de - fy, Of Den - mark's Juel who can de - fy the pow'r?
each to Heav'n commend his soul, Let each to Heav'n commend his soul and fly.
war and vic - t'ry, be thine arms, 'Mid war and vic - t'ry be thine arms my grave!

# Sally Come Up

T. M. SEWELL, arr.

1. Mas - sa's gone de news to hear, An' he has lef' de o - ber-seer To
2. Mon - day night I gave a ball, And I in - vite de nig - gars all; De
3. De fiddle was played by Pom - pey Jones, Un - cle Ned he shook de bones;

look to all de nig - gers here, While I make lub to Sal - ly.
thick, de thin, de short, de tall, But none come to Sal - ly.
Joe he played de pine stick stones, But I made lub to Sal - ly.

*poco piu lento*

She's such a belle, A real dark swell, She dress so slick, and look so well, Dar's

*a tempo*

not a gal like Sal - ly. Sal - ly come up, Sal - ly go down,

Copyright, Underwood & Underwood

**EMMA EAMES**

The eminent American prima donna. She was born in Shanghai, China, in 1867, studied music in Boston and in Paris, and made her debut in the latter city, 1889. Two years later she made tremendous successes at Covent Garden and in New York, and has since been a leading member of American and European opera companies. Her popular encore is "Dixie"—Heart Songs, p. 166.

LILLIAN NORDICA

The beloved American opera singer. She is a New England girl, born in Farming-
ton, Maine, 1859. She studied at the New England Conservatory of Music, later
at Milan, and first appeared in Grand Opera at Brescia. Her popular encore is
"John Anderson, My Jo"—Heart Songs, p. 378.

## Sally Come Up

Sal - ly come twist your heel a-round; De ol' man he's gone down to town, Oh

Sal - ly, come down the mid - dle.

*Interlude ad lib.*

## Little Bo-Peep

J. W. ELLIOTT

*Andante quasi allegretto*

1. Lit - tle Bo - Peep has lost her sheep, And can't tell where to find them;
2. Lit - tle Bo - Peep fell fast a - sleep, And dreamt she heard them bleat - ing;
3. Then up she took her lit - tle crook, De - ter - mined sure to find them;

*cres.*      *f*      *dim.*

Leave them a - lone, and they'll come home, Wag-ging their tails be - hind them.
When she a - woke 'twas all a joke, Ah! cru - el vi-sion so fleet - ing.
What was her joy to be - hold them nigh, Wag-ging their tails be - hind them.

*cres.*      *fz*      *dim.*

## Farewell, My Own

From SULLIVAN's "Pinafore"

RALPH

Fare - well, my own, Light of my life, fare-well!

*Allegretto moderato*

For crime un-known I go to a dun - geon cell.

JOSEPHINE

I will a-tone; In the meantime, fare-well! And all a-

lone Re-joice in your dun - geon cell! . A bone, .. a bone, . I'll

FINE    Sir J. PORTER

FINE

pick with this sai-lor fell ;    Let him be shown at once to his dun - geon cell.

*p* SOPRANO & ALTO.

.He'll hear no   tone   Of the maid - en   he loves   so well !  No   tel - e -
TENOR & BASS

LITTLE BUTTERCUP (*Mysteriously*)

phone Com - mu - ni - cates with   his cell !    But   when   is   known   The

D.S.

se - cret  I have to   tell,    Wide will be thrown The  door  of  his dun - geon cell.

# Old Rosin, the Beau

1. I .. live for the good of my na-tion, And my sons are all grow-ing low, But I hope that my next gen-e-ra-tion Will re-sem-ble old Ros-in, the beau... I've trav-el'd this coun-try all o-ver, And now to the next I will go: For I

2. In the gay round of pleas-ure I've trav-eled, Nor will I be-hind leave a foe; And when my com-pan-ions are jo-vial, They will drink to old Ros-in, the beau... But my life is now drawn to a clos-ing, And all will at last be so: So we'll

3. When I'm dead and laid out on the coun-ter, The peo-ple all mak-ing a show, Just sprin-kle plain whis-key and wa-ter On the corpse of old Ros-in, the beau... I'll have to be bur-ied, I reck-on, And the la-dies will all want to know, And they'll

4. Oh! when to my grave I am go-ing, The chil-dren will all want to go; They'll run to the doors and the win-dows, Say-ing, "There goes old Ros-in, the beau." . . Then pick me out six trust-y fel-lows, And let them all stand in a row, And

5. Then shape me out two lit-tle do-nochs,* Place one at my head and my toe, And do not for-get to scratch on it The name of old Ros-in, the beau... Then let those six trust-y good fel-lows, Oh! let them all stand in a row, And

* Drinking-mugs.

know that good quar-ters a-wait me, | To wel-come old Ros-in, the beau...
take a full bump-er at part-ing, | To the name of old Ros-in, the beau...
lift up the lid of my cof-fin, | Saying,"Here lies old Ros-in, the beau."
dig a big hole in a cir-cle, | And in it toss Ros-in, the beau...
rake down that big bel-lied bot-tle, | And drink to old Ros-in, the beau...

## Old Black Joe

STEPHEN C. FOSTER

*Poco adagio*

1. Gone are the days when my heart was young and gay; Gone are my friends
2. Why do I weep when my heart should feel no pain? 'Why do I sigh
3. Where are the hearts once so hap-py and so free? The chil-dren so dear,

from the cot-ton-fields a-way; Gone from the earth to a bet-ter land, I know,
that my friends come not a-gain, Griev-ing for forms now de-part-ed long a-go?
that I held up-on my knee? Gone to the shore where my soul has longed to go,

CHORUS

I hear their gen-tle voi-ces call-ing,"Old Black Joe."I'm com-ing, I'm com-ing,

For my head is bend-ing low; I hear those gen-tle voi-ces call-ing,"Old Black Joe!"

# The Hazel Dell

G. F. ROOT

1. In the Ha - zel Dell my Nel-ly's sleep - ing, Nel-ly lov'd so long! And my
2. In the Ha - zel Dell my Nel-ly's sleep - ing, Where the flow - ers wave, And the
3. Now I'm wea - ry, friendless and for - sak - en, Watch-ing here a - lone, Nel - ly,

lone - ly, lone - ly watch I'm keep - ing, Nel-ly lost and gone; Here in
si - lent stars are night - ly weep - ing, O'er poor Nel - ly's grave; Hopes that
thou no more will fond - ly cheer me, With thy lov - ing tone; Yet for -

moon - light oft - en we have wan - der'd Thro' the si - lent shade, Now where
once my bos - om fond - ly cher - ish'd Smile no more for me, Ev - 'ry
ev - er shall thy gen - tle im - age In my mem - 'ry dwell, And my

leaf - y branch-es droop-ing down - ward, Lit-tle Nel - ly's laid.
dream of joy, a - las! has per - ish'd, Nel - ly dear, with thee.
tears thy lone - ly grave shall moist - en, Nel - ly dear, fare - well.

Chorus *2nd time* pp

All a - lone my watch I'm keep - ing In the Ha - zel Dell, For my

dar - ling Nel - ly's near me sleep - ing, Nel - ly dear, fare - well.

# The Bowld Sojer Boy

SAMUEL LOVER

1. O, there's not a thrade that's go - ing, Worth show - ing or know - ing Like
2. But when we get the rout, How they pout and they shout, While
3. Then come a - long with me, Gra - ma - chree, and you'll see How

that from glo - ry grow-ing For a bowld so - jer boy! Where right or left we go, Sure you
to the right a - bout, Goes the bowld so - jer boy; 'Tis then that la-dies fair, In de -
hap - py you will be, With your bowld so - jer boy; Faith if you're up to fun, With me

know, friend or foe, Will have the hand or toe From the bowld so - jer boy, There's
spair tear their hair, But the Div'l a one I care, Says the bowld so - jer boy; For the
run, 'twill be done In the snap-ping of a gun, Says the bowld so - jer boy. And 'tis

not a town we march thro' But          la-dies look-ing arch thro' The     win-dow-panes, will
world is  all  be-fore  us, Where the land-la-dies  a-dore  us,  And   ne'er  re-fuse  to
then that with-out scan-dal,  My  -  self will proud-ly dan-dle  The    lit-tle farth-ing

sarch thro'  The  ranks  to   find their  joy,    While  up  the street, each girl  you meet With
score  us,  But  chalk  us   up  with  joy;    We  taste her  tap, we tear her cap, "O
can-dle  Of our  mu-tual  flame, my  joy;    May  his light shine as bright as mine 'Til

look  so  sly  will cry "My eye! Oh,  is-n't he   a  dar-ling, The bowld so-jer boy!"
that's the  chap  for me," says she, "Oh!  is-n't  he   a  dar-ling, The bowld so-jer boy!"
in  the  line  he'll blaze and raise The  glo-ry  of his corps, Like a bowld so-jer boy!

## The Bonnie Banks o' Loch Lomon'

Scotch Folksong

1. By yon bon - nie banks, and by yon bon - nie braes, Where the
2. 'Twas there that we part - ed in yon sha - dy glen, On the
3. The wee bird - ies sing, and the wild flow - ers spring, An' in

sun shines bright on Loch Lo - mon', Where I and my love were
steep, steep side o' Ben Lo - mon', Where in pur - ple hue, the
sun - shine the wa - ters are sleep - in': But the bro - ken heart it

ev - er wont to gae, On the bon - nie, bon - nie banks o' Loch Lo - mon'.
high-land hills we view, An' the moon com - in' oot in the gloam - in'.
kens nae se - cond spring, Tho' the wae - fu' may cease frae' their greet - in'.

First, SOLO; *then* CHORUS
Poco piu mosso

O, you'll tak' the high road, and I'll tak' the low, An'

Poco piu mosso

*First time p, second f*

I'll be in Scot-land a - fore ye; But I and my true love will

*rall.* . . . . . . . . *a tempo.*

nev - er meet a - gain, On the bon-nie, bon-nie banks o' Loch Lo - mon'.

*rall.* . . . . . . . *a tempo*

# The Rose of Alabama

S. S. STEELE

*With spirit*

1. A - way from Mis - sis - sip - pi's vale, Wid my ole hat dar for a sail, I
2. I land - ed on de sand bank, I sat up - on a hol - ler plank, An'
3. Oh, ar - ter d'reck-ly, by an' bye, De moon rose white as Rose's eye, Den
4. De riv - er rolled, de crick - ets sing, De light-nin'-bug he flash'd his wing, And

cross'd up - on a cot - on bale, To Rose ob Al - a - ba - ma.
dare I made the ban - jo twank, For Rose ob Al - a - ba - ma.
like a young coon out so sly, Stole Rose ob Al - a - ba - ma.
like a rope my arms I fling Round Rose ob Al - a - ba - ma.

Oh, brown Ro-sey, The Rose of Al - a - ba-ma, A sweet to-bac-co po-sey Is de

Rose of Al - a - ba - ma,  A sweet to-bac - co  po-sey  Is  de  Rose of Al - a - ba - ma.

## The Hardy Norseman

Norse National Song

*Risoluto f*

1. The har - dy Norseman's home of yore  Was  on  the foam-ing  wave! And there he gathered
2. What tho' our pow'r be  weak-er now  Than it  was wont to  be,  When bold-ly forth our

bright re - nown, The brav - est  of  the  brave. Oh! ne'er should we  for - get our sires, When
fa - thers sail'd, And  conquer'd Nor-man - die!  We still may sing their deeds of fame  In

*cres.*

ev - er we may be;  They brave-ly won  a  gal-lant name And rul'd the stormy  sea.
thrilling har - mo - ny;  For  they did win  a  gal-lant name And rul'd the stormy  sea.

# Who is Sylvia

SHAKESPEARE     *"One of the world's purest vocal gems"*     SCHUBERT

1. Who   is   Syl - via?    What   is   she,   That
2. Is   she   kind, as    she   is   fair?   For
3. Then   to   Syl - via    let   us   sing,   That

all our swains commend   her?     Ho - ly,   fair,   and
beauty lives with kind - ness;     To   her   eyes   love
Syl-via is ex - cel - ling;     She   ex - cels   each

wise   is   she;   The heav'ns such grace did   lend   her,
doth   re - pair,   To   help him of his   blind - ness;
mor - tal thing   Up - on the dull earth dwell - ing;

That a - dor - ed she might
And, be - ing help'd, in - hab - its
To her gar - lands let us

be, That a - dor - ed She might be.
there, And, be - ing help'd, in - hab - its there.
bring, To her gar - lands let us bring.

FINE

## Soldier's Farewell

MALE VOICES

JOHANNA KINKEL

poco riten.

*p Andante*

*p*

*Crescendo e poco accel. al fine*

1. How can I bear to leave thee, One part-ing kiss I give thee; And then what-e'er befalls me,
2. Ne'er more may I be-hold thee, Or to this heart en-fold thee; With spear and pennon glancing,
3. I think of thee with longing, Think thou when tears are thronging, That with my last faint sighing,

*p Tempo 1. Tranquillo e molto espress.*

*f*     *p*     *pp*

I go where honor calls me. Farewell, farewell, my own true love, Farewell, farewell, my own true love.
I see the foe advancing. Farewell, farewell, my own true love, Farewell, farewell, my own true love.
I'll whisper soft when dying. Farewell, farewell, my own true love, Farewell, farewell, my own true love.

# Ever of Thee

George Linley

Foley Hall

1. Ev - er of thee I'm fond - ly dreaming, Thy gen-tle voice my spir-it can cheer;
2. Ev - er of thee, when sad and lone-ly, Wand'ring a - far my soul joy'd to dwell,

Thou wert the star that mild - ly beam-ing, Shone o'er my path when
Ah! then I felt I lov'd thee on - ly All seem'd to fade be -

all was dark and drear.
fore af - fec - tion's spell.

Still in my heart thy form I cher - ish, Ev - 'ry kind thought like a
Years have not-chill'd the love I cher - ish, True as the stars hath my

bird, flies to thee; Ah! nev-er till life and mem-'ry per-ish, Can I for-get how
heart been to thee; Ah! nev-er till life and mem-'ry per-ish, Can I for-get how

dear thou art to me; Morn, noon, and night, Wher-e'er I may be, . .

Fond-ly I'm dream-ing ev-er of thee, Fond-ly I'm dream-ing

ev-er of thee!

# Beautiful Isle of the Sea

GEORGE COOPER                                    J. R. THOMAS

1. Beau - ti - ful isle of the sea! Smile .. on the brow of the
2. Oft ... on your shell-gird-led shore, Eve - ning has found me re -

wa - ters,      Dear .. are your mem'ries to me,
clin - ing,      Vi - - sions of youth dreaming o'er,

Sweet as the songs of your daughters ; O - ver your mountains and vales,
Down where the lighthouse was shin-ing ; Far from the glad-ness you gave,

Down by each murmur-ing riv - er,      Cheer'd by the flow'r-lov-ing
Far ... from all joys worth pos-sess - ing,  Still .. o'er the lone wea-ry

gales, . . . . . . Oh, . . could I wan-der for - ev - er!
wave, . . . . . . Comes, to the wand'rer your bless - ing.

Land . . of the True and the Old, Home . . ev - er dear un - to

me; . . . . . Foun - tain of pleas-ures un - told, . . .

. Beau - ti - ful isle of the sea! Foun - tain of pleas-ures un -

told, ...      Beau - ti - ful, beau - ti - ful isle of the sea!

## Integer Vitæ

HORACE, Ode XXII. Translated by W. N. EAYRS      F. FLEMMING

1. He who is up - right, kind, and free from er - ror, Needs not the aid of arms of men to guard him; Safe - ly he moves, a child to guilt - y ter - rors, Strong in his vir - tues.

2. What tho' he jour - ney o'er the burn - ing des - ert, Or climb a - lone the dread -ful, dan- g'rous moun-tains, Or taste the wa - ters of the famed Hy - das - pes, Gods will at - tend . . him.

3. Place me where fate de - nies to man a dwell - ing, Con - scious of right, all oth - er cares neg - lect - ing; There could I live, thy charms and vir - tues tell - ing, Sweet smil - ing maid - den.

1 Integer vitæ scelerisque purus
  Non eget Mauris jaculis nec arcu
  Nec venenatis gravida sagittis,
      Fusce, pharetra.

2 Sive per Syrtes iter æstuosas
  Sive facturus per inhospitalem
  Caucasum vel quæ loca fabulosus
      Lambit Hydaspes.

3 Pone sub curru nimium propinqui
  Solis in terra domibus negata :
  Dulce ridentem Lalagen amabo,
      Dulce loquentem.

# Dost Thou Love Me, Sister Ruth

Adapted by JOHN PARRY

From HAYDN'S "Surprise Symphony"

1. Dost thou love me, Sis-ter Ruth? Say, say, say! As I fain would speak the truth,
2. Wilt thou prom-ise to be mine, Maid-en fair? Take my hand, my heart is thine,
3. Love like ours can nev-er cloy, Humph! humph! humph! While no jeal-ous fears an-noy,

Yea! yea! yea! Long my heart hath yearn'd for thee, Pret-ty Sis-ter Ruth;
There, there, there. Let us thus the bar-gain seal, O! dear me, high-ho!
Humph! humph! humph! O! how blest we both should be, Hey down, ho down hey!

That has been the case with me, Dear engaging youth!
Lauk! how ver-y odd I feel! O! dear me, high-ho!
I could almost dance with glee, Hey down, ho down hey!

*Rising alternately on their tip-toes.*

# Flee as a Bird

Written and adapted by Mrs. M. S. B. Dana

*Moderato*

1. Flee as a bird to your moun - tain, Thou who art wea - ry of
2. He will protect thee for ev - er, Wipe ev - 'ry fall - ing

sin; . . Go to the clear flow-ing foun - tain, Where you may wash and be
tear; . He will for-sake thee, O nev - er, Shel - tered so ten - der - ly

clean; Fly, for th' aven - ger is near . . thee; Call and the Sav-iour will
there; Haste, then, the hours are fly - ing, Spend not the moments in

hear thee, He on His bo - som will bear . . thee, Thou who art wea - ry of
sigh - ing, Cease from your sor - row and cry - ing, The Sav-iour will wipe ev - 'ry

*un poco ritenuto*

sin, O thou,who art wea - ry of sin.
tear, The Sav- iour will wipe ev -'ry tear.

*colla voce*

## O Paradise

Rev. F. W. FABER                                        JOSEPH BARNBY

1. O Par - a- dise! O  Par - a -dise! Who doth not crave for rest? Who would not seek the
2. O Par - a- dise! O  Par - a -dise. We're looking,waiting here ;  We long  to  be where
3. O Par - a- dise! O  Par - a -dise! We want to sin  no more,  We want  to  be  as
4. Lord Je - sus,Prince of Par - a - dise! Oh,keep us  in Thy love, And guide us to that

CHORUS
Where loy - al hearts and true

hap - py land Where they that loved,are blest? Where loy -      al hearts and true Stand
Je - sus is, To feel, and see Him near.
pure  on earth As  on thy spot-less shore.
hap - py land Of per - fect rest a  bove.

ev - er  in the light, All  rap-ture thro' and thro',In God's most ho - ly sight. A -men.

# Come Home, Father

Words and Music **by** Henry C. Work

1. Fa -ther, dear fa-ther, come home with me now! The clock in the steeple strikes one; You
2. Fa -ther, dear fa-ther, come home with me now! The clock in the steeple strikes two; The
3. Fa -ther, dear fa-ther, come home with me now! The clock in the steeple strikes three; The

said you were com-ing right home from the shop, As soon as your day's work was done. Our
night has grown cold- er, and Ben- ny is worse, But he has been call- ing for you. In-
house is so lone-ly—the hours are so long For poor weeping moth-er and me. Yes,

fire has gone out— our house is all dark—And moth-er's been watch-ing since tea, . . With
deed he is worse—Ma says he will die, Per-haps be-fore morn-ing shall dawn; And
we are a -lone— poor Ben- ny is dead, And gone with the an-gels of light; And

poor broth-er Ben - ny so sick in her arms, And no one to help her but me. . . Come
this is the mes-sage she sent me to bring—"Come quickly, or he will be gone." Come
these were the ver - y last words that he said—"I want to kiss Pa-pa good-night."Come

home! come home! come home! . Please,fa - ther, dear fa - ther, come home. . .

**Chorus**

Hear the sweet voice of the child, . Which the nightwinds re-peat as they roam! . Oh,

## Come Home, Father

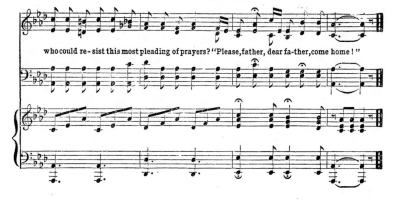

who could re-sist this most pleading of prayers? "Please, father, dear fa-ther, come home!"

## The Three Sailor Boys

THEO. MARZIALS

*Merrily*

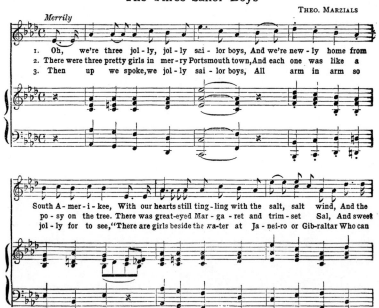

1. Oh, we're three jol-ly, jol-ly sai-lor boys, And we're new-ly home from
2. There were three pretty girls in mer-ry Portsmouth town, And each one was like a
3. Then up we spoke, we jol-ly sai-lor boys, All arm in arm so

South A-mer-i-kee, With our hearts still ting-ling with the salt, salt wind, And the
po-sy on the tree. There was great-eyed Mar-ga-ret and trim-set Sal, And sweet
jol-ly for to see, "There are girls beside the wa-ter at Ja-nei-ro or Gib-raltar Who can

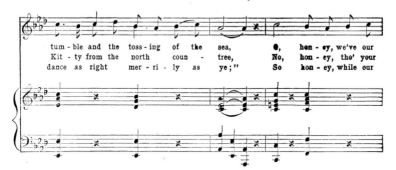

tum - ble and the toss - ing of the sea,　　O, hon - ey, we've our
Kit - ty from the north coun - tree,　　No, hon - ey, tho' your
dance as right mer - ri - ly as ye;"　　So hon - ey, while our

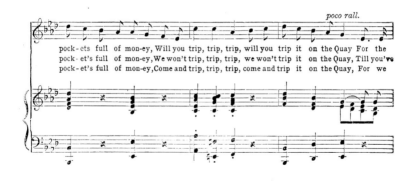

*poco rall.*

pock - ets full of mon - ey, Will you trip, trip, trip, will you trip it on the Quay For the
pock - et's full of mon - ey, We won't trip, trip, trip, we won't trip it on the Quay, Till you've
pock - et's full of mon - ey, Come and trip, trip, trip, come and trip it on the Quay, For we

*a tempo*

wind's in the sail and the thunder in the gale And our good ship plunging to be free.
set the clerk a-singing, and the wedding bells a-ringing, And the parson has pocketed the fee.
sailors love the ocean and the change, and the commotion, And the good ship plunging on the sea.

234

# My Trundle-Bed

J. C. BAKER

1. As I rum-mag'd thro' the at-tic, List-'ning to the fall-ing
2. So I drew it from the re-cess, Where it had re-main'd so
3. As I lis-ten'd, rec-ol-lec tions,That I thought had been for-
4. Then it was with hands so gent-ly Placed up-on my in-fant
5. Years have pass'd, and that dear moth-er Long has mould-er'd 'neath the
6. This she taught me, then she told me Of its im-port,great and

rain, As it pat-ter'd on the shin-gles And a-
long, Hear-ing all the while the mu-sic Of my
got, Came with all the gush of mem-'ry, Rush-ing,
head, That she taught my lips to ut-ter Care-ful-
sod, And I trust her saint-ed spir-it Rev-els
deep— Af-ter which I learned to ut-ter "Now I

gainst the win-dow pane; Peep-ing o-ver chests and box-es,
moth-er's voice in song; As she sung in sweet-est ac-cents,
throng-ing to the spot; And I wan-der'd back to child-hood,
ly the words she said; Nev-er can they be for-got-ten,
in the home of God: But that scene at sum-mer twi-light,
lay me down to sleep:" Then it was with hands up-lift-ed,

Which with dust were thick - ly spread; Saw I in the farth - est cor - ner
What I since have oft - en read— (*Omit.* . . . . . . . . . . . . . . . . )
To those mer - ry days of yore, When I knelt be - side my moth - er,
Deep are they in mem -'ry riven— (*Omit.* . . . . . . . . . . . . . . . . )
Nev - er has from mem -'ry fled, And it comes in all its fresh - ness
And in ac - cents soft and mild, (*Omit.* . . . . . . . . . . . . . . . . )

What was once my trun - dle - bed.
By this bed up - on the floor.
When I see my trun - dle - bed.

2. "Hush, my dear, lie still and slum - ber, Ho - ly an - gels guard thy bed."
4. "Hallowed be Thy name, O Fa - ther! Fa - ther! Thou who art in heaven."
6. That my moth - er asked—"Our Fa - ther! Fa - ther! do Thou bless my child!"

# Tom Bowling

T. DIBDIN

§: *Andante*

1. Here a sheer hulk, lies poor Tom Bow-ling, The dar-ling of our crew, No
2. Tom nev-er from his word de-part-ed, His vir-tues were so rare, His
3. Yet shall poor Tom find pleas-ant weath-er, When He who all com-mands Shall

*p*

more he'll hear the tem-pest howling, For death has broach'd him to. His form was of the
friends were ma-ny and true-heart-ed, His Poll was kind and fair; And then he'd sing so
give, to call life's crew to-geth-er, The word to pipe all hands; Thus Death who kings and

. man-liest beau-ty, His heart was kind and soft, . . Faith-ful be-low he
blithe and jol-ly, Ah! many's the time and oft; . . But mirth is turn'd to
tars dis-patches, In vain Tom's life has doff'd; . For tho' his bod-y's

did his du - ty, And now he's gone a - loft, . . And now he's gone a - loft.
mel - an - cho - ly, For Tom has gone a - loft, . . For Tom has gone a - loft.
un - der hatch-es, His soul has gone a - loft, . . His soul has gone a - loft.

## Pirates' Chorus

*Moderato*                                      BALFE

Ev - er be hap - py and light as thou art, Pride of the Pi-rate's heart!

Long be thy reign, O'er land and main, By the glaive, by the chart, Queen

of the Pirate's heart! Queen! Ev-er be hap- py and light as thou art, Pride of the Pi - rate's

heart! Pride, pride of the Pi - rate's heart! Pride, pride of the Pi - rate's heart.

# The Blue Alsatian Mountains

CLARIBEL

STEPHEN ADAMS

*Not too slow*

1. By the blue Al - sa - tian moun-tains Dwelt a maid - en young and fair, . Like the
2. By the blue Al - sa - tian moun-tains Came a stran - ger in the Spring, And he
3. By the blue Al - sa - tian moun-tains Ma - ny spring-times bloom'd and pass'd, And the

care-less - flow - ing foun-tains Were the rip - ples of her hair, Were the rip - ples
lin-ger'd by the foun-tains Just to hear the maid - en sing, Just to hear the
maid - en by the foun-tains Saw she lost her hopes at last, She lost her

of her hair; An-gel mild her eyes so win - ning, An-gel bright her hap - py smile,
maid - en sing; Just to whis - per in the moonlight, Words the sweetest she had known,
hopes at last. And she with - ered like a flow - er That is wait - ing for the rain;

When be - neath the foun-tains spin - ning, You could hear her song the while. A-
Just to charm a - way the hours, Till her heart was all his own. A-
She will nev - er see the stran-ger, Where the foun-tains fall a - gain. A-

dé, A - dé, A - dé, . . Such songs will pass a - way, Tho' the blue Al - sa - tian
dé, A - dé, A - dé, . . Such dreams may pass a - way, But the blue Al - sa - tian
dé, A - dé, A - dé, . . The years have passed a - way, But the blue Al - sa - tian

CHORUS

moun-tains Seem to watch and wait al - way. A - dé, A - dé, A - dé, Such songs will

[A-day,]

pass a - way, Tho' the blue Al - sa-tian mountains Seem to watch and wait al - way.

## Lulu is Our Darling Pride

Arr. by C. JARVIS

*p A little lively*

1. Lu - lu is our dar - ling pride, Lu - lu bright, Lu - lu gay, Danc-ing light-ly
2. As the flow'rs of ear - ly spring Seem more gay, seem more light, As their per - fume
3. When the clouds of trou - ble come, Lu - lu soothes all our care; Ah! how dark would

FINE

at our side All the live - long day. Not a bird that wings the air,
first they fling Fra - grant at our feet. So tho' oth - ers loved there be,
be our home, Were not Lu - lu there! Lu - lu with her sun - ny smiles,

D.C.

Soar-ing to the sun, Free - er is from ev - 'ry care, Than our dar - ling one. Oh!
Bloom-ing in our bower, Lu - lu wins our hearts, for she Is our loveliest flow'r. Oh!
Cheer-ing ev - 'ry heart, Till each trou - ble she be-guiles, And the clouds de-part. Oh!

# They All Love Jack

F. E. WEATHERLY

STEPHEN ADAMS

1. When the ship is trim and rea-dy, And the jol-ly days are done, When the
2. Where he goes their hearts go with him, E'en his ship he calls her "she;" Up a-
3. When he's sail'd the world all o-ver, And a-gain he steps a-shore, There are

last good-byes are whisper'd, And Jack a-board is gone; The lass-es fall a-
loft that "lit-tle che-rub" Sure a maid-en she must be. And as o'er the sea he
scores of lass-es wait-ing To love him all the more; He may lose his gold-en

weep-ing, As they watch his ves-sel's track, For all the lands-men lov-ers Are
trav-els, The mer-maids down be-low Would give their crys-tal kingdoms For the
gui-neas, But a wife he'll nev-er lack, If he'd wed them all, they'd take him, For they

noth - ing af - ter Jack,        For all  the lands-men lov - ers Are    noth-ing af - ter
love  of Jack, I trow,        Would give their crys - tal kingdoms For the  love  of Jack,  I
all        love    Jack!      If he'd wed them all, they'd take him, For they all, they  all love

Jack.  For his heart  is like the sea.    Ev - er  o - pen, brave, and free,   And the
trow.  For his heart  is like the sea.    Ev - er  o - pen, brave, and free,   And the
Jack!  For his heart  is like the sea,    Ev - er  o - pen, brave, and free,   And the

girls must lonely  be,     Till his ship comes back ; But  if love's the best of   all .  . That

They All Love Jack

can  a man be - fall, . .Why,Jack's the king of  all, . . For they all love  Jack!

## Lorena

Rev. H. D. L. WEBSTER                                   J. P. WEBSTER

1. The years creep slow-ly by, Lo - re - na, The snow is on the grass a - gain, The
2. A hundred months have pass'd,Lo - re - na, Since last  I held that hand in mine, And
3. We loved each oth - er then, Lo - re - na, More than we ev - er dared to  tell; And
4. The sto - ry  of that past, Lo - re - na, A - las!  I care not to re-peat, Tha
5. Yes, these were words of thine,Lo - re - na, They burn with-in  my mem-'ry yet; They
6. It mat-ters lit - tle now, Lo - re - na, The past— is in th' e-ter-nal Past,  Ou

sun's  low down the sky, Lo - re - na,The frost gleams where the flow'rs have been.But the
felt  that pulse beat fast, Lo - re - na,  Tho' mine beat fast - er far than thine.    A
what we might have been.Lo - re - na,  Had but our lov-ings prosper'd well —  But
hopes that could not  last, Lo - re - na,  They lived, but on - ly lived to cheat.   I
touched some tender chords,Lo - re - na, Which thrill and tremble with re · gret.  'Twas
heads  will soon lie  low, Lo - re - na, Life's tide is ebb - ing out so  fast.   There

heart throbs on as warmly now,
hundred months,'twas flow-'ry May,
then, 'tis past—the years are gone,
would not cause e'en one re-gret
not thy woman's heart that spoke;
is a Fu-ture! O thank God,

As when the summer days were nigh;
When up the hill-y slope we climbed,
I'll not call up their shadowy forms;
To ran - kle in your bo - som now;
Thy heart was al-ways true to me;
Of life this is so small a part;

Oh! the
To
I'll
For
A
'Tis

sun can nev-er dip so low,
watch the dy-ing of the day . .
say to them, "lost years, sleep on!
"if we try, we may for-get" .
du - ty stern and press-ing, broke
dust to dust be-neath the sod; .

A-down af - fection's cloud-less sky;
And hear the dis-tant church-bells chimed;
Sleep on! nor heed life's pelt - ing storm;"
Were words of thine long years a - go;
The tie which linked my soul with thee;
But there, up there, tis heart to heart:

The
To
I'll
For
A
'Tis

sun can nev-er dip so low, . . .
watch the dy-ing of the day . . .
say to them, "lost years, sleep on! . . .
"if we try, we may for-get" . . .
du - ty stern and pressing, broke . .
dust to dust be-neath the sod; . . .

A-down af-fec-tion's cloud - less sky.
And hear the dis-tant church - bells chimed.
Sleep on! nor heed life's pelt - ing storm."
Were words of thine long years a - go.
The tie which linked my soul with thee.
But there, up there, 'tis heart to heart.

# I Dreamt That I Dwelt in Marble Halls

From BALFE'S "Bohemian Girl"

1. I dreamt that I dwelt in mar - ble halls, With
   vas - sals and serfs at my side, . . . And of all who as-sem-bled with-in those
   walls That I was the hope and the pride. . . . I had rich-es too great to
   count; could boast Of a high an - ces - tral name; . . . But I al - so

2. I dreamt that suit - ors sought my hand; That
   knights up - on bend - ed knees, . . And with vows no maid-en heart could with-
   stand, They pledg'd their faith to me, . . . And I dreamt that one of that
   no - ble host Came forth my hand to claim; . . . But I al - so

dreamt, which pleas'd me most, That you lov'd me still the same, that you lov'd me, you
dreamt, which charm'd me most, that you lov'd me still the same, that you lov'd me, you

lov'd me still the same, That you lov'd me, you lov'd me, still the same.  same.

## Retreat

H. Stowell                               T. Hastings

1. From ev - 'ry storm-y wind that blows, From ev - 'ry swell-ing tide of woes,
2. There is a place where Je - sus sheds The oil of glad-ness on our heads,
3. There is a scene where spi - rits blend, Where friend holds fel-low-ship with friend;
4. There, there, on ea - gle wings we soar, And sense and sin mo - lest no more,

There is a calm, a sure re-treat; 'Tis found - neath the mer - cy - seat.
A place than all be-sides more sweet; It is blood-bought mer-cy - seat.
Though sundered far, by faith they meet A-round one com-mon mer-cy - seat.
And heav'n comes down our souls to greet, And glo - ry crowns the mer - cy - seat!

# My Mary Anne

M. Tyte

**Moderato**

1. Fare-you-well, my own Ma-ry Anne, Fare-you-well a-while, For the
2. Don't you see that tur-tle dove, Sit-ting on yon pine, La-
3. A lob-ster in a lob-ster pot, A blue fish wrig-gling on a hook, May
4. The pride of all the pro-duce rare, That in the kit-chen gar-den grow'd, Was

ship it is read-y, And the wind it is fair, And I am bound for the
ment-ing the loss of its own true love? And so am I for
suf-fer some, but oh, no, not What I do feel for
pump-kins, but none could com-pare, In an-gel form to

sea, Ma-ry Anne, I am bound for the sea. . .
mine, Ma-ry Anne, So am I for mine. .
my Ma-ry Anne! What I feel for Ma-ry Anne. .
my Ma-ry Anne! Could compare with Ma-ry Anne. .

# Barbara Allen

Old Song

*Andante*

1. In Scar - let town, where I was born, There was a fair maid dwell-in', Made
2. And death is print - ed on his face, And o'er his heart is steal-in', Then
3. When he was dead and in his grave, Her heart was struck with sor - row; "O

ev -'ry youth cry "well - a - way;" Her name was Barb'ra Al - len. All in the mer - ry
haste a - way to com - fort him, O love - ly Bar-b'ra Al - len. So slow-ly, slow - ly
moth-er, moth - er, make my bed, For I shall die to - mor-row. Fare-well," she said, "ye

month of May, When green buds then were swell-in', Young Jem - my Grove on his
she came up, And slow - ly she came nigh him; And all she said, when
vir - gins all, And shun the fault I fell in; Hence - forth take warn - ing

death - bed lay, For love of Bar - b'ra Al - len.
there she came, "Young man, I think you're dy - ing."
by the fall Of cru - el Bar - b'ra Al - len."

*mf*

# Believe Me if All Those Endearing Young Charms

TOM MOORE

1. Be - lieve me if all those en - dearing young charms Which I gaze on so fond - ly to -
2. It is not while beauty and youth are thine own, And thy cheeks unpro-fan'd by a

day, Were to change by to - mor - row, and fleet in my arms, Like fai - ry gifts
tear, That the fer - vor and faith of a soul can be known, To which time will but

fad - ing a - way, . Thou would'st still be a - dor'd, as this mo - ment thou art, Let thy
make thee more dear. . . Oh! the heart that has tru - ly lov'd nev - er for - gets, But as

love - li - ness fade as it will; . . And a - round the dear ru - in each
tru - ly loves on to the close; . . As the sun - flow - er turns on her

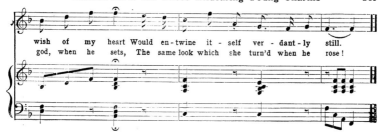

wish   of   my   heart   Would   en - twine   it - self   ver - dant - ly   still.
god,   when   he   sets,   The   same   look   which   she   turn'd   when   he   rose !

## Fair Harvard

1 Fair Harvard! thy sons to thy jubilee throng,
    And with blessings surrender thee o'er,
  By these festival rites, from the age that is past,
    To the age that is waiting before.
  O relic and type of our ancestor's worth,
    That has long kept their memory warm,
  First flower of their wilderness! star of their night,
    Calm rising through change and through storm !

2 To thy bowers we were led in the bloom of our youth,
    From the home of our infantile years,
  When our fathers had warned, and our mothers had prayed,
    And our sisters had blest, through their tears ;
  Thou then wert our parent, the nurse of our souls,
    We were moulded to manhood by thee,
  Till freighted with treasure-thoughts friendships, and hopes,
    Thou did'st launch us on Destiny's sea.

3 Farewell! be thy destinies onward and bright!
    To thy children the lesson still give,
  With freedom to think, and with patience to bear,
    And for right ever bravely to live.
  Let not moss-covered error moor thee at its side,
    As the world on truth's current glides by ;
  Be the herald of light, and the bearer of love,
    Till the stock of the Puritans die.

## The Graduates' Farewell
### W. T. ADAMS

2 How sad mid the sunshine that gladdens this scene,
    Comes the thought that to-day we must part ;
  That the bond which affection has ever kept green
    Must be severed to-day in the heart ;
  That we meet in this home of our childhood no more,
    As we lovingly meet to the last ;
  That we never again on this time-bounded shore
    May unite in the songs of the past !

2 But fondly our thoughts will return to the spot
    On the wings of remembrance borne up ;
  And our hearts shall rejoice, while we cherish the lot
    That permits us to drink of this cup.
  Then farewell to our school, and farewell to the friends
    Who have lighted our pathway with love ;
  Though to-day we must part, yet our prayers will ascend
    That our school be united above !

# Tom-Big-Bee River

S. S. STEELE

1. On Tom-big-bee riv - er so bright I was born, In a hut made eb
2. All de day in de field de soft cot - ton I hoe, I tink ob my

husks ob de tall yal - ler corn, And dar I fust meet wid my Ju - la so
Ju - la an sing as I go; Oh, I catch her a bird, wid a wing ob true

true, An I row'd her a - bout In my gum - tree ca - noe. Sing-ing row a-way,
blue, An at night sail her round In my gum - tree ca - noe.

CHORUS

row, O'er de wa - ters so blue. Like a fea - ther we'll float, In my gum-tree ca-noe.

3 Wid my hands on de banjo and toe on de oar,
   I sing to de sound ob de river's soft roar;
   While de stars dey look down at my Jula so true,
   An' dance in her eye in my gum-tree canoe.
   Singing row away, etc.

4 One night de stream bore us so far away,
   Dat we couldn't cum back, so we thought we'd
      jis stay,
   Oh, we spied a tall ship wid a flag ob true blue,
   An' it took us in tow wid my gum-tree canoe.
   Singing row away, etc.

## Swing Low, Sweet Chariot

Slave Hymn

Swing low, sweet char - i - ot,——Com-ing for to car - ry me home,

Swing low, sweet char - i - ot, Com-ing for to car - ry me home.

1. I looked o - ver Jor - dan, and what did I see, Com-ing for to car - ry me
2. If you get there be - fore I do, Com-ing for to car - ry me
3. The bright - est day that ev - er I saw, Com-ing for to car - ry me
4. I'm some - times up and some - times down. Com-ing for to car - ry me

home? A band of an - gels com-ing af-ter me, Com-ing for to car - ry me home.
home? Tell all my friends I'm com - ing too, Com-ing for to car - ry me home.
home? When Je - sus wash'd my sins a - way, Com-ing for to car - ry me home.
home? But still my soul feels heav-en - ly bound, Com-ing for to car - ry me home.

# Good-Bye

J. C. ENGELBRECHT

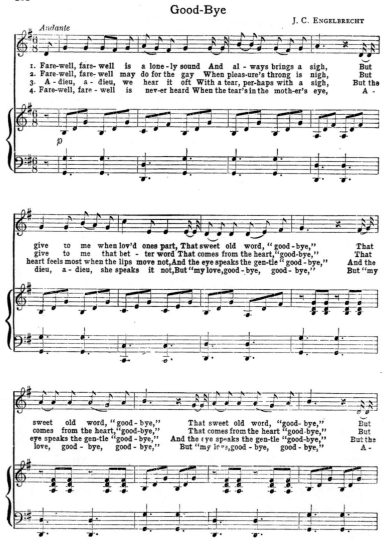

*Andante*

1. Fare-well, fare-well is a lone-ly sound And al - ways brings a sigh, But
2. Fare-well, fare-well may do for the gay When pleas-ure's throng is nigh, But
3. A - dieu, a - dieu, we hear it oft With a tear, per-haps with a sigh, But the
4. Fare-well, fare - well is nev-er heard When the tear's in the moth-er's eye, A -

give to me when lov'd ones part, That sweet old word, " good - bye," That
give to me that bet - ter word That comes from the heart, "good - bye," That
heart feels most when the lips move not, And the eye speaks the gen-tle " good - bye," And the
dieu, a - dieu, she speaks it not, But "my love, good - bye, good - bye," But "my

sweet old word, " good - bye," That sweet old word, "good - bye," But
comes from the heart, "good-bye," That comes from the heart "good-bye," But
eye speaks the gen-tle "good-bye," And the eye speaks the gen-tle "good-bye," But the
love, good - bye, good - bye," But "my love, good - bye, good - bye," A -

# Good-Bye

give to me when lov'd ones part, That good old word "good-bye."
give to me that bet-ter word That comes from the heart,"good-bye."
heart feels most when the lips move not,And the eye speaks the gen-tle "good-bye."
dieu, a-dieu, she speaks it not,But "my love, good-bye, good-bye."

## Ariel

S. MEDLEY

ARR. by L. MASON

1. Oh, could I speak the match-less worth, Oh, could I sound the glo-ries forth,
2. I'd sing the pre-cious blood he spilt, My ran-som from the dread-ful guilt,
3. I'd sing the char-ac-ters he bears, And all the forms of love he wears,
4. Well—the de-light-ful day will come, When my dear Lord will bring me home,

Which in my Sav-iour shine! I'd soar,and touch the heav'nly strings, And vie with Ga-briel,
Of sin and wrath di-vine! I'd sing his glo-rious right-eous-ness, In which all-per-fect
Ex-alt-ed on his throne: In loft-iest songs of sweet-est praise, I would to ev-er-
And I shall see his face: Then with my Sav-iour,Broth-er,Friend, A blest e-ter-ni-

while he sings In notes al-most di-vine, In notes al-most di-vine.
heav'n-ly dress My soul shall ev-er shine, My soul shall ev-er shine.
last-ing days Make all his glo-ries known, Make all his glo-ries known.
ty I'll spend, Tri-um-phant in his grace, Tri-um-phant in his grace.

# I Wandered by the Sea-Beat Shore

J. W. CHERRY

*Moderato con espressione*

1. One sum-mer eve, with pen-sive thought, I wander'd on the sea-beat
2. I stoop'd up-on the peb-bly strand To cull the toys that round me

shore, Where oft in heed - less in-fant sport I gath-er'd shells in days be-
lay, But as I took them in my hand, I threw them one by one a-

fore, I gath-er'd shells in days be-fore. The plash-ing waves like mu-sic
way, I threw them one by one a-way. "Oh! thus," I said, "in ev-'ry

fell, Re-spon-sive to my fan-cy wild, A dream came o'er me like a
stage By toys our fan - cy is be-guil'd, We gath-er shells from youth to

spell,  I thought I  was    a - gain  a  child;   A dream came o'er   me  like a
age,  And then we leave  them like  a  child;   We gath- er shells from youth to

*espressivo*                                    *ad lib.*

spell,   I thought   I    was   a - gain,   a - gain   a   child.
age,  And then   we   leave them, leave   them   like   a   child."

*colla voce*

## The Independent Farmer

W. W. FOSDICK                                          G. F. ROOT

*Allegretto*

Let  sail - ors  sing   of    o - cean deep, Let  sol - diers praise their  ar  -  mor, But

1ST DIVISION

in  my heart this toast I'll keep, The  In - de-pend-ent  Farm - er.   He cares not how the

# The Independent Farmer

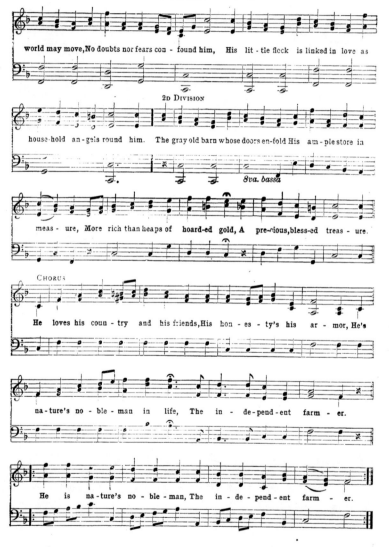

world may move, No doubts nor fears con - found him, His lit - tle flock is linked in love as

**2D DIVISION**

house-hold an - gels round him. The gray old barn whose doors en-fold His am - ple store in

*8va. bassa*

meas - ure, More rich than heaps of hoard-ed gold, A pre-cious, bless-ed treas - ure.

**CHORUS**

He loves his coun - try and his friends, His hon - es - ty's his ar - mor, He's

na - ture's no - ble - man in life, The in - de - pend - ent farm - er.

He is na - ture's no - ble - man, The in - de - pend - ent farm - er.

# Onward, Christian Soldiers

## You Never Miss the Water

HARRY LINN                                    R. HOWARD

1. When a child, I lived at Lin - coln with my par - ents at the farm, The
2. As years roll'd on, I grew to be a mis - chief - mak - ing boy, De -
3. When I ar - riv'd at man - hood, I em - bark'd in pub - lic life, And
4. Then I stud - ied strict e - con - o - my, and found to my sur - prise, My
5. I'm mar - ried now and hap - py, I've a care - ful lit - tle wife, We

les - sons that my moth - er taught to me were quite a charm; She would
struc - tion seem'd my on - ly sport, it was my on - ly joy; And
found it was a rug - ged road, be - strewn with care and strife; I
funds in - stead of sink - ing, ve - ry quick - ly then did rise; I
live in peace and har - mo - ny, de - void of care and strife; Kind

of - ten take me on her knee when tir'd of child - ish play, And
well do I re - mem - ber, when oft - times well chas - tised, How
spec - u - la - ted fool - ish - ly, my loss - es were se - vere, But
grasp'd each chance, and al - ways struck the i - ron while 'twas hot, I
For - tune smiles up - on us, we have lit - tle chil - dren three, The

as she press'd me to her breast, I've heard my moth - er say:
fa - ther sat be - side me then, and thus has me ad - vised:
still a ti - ny lit - tle voice kept whis-p'ring in my ear:
seiz'd my op - por-tu - ni - ties, and nev - er once for - got:
les - son that I teach them, as they prat - tle round my knee:

CHORUS

Waste not, want not, is the max-im I would teach, Let your watch-word be des-patch, and

prac - tise what you preach; Do not let your chan - ces like

sun-beams pass you by, For you nev - er miss the wa - ter till the well runs dry.

# Co-ca-che-lunk

**Solo**

1. When we first came on this cam - pus, Fresh - men we, as green as grass;
2. We have fought the fight to - geth - er, We have strug-gled side by side;
3. Some will go to Greece or Hart-ford, Some to Nor - wich or to Rome;
4. When we come a - gain to - geth - er, Vi - gin - ten - ni - al to pass,

New, as grave and rev - er - end sen - iors, Smile we o - ver the ver - dant past.
Bro - ken is the bond that held us— We must cut our sticks and slide.
Some to Green-land's i - cy mountains—More, per - haps, will stay at home.
Wives and chil - dren all in - clud - ed,—Won't we be an up - roar - ious class?

**Chorus (Male Voices)**

Co - ca - che - lunk - che - lunk - che - la - ly, Co - ca - che - lunk - che - lunk - che - lay,

Co - ca - che - lunk - che - lunk - che - la - ly, Hi! O chick - a - che - lunk - che - lay.

## Lead, Kindly Light

Cardinal NEWMAN

J. B. DYKES

*mf* *p*

1. Lead, kind-ly Light, a-mid th'encir - cling gloom, Lead thou me on; The night is
2. I was not ev - er thus, nor pray'd that Thou Should'st lead me on; I lov'd to
3. So long thy pow'r hath blest me, sure it still Will lead me on; O'er moor and

*p* *cres.*

dark, and I am far from home, Lead thou me on; Keep thou my feet; I
choose and see my path; but now Lead thou me on; I lov'd the gar - ish
fen, o'er crag and tor-rent, till The night is gone, And with the morn those

*dim.* *p*

do not ask to see . . The dis - tant scene; one step e - nough for me.
day; and, spite of fears, . . Pride ruled my will; re - mem - ber not past years.
an - gel fa - ces smile, . Which I have loved long since and lost a - while.

λ

# It's a Way We Have at Old Harvard *

1. It's a way we have at old Har-vard, It's a way we have at old Har-vard, It's a
2. For we think it is .. no sin, sir, To take the Fresh-men in, sir, And
3. For we think it is .. but right, sir, On Wednesday and Saturday night, sir, To ..

way we have at old Har-vard, To drive dull care a - way;     To drive dull care a -way,     To
ease them of their tin, sir, To drive dull care a - way;     To drive dull care a -way,     To
get most glorious-ly tight sir, To drive dull care a - way;     To drive dull care a -way,     To

CODA

drive dull care a - way, .. It's a way we have at old Har-vard, It's a way we have at old

* The name " Harvard " may be changed to that of any college

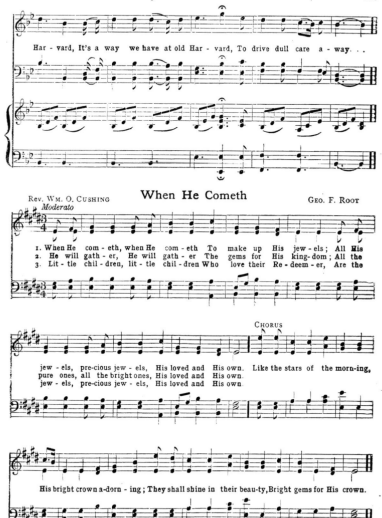

Har - vard, It's a way we have at old Har - vard, To drive dull care a - way...

Rev. Wm. O. Cushing                  **When He Cometh**                  Geo. F. Root
*Moderato*

1. When He com - eth, when He com - eth To make up His jew - els; All His
2. He will gath - er, He will gath - er The gems for His king - dom; All the
3. Lit - tle chil - dren, lit - tle chil - dren Who love their Re - deem - er, Are the

CHORUS

jew - els, pre-cious jew - els, His loved and His own. Like the stars of the morn-ing,
pure ones, all the bright ones, His loved and His own.
jew - els, pre-cious jew - els, His loved and His own.

His bright crown a-dorn - ing; They shall shine in their beau-ty, Bright gems for His crown.

# Tapping at the Garden Gate

J. LOKER

S. W. NEW

1. Who's that tap-ping at the gar-den gate? Tap, tap, tap-ping at the gar-den gate?
2. Oh, you sly lit-tle "Fox" you know, Fid-get-ting a-bout un-til you go,

Ev-'ry night I have heard of late, Some-bod-y tap-ping at the gar-den gate.
Drop'd the sugar spoon! Why, there it lies! Bless the girl, where are your eyes?

What? you, sly lit-tle puss, don't know Why do you blush and fal-ter so?
Were I a-ble to leave my chair, Soon would I find out who is there;

What are you look-ing for un-der the chair? The tap, tap, tap-ping comes not from there.
Don't tell me you think it's the cat, Cats don't tap, tap, tap like that.

## Tapping at the Garden Gate

Ev - 'ry night a - bout half past eight There's tap, tap, tap-ping at the gar - den gate,
Cats don't know when it's half past eight, And come tap, tap-ping at the gar - den gate,

Ev - 'ry night a - bout half past eight, There's tap, tap, tap-ping at the gar - den gate.
Cats don't know when it's half past eight, And come tap, tap-ping at the gar - den gate.

## Take Back the Heart

CLARIBEL

1. Take back the heart that thou gav - est, What is my an-guish to thee? . .
2. Then, when at last o - ver - tak - en, Time flings its fet-ters o'er thee, . .

Take back the free-dom thou crav - est, Leav - ing the fet - ters to me. . .
Come with a trust still un-shak - en, Come back a cap-tive to me. . .

Take back the vows thou hast spo - ken, Fling them a - side and be free. . . . .
Come back, in sad - ness or sor - row, Once more my dar - ling to be ; . . . . .

*Stringendo* ... *rall.*

Smile o'er each pit - i - ful to - ken, Leav - ing the sor - row for me. . . . . .
Come as of old, love, to bor - row Glimp - ses of sun - light from me. . . . . .

*rall. colla parte*

Drink deep of life's fond il - lu - sion, Gaze on the storm-cloud, and flee, . . . .
Love shall re - sume her do - min - ion, Striv - ing no more to be free, . . . .

*rit.* ... *lento*

Swift - ly thro' strife and con - fu - sion, Leav - ing the bur - den to me. . .
When on her world wea - ry pin - ion Flies back my lost love to me. . .

# My Ain Countrie

Mary Lee Demarest

1. { I am far frae my hame, an' I'm wea-ry aft-en-whiles, For the
   { An' I'll ne'er be fu' con-tent, un - til mine een do see The
D.C. *But these sights an' these soun's will as naeth-ing be to me, When I*

langed-for hame-bring-in', an' my Fai-ther's wel-come smiles, } ain coun - trie.
gow-den gates o' heav'n an' my { Omit . . . . . . . . }
*hear the an - gels sing-in' in my { Omit . . . . . . . . } ain coun - trie.*

{ The earth is fleck'd wi' flow - ers, mon - y tint - ed, fresh an' gay. }
{ The bird - ies war - ble blithe - ly, for my Fai - ther made them sae : }

2 I've His gude word o' promise that some gladsome day, the King
To His ain royal palace His banished hame will bring ;
Wi' een an' wi' hert rinnin' ower, we shall see
The King in His beauty, in oor ain countrie.
My sins hae been mony, an' my sorrows hae been sair,
But there they'll never vex me, nor be remembered mair,
For His bluid has made me white, and His han' shall dry my e'e,
When He brings me hame at last, to my ain countrie.

3 Sae little noo I ken o' yon blessed, bonnie place,
I only ken it's Hame, whaur we shall see His face ;
It wad surely be eneuch forever mair to be
In the glory o' His presence, in oor ain countrie.
Like a bairn to his mither, a wee birdie to its nest,
I wad fain be gangin' noo unto my Saviour's breast,
For He gathers in His bosom witless, worthless lambs like me,
An' carries them Himsel', to His ain countrie.

4 He is faithfu' that hath promised, an' He'll surely come again,
He'll keep His tryst wi' me, at what hour I dinna ken ;
But He bids me still to wait, an' ready aye to be,
To gang at ony moment to my ain countrie.
Sae I'm watching aye, and singin' o' my hame, as I wait
For the soun'ing o' His footfa' this side the gowden gate.
God gie His grace to ilka ane wha' listens noo to me,
That we a' may gang in gladness to oor ain countrie.

# My Last Cigar

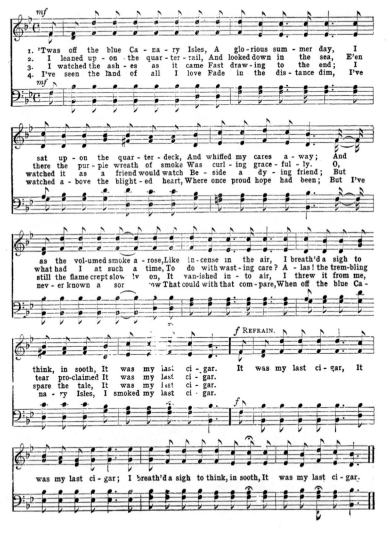

1. 'Twas off the blue Ca-na-ry Isles, A glo-rious sum-mer day, I
2. I leaned up-on the quar-ter-rail, And looked down in the sea, E'en
3. I watched the ash-es as it came Fast draw-ing to the end; I
4. I've seen the land of all I love Fade in the dis-tance dim, I've

sat up-on the quar-ter-deck, And whiffed my cares a-way; And
there the pur-ple wreath of smoke Was curl-ing grace-ful-ly. O,
watched it as a friend would watch Be-side a dy-ing friend; But
watched a-bove the blight-ed heart, Where once proud hope had been; But I've

as the vol-umed smoke a-rose, Like in-cense in the air, I breath'd a sigh to
what had I at such a time, To do with wast-ing care? A-las! the trem-bling
still the flame crept slow-ly on, It van-ished in-to air, I threw it from me,
nev-er known a sor-row That could with that com-pare, When off the blue Ca-

*f* REFRAIN.

think, in sooth, It was my last ci-gar. It was my last ci-gar, It
tear pro-claimed It was my last ci-gar.
spare the tale, It was my last ci-gar.
na-ry Isles, I smoked my last ci-gar.

was my last ci-gar; I breath'd a sigh to think, in sooth, It was my last ci-gar.

# My Moustache

(MALE VOICE

*Tune in Second Tenor*

1. My mous-tache is grow-ing, Its ge-nial warmth be-stow-ing; Its
2. But when I am drink-ing, I oft-times am think-ing, There's

beau-ty charms the eye of all Broad-way. Come forth like a fair-y so
one thing you will hin-der ve-ry much; The rap-tur-ous bliss-es of

light and so air-y, And ram-ble o'er my up-per lip so gay.
sweet stol-en kiss-es, You'll scarce-ly let the girls our two lips touch.

REFRAIN

Come! come! mous-tache come, Come e'er the dye on thee fades; Come

O come, come, come, come

forth like a fai-ry, so light and so air-y, And ram-ble o'er my up-per lip so gay.

# The Old Arm Chair

ELIZA COOKE                                              HENRY RUSSELL

*Andante con espressione*

1. I love it, I love it, and who shall dare To
2. I sat and watch'd her man - y a day, When her
3. 'Tis past! 'tis past! but I gaze on it now With

chide me for lov - ing that old arm chair? I've treas-ured it long as a
eye grew dim, and her locks were grey, And I al - most wor-shipp'd her
quiv - er - ing breath and throb-bing brow: 'Twas there she nurs'd me, 'twas

ho - ly prize, I've be - dew'd it with tears, and em - balm'd it with sighs; 'Tis
when she smil'd, And turn'd from her bi - ble to bless her child.
there she died; And mem- 'ry flows with la - va tide.

bound    by a    thou  -  sand   bonds   to   my heart,   Not   a
Years    roll'd  on,    but the   last   one   sped,      My
Say      it is   fol  -  ly, and  deem   me   weak,       While the

tie     will break, not a   link    will start! Would ye learn   the spell?   A
i-dol   was shatter'd, my earth  -  star fled;  I   learnt   how much   the
scald  -  ing drops  start down   my cheek; But  I  love it,  I love it,   and

moth-er   sat there,  And  a   sa  -  cred thing is that old   arm   chair.
heart     can bear,   When I   saw   her   die   in that old   arm   chair.
can  -  not tear   My   soul from a moth - er's   old   arm   chair.

# Love Not

CAROLINE NORTON

JOHN BLOCKLEY

*Andantino*

1. Love not! love not! ye hap-less sons of clay; Hope's gay-est
2. Love not! love not! the thing you love may die, May per-ish
3. Love not! love not! the thing you love may change, The ro - sy
4. Love not! love not! O warn-ing vain-ly said! In pres-ent

wreaths are made of earth - ly flow'rs; Things that are made to
from the gay and glad - some earth; The si - lent stars, the
lip may cease to smile on you, The kind - ly beam - ing
hours, as in the years gone by, Love flings a ha - lo

fade and fall a-way, Ere they have blossomed, for a few . . short hours,
blue and smiling sky, Beams on its grave as once up - on . . its birth,
eye grow cold and strange, The heart still warmly beat, yet not . . be true,
round the dear one's head, Fault - less, im - mor-tal, till they change or die,

Love Not
273

ad lib.

| Ere | they have blossomed | for a few | short | hours. | Love not! love not! |
| Beams | on its grave as | once up-on | its | birth. | Love not! love not! |
| The | heart still warmly | beat, yet not | be | true. | Love not! love not! |
| Fault - less, im - mor-tal, | till they change | or | die. | | Love not! love not! |

SCHMOLKE
Tr. BORTHWICK

## My Jesus, as Thou Wilt

WEBER

1. My Je - sus, as Thou wilt: O may Thy will be mine; In - to Thy
2. My Je - sus, as Thou wilt: Though seen thro' ma - ny a tear, Let not my
3. My Je - sus, as Thou wilt: All shall be well for me; Each chang-ing

hand of love I would my all re - sign. Thro' sor - row or thro' joy,
star of hope Grow dim or dis - ap - pear. Since Thou on earth hast wept
fu - ture scene I glad-ly trust with Thee. Straight to my home a - bove,

Con - duct me as Thine own, And help me still to say, "My Lord, Thy will be done."
And sor - row'd oft a - lone, If I must weep with Thee, "My Lord, Thy will be done."
I trav - el calm-ly on, And sing in life or death, "My Lord, Thy will be done."

# Your Mission

JESSIE R. GATES  
Moderato

S. M. GRANNIS

1. If you can not on the o - cean Sail a - mong the swift - est fleet, Rock-ing
2. If you are too weak to jour - ney Up the moun - tain, steep and high; You can
3. If you have not gold and sil - ver Ev - er read - y to comm _d; If you
4. If you can not in the con - flict Prove your - self a sol - dier true, If, where
5. Do not, then, stand i - dly wait - ing, For some great - er work to do; For - tune

on the high - est bil - lows, Laugh-ing at the storms you meet; You can
stand with - in the val - ley, While the mul - ti - tudes go by; You can
can not t'wards the need - y, Reach an ev - er o - pen hand; You can
fire and smoke are thick - est, There's no work for you to do; When the
is a la - zy god - dess, She will nev - er come to you. Go and

cres.      dim.

ritard.

stand a - mong the sail - ors, An - chor'd yet with - in the bay, You can
chant in hap - py meas - ure, As they slow - ly pass a - long, Though they
vis - it the af - flict - ed, O'er the err - ing you can weep, You can
bat - tle - field is si - lent, You can go with care - ful tread, You can
toil in an - y vine - yard, Do not fear to do or dare, If you

## Your Mission

lend a hand to help them, As they launch their boats away, As they launch their boats away.
may for-get the sing-er, They will not for-get the song, They will not for-get the song.
be a true dis-ci-ple, Sit-ting at the Sav-iour's feet, Sit-ting at the Saviour's feet.
bear a-way the wounded, You can cov-er up the dead, You can cov-er up the dead.
want a field of la-bor, You can find it an-y-where, You can find it an-y-where.

## God Speed the Right

W. E. HICKSON                                          German Air
*Maestoso*

1. Now to heav'n our pray'r as-cend-ing, God speed the right; In a no-ble
2. Be that pray'r a-gain re-peat-ed, God speed the right; Ne'er de-spair-ing,
3. Pa-tient, firm, and per-se-ver-ing, God speed the right; Ne'er th'e-vent nor

cause con-tend-ing, God speed the right; Be our zeal in heav'n re-cord-ed,
tho' de-feat-ed, God speed the right; Like the good and great in sto-ry,
dan-ger fear-ing, God speed the right; Pains, nor toils, nor tri-als heed-ing,

With suc-cess on earth re-ward-ed, God speed the right, God speed the right.
If we fail, we fail with glo-ry, God speed the right, God speed the right.
In the strength of heav'n suc-ceed-ing, God speed the right, God speed the right.

# Love's Old, Sweet Song

G. Clifton Bingham

J. L. Molloy

1. Once in the drear dead days be-yond re-call, When on the world the mist be-gan to fall,
2. E - ven to - day we hear Love's song of yore, Deep in our hearts it dwells for-ev -er more;

Out of the dreams that rose in happy throng Low in our hearts love sang an old sweet song;
Foot-steps may fal - ter, wea-ry grow the way, Still we can hear it at the close of day;

And in the dusk where fell the firelight gleam, Softly it wove itself in - to our dream.
So till the end, when life's dim shadows fall, Low will be found the sweetest song of all.

Just a song at twi- light, when the lights are low, And the flick-'ring sha -dows

sempre Ped.    * Ped.    * Ped

soft - ly come and  go,  Tho' the heart be wea - ry,  sad the day and long,

Still to us  at twi - light comes Love's old song, comes Love's old, sweet song.

## Jack and Gill

H. L. HANDY

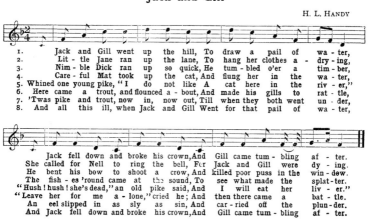

1.     Jack and Gill went  up  the hill, To  draw  a  pail of  wa - ter,
2.     Lit - tle Jane ran  up  the lane, To  hang her clothes a - dry - ing,
3.     Nim - ble Dick ran  up  so quick, He  tum - bled o'er  a  tim - ber,
4.     Care - ful Mat took  up  the cat, And  flung her  in  the  wa - ter,
5. Whined one young pike, "I  do  not like A  cat here  in  the  riv - er,"
6. Here came  a  trout, and flounced a - bout, And  made his  gills  to  rat - tle,
7. 'Twas pike and trout, now  in,  now out, Till  when they  both went  un - der,
8. And  all  this  ill, when Jack and Gill Went  for that  pail of  wa - ter,

    Jack fell down and broke his crown, And  Gill came tum - bling  af - ter.
She called for Nell  to  ring the bell, For  Jack and Gill  were  dy - ing.
He  bent his  bow  to  shoot  a  crow, And  killed poor puss in the  win - dow.
The  fish - es 'round came at the sound, To  see what made the  splat - ter.
"Hush! hush! she's dead," an  old  pike said, And  I  will  eat  her  liv - er."
"Leave her  for  me  a - lone," cried he; And  then there came  a  bat - tle.
An  eel slipped in as  sly  as  sin, And  car - ried off  the  plun - der.
And  Jack fell down and broke  his crown, And  Gill came tum - bling  af - ter.

## I'll Hang My Harp on a Willow Tree

W. Guernsey.

*Andante moderato*

1. I'll hang my harp on a wil - low tree, I'll off to the wars a -
2. She took me a - way from my war - like lord, And gave me a silk - en
3. Then I'll hide in my breast ev - 'ry self - ish care, I'll flush my pale cheek with
4. But one gold - en tress of her hair I'll twine, In my hel - met's sa - ble

gain, My peace-ful home has no charms for me, The bat - tle field no pain; The
suit, I tho't no more of my mas - ter's sword, But play'd my mas - ter's lute; She
wine; When smiles a - wake the bri - dal pair, I'll has - ten to give them mine. I'll
plume, And then on the field of Pal - es - tine I'll seek an ear - ly doom; And

la - dy I love will soon be a bride, With a di - a - dem on her brow. Oh!
seem'd to think me a boy a - bove Her pa - ges of low de - gree, Oh!
laugh and I'll sing tho' my heart may bleed, And I'll walk in the fes - tive train, And
if by the Sar - a - cen's hand I fall, 'Mid the no - ble and the brave, A

why did she flat-ter my boy-ish pride, She's go-ing to leave me now, Oh! now.
had I but lov'd with a boy-ish love, It would have been better for me, Oh! me.
if I sur-vive it I'll mount my steed, And off to the wars a-gain, And gain.
tear from my La - dy love is all I ask for the war-rior's grave, A grave.

## Rest for the Weary

S. Y. HARMER. Rev. J. W. DADMUN

1. In the Christian's home in glo - ry, There re - mains a land of rest, There my
2. He is fit - ting up my man-sion, Which e - ter - nal-ly shall stand, For my
3. Pain nor sick-ness ne'er shall en - ter, Grief nor woe my lot shall share; But in
4. Death it - self shall then be vanquished, And his sting shall be with-drawn; Shout for
5. Sing, O sing, ye heirs of glo - ry, Shout your tri-umph as you go; Zi - on's

CHORUS

Saviour's gone be-fore me, To ful - fil my soul's re - quest. There is rest for the
stay shall not be tran-sient In that ho - ly, hap - py land. On the oth - er side of
that ce - les - tial cen - tre, I a crown of life shall wear.
gladness, O, ye ransomed, Hail with joy the ris - ing morn.
gate will o - pen for you, You shall find an entrance through.

wea-ry, There is rest for the wea-ry, There is rest for the wea-ry, There is rest for you.
Jor - dan, In the sweet fields of E-den, Where the tree of life is blooming, There is rest for you.

# Twenty Years Ago

WILLIAM WILLING

*Not too fast*

1. I've wan-der'd to the vil-lage, Tom, I've sat be-neath the tree, Up-
2. The grass is just as green, dear Tom, bare-foot-ed boys at play Were
3. The riv-er's run-ning just as still; the wil-lows on its side Are
4. The spring that bub-bled 'neath the hill, close by the spread-ing beech, Is
5. Near by the spring, up-on an elm, you know I cut your name, Your
6. My lids have long been dry, dear Tom, but tears came in my eyes; I
7. Some now are in the church-yard laid, some sleep be-neath the sea, But

on the school-house play-ing ground, which shel-ter'd you and me. But
sport-ing just as we did then, with spir-its just as gay; But the
larg-er than they were, dear Tom, the stream ap-pears less wide. The
ve-ry low, 'twas once so high that we could al-most reach; And
sweet-heart's just be-neath it, Tom, and you did mine the same; Some
thought of her I loved so well, those ear-ly bro-ken ties; I
few are left of our old class, ex-cept-ing you and me; And

none were there to greet me, Tom; and few were left to know, That
Mas-ter sleeps up-on the hill which, coat-ed o'er with snow, Af-
grape-vine swing is ru-ined, now, where once we played the beau, And
kneel-ing down to get a drink, dear Tom, I start-ed so, Just
heart-less wretch had peeled the bark, 'twas dy-ing sure but slow, Up-
vis-it-ed the old church-yard, and took some flow'rs to strew Up-
when our time shall come, dear Tom, and we are called to go, I

play'd with us up - on the grass, some twen - ty years a - go.
ford - ed us a slid - ing place just twen - ty years a - go.
swung our sweet-hearts, "pret - ty girls," just twen - ty years a - go.
see how much that I was changed since twen - ty years a - go.
as that one, whose name was cut, died twen - ty years a - go.
on the graves of those we loved some twen - ty years a - go.
hope they'll lay us where we played just twen - ty years a '- go.

## O Weary Feet

CLARA L. HAYES

ALFRED BEIRLY

1. O wea - ry feet, the way seems drear and long; O tir - ed
2. In self - ish toil you can - not find the way; To seek re -
3. Be strong in hope, nor doubt your Fa - ther's care; Bright is God's

eyes, you peer in - to the night; Soul, sing a - gain hope's
ward will nev - er bring you gain; O trust God's love, your
world, the clouds are all your own; Sun - shine, and joy, and

long - for - got - ten song; Look up, dear heart, be - hold the per - fect Light.
ef - fort He'll re - pay, He giv - eth smiles for tears, and joy for pain.
glo - ry ev - 'ry - where, Make earth a heav'n where dark-ness is un - known.

282

# I Cannot Sing the Old Songs

CLARIBEL

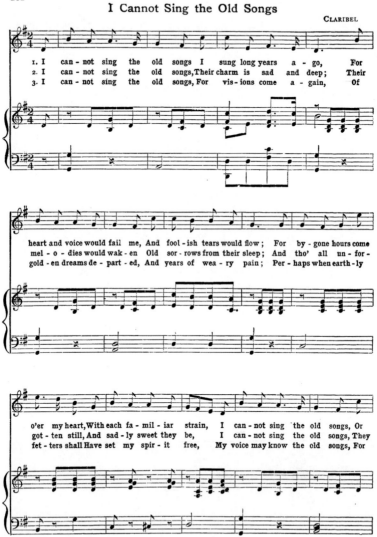

1. I can-not sing the old songs I sung long years a - go, For
2. I can-not sing the old songs, Their charm is sad and deep; Their
3. I can-not sing the old songs, For vis-ions come a - gain, Of

heart and voice would fail me, And fool-ish tears would flow; For by-gone hours come
mel - o - dies would wak - en Old sor - rows from their sleep; And tho' all un - for
gold - en dreams de - part - ed, And years of wea - ry pain; Per - haps when earth-ly

o'er my heart, With each fa - mil - iar strain, I can-not sing the old songs, Or
got - ten still, And sad - ly sweet they be, I can-not sing the old songs, They
fet - ters shall Have set my spir - it free, My voice may know the old songs, For

dream those dreams a-gain, I can-not sing the old songs, Or dream those dreams a-gain.
are too dear to me, I can-not sing the old songs, They are too dear to me.
all e - ter - ni - ty, My voice may know the old songs, For all e - ter - ni - ty.

## Shall We Meet

H. L. Hastings

Elisha S. Rice

1. Shall we meet be - yond the riv - er, Where the surg - es cease to roll,
2. Shall we meet in that blest har - bor, When our storm - y voyage is o'er?
3. Shall we meet in yon - der cit - y, Where the tow'rs of crys - tal shine,
4. Shall we meet there ma - ny loved ones, That were torn from our em - brace?
5. Shall we meet with Christ, our Sav - iour, When He comes to claim His own?

Where in all the bright for - ev - er, Sor - row ne'er shall press the soul?
Shall we meet and cast the an - chor By the bright, ce - les - tial shore?
Where the walls are all of jas - per, Built by work - man-ship di - vine?
Shall we lis - ten to their voi - ces, And be - hold them face to face?
Shall we know His bless - ed fa - vor, And sit down up - on His throne?

D. S. Shall we meet be - yond the riv - er, Where the surg - es cease to roll?

CHORUS

D. S.

Shall we meet, shall we meet, Shall we meet be - yond the riv - er?

## When Shall We Three Meet Again

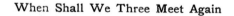

1. When shall we three meet again? When shall we three meet a-gain? Oft shall glowing hope ex-pire,
2. Tho' in dis-tant lands we sigh, Parch'd beneath the burning sky; Tho' the deep beneath us rolls,
3. When around the youthful pine Moss shall creep, and ivy twine; When these burnish'd locks are gray,
4. When the dreams of life are fled, When its wast-ed lamp is dead; When in cold ob - livion's shade

Oft shall wearied love re-tire, Oft shall death and sor-row reign, Ere we three shall meet a-gain.
Friendship shall unite our souls; Still in Fan-cy's rich domain Oft shall we three meet a-gain.
Thinned by ma-ny a toil-spent day, May this long-lov'd bow'r remain, Here may we three meet again.
Beau-ty, wealth, and pow'r are laid, Where immortal spirits reign, There shall we three meet again.

## When This Cruel War is Over

CHAS. C. SAWYER

HENRY TUCKER

Moderato e cantabile

1. Dear - est one, do you re - mem - ber When we last did meet?
2. When the sum-mer breeze is sigh - ing Mourn-ful - ly a - long;
3. If a - mid the din of bat - tle, No - bly you should fall,
4. But our coun-try called you, loved one, An - gels guide your way;

When you told me how you loved me, Kneel-ing at my feet?
Or when autumn leaves are fall - ing, Sad - ly breathes the song.
Far a-way from those who love you, None to hear you call:
While our "Southern boys" are fight - ing, We can on - ly pray.

Oh! how proud you stood be - fore    me,    In    your suit    of   gray; . .
Oft    in dreams I  see  you  ly  -  ing    On    the  bat - tle  plain; . .
Who would whis-per words of  com  - fort?  Who  would soothe your pain ?—. .
When  you strike for God and  Free - dom,   Let   all   na - tions see . . .

When  you vowed from me and  coun - try    Ne'er  to   go   a - stray!
Lone - ly, wound-ed, ev - en   dy  -  ing,   Call - ing, but  in   vain.
Such  are  ma - ny  cru - el   fan - cies    Ev - er   in  my  brain!
How  you love our South-ern  ban - ner,  Em - blem of  the  free.

CHORUS

Weep - ing,  sad  and  lone - ly,    Sighs  and tears, how  vain;

When this cru - el war is  o - ver,  Pray - ing then to meet a - gain!

## Paddle Your Own Canoe

H. CLIFTON

M. HOBSON

1. I've trav-ell'd a - bout a bit in my time And of
2. I have no wife to both - er my life, No
3. It's all ve - ry well to de - pend on a friend,— That
4. If a hur - ri - cane rise in the mid - day skies, And the

trou - bles I've seen a few, . . . . But found it bet - ter in
lov - er to prove un - true, . . . But the whole day long with a
is, if you've prov'ed him true,— . . . But you'll find it bet - ter by
sun is lost to view, . . . Move stead - i - ly by with a

ev - 'ry clime To pad - dle my own ca - noe. . . My wants are small, I
laugh and a song, I pad - dle my own ca - noe. . . I rise with the lark, and from
far, in the end, To pad - dle your own ca - noe. . . "To bor-row is dear - er by
stead - fast eye, And pad - dle your own ca - noe. . . The dai-sies that grow in the

care not   at   all   If   my   debts   are   paid   when   due.   .   .   .   I
day - light   till   dark   I   do what   I   have   to   do.   .   .   .   I'm
far   than   to   buy,"—   A   max - im.   tho' old,   still   true ;   .   .   .   You
bright   green   fields,   Are bloom - ing   so   sweet   for   you.   .   .   .   So

drive a - way strife, in   the   o - cean of   life While I   pad - dle my   own   ca - noe.
care-less of wealth, if   I've on - ly   the   health   To   pad - dle my   own   ca - noe.
nev - er   will sigh, if   you on - ly   will   try   To   pad - dle your   own   ca - noe.
nev - er   sit down, with   a   tear   or   a   frown, But   pad - dle your   own   ca - noe.

*rit.*

**CHORUS**

Then love your neigh-bor   as   your-self,   As   the world you go   trav - el - ing   through,   And

nev - er   sit down, with a   tear   or   a   frown, But   pad-dle your own   ca - noe.   .   .

## Robin Adair

*Andante affettuoso*

1. What's this dull town to me? Rob-in's not near; What was't I wish'd to see?
2. What made th' As-sembly shine? Rob-in A - dair! What made the ball so fine?
3. But now thou'rt cold to me, Rob-in A - dair! But now thou'rt cold to me,

What wish'd to hear? Where's all the joy and mirth Made this town a
Rob - in was there! What, when the ball was o'er, What made my
Rob - in A - dair! You that I lov'd so well Still in my

Heav'n on earth? Oh! they're all fled with thee, Rob-in A - dair!
heart so sore?—Oh! it was part-ing with Rob-in A - dair!
heart shall dwell! Oh! I can ne'er for-get Rob-in A - dair!

# Miss Lucy Long

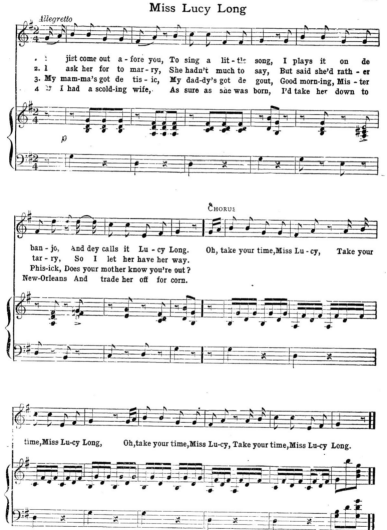

jist come out a-fore you, To sing a lit-tle song, I plays it on de
2. I ask her for to mar-ry, She hadn't much to say, But said she'd rath-er
3. My mam-ma's got de tis-ic, My dad-dy's got de gout, Good morn-ing, Mis-ter
4. If I had a scold-ing wife, As sure as she was born, I'd take her down to

ban-jo, And dey calls it Lu-cy Long. Oh, take your time, Miss Lu-cy, Take your
tar-ry, So I let her have her way.
Phis-ick, Does your mother know you're out?
New-Orleans And trade her off for corn.

time, Miss Lu-cy Long, Oh, take your time, Miss Lu-cy, Take your time, Miss Lu-cy Long.

## Stonewall's Requiem

M. DEEVES

1. The muf - fled drum is beat - ing, There's a sad and sol - emn tread, Our
2. They've borne him to an hon - or'd grave, The lau - rel crowns his brow, By

Ban-ner's draped in mourn-ing, As it shrouds "th'illustrious dead." Proud forms are bent with
hal-low'd James's si - lent wave He's sweet-ly sleep - ing now; Vir - gin - ia to the

*very slow*

sor- row, And all South-ern hearts are sore, The He - ro now is sleep-ing, No - ble
South is dear, She holds a sa - cred trust, Our fall - en braves from far and near Are

*a tempo*

Stone - wall is no more. 'Mid the rat - tling of the mus - kets And the
cov - ered with her dust; She .. shrines the spot where now is laid The

# Stonewall's Requiem

can - non's thun - drous roar,     He stained the field of  glo - ry With his
brav - est of  them all,     The mar - tyr of  our  coun-try's cause, Our

*ritard.*

brave life's pre - cious gore,  And though  our  flag waved proud - ly, We  were
i - dol - ized  Stone-wall;  But though  his  spir - it's waft - ed  To  the

*ritard.*

vic - tors ere sun - set,  The gal-lant deeds of Chance-lors-ville Will min - gle with re - gret.
hap-py realms a - bove,  His name shall live for - ev - er link'd With rev - er - ence and love.

# The Lord's Prayer

1 Our Father, who art in *heaven*, | hallowed | be Thy | name ; || Thy kingdom come, Thy will be
*done* in | earth, as it | is in | heaven ;

2 Give *us* this | day our | daily | bread ; || and forgive us our trespasses, as we for*give* | them that
| trespass a- | gainst us.

3 And lead us not into temptation, *but* de- | liver | us from | evil ; || for Thine is the kingdom, and
**the** power, *and* the | glory, for- | ever. A- | men.

# The First Nowell

Ancient Song

Moderato

1. The first Now-ell the an-gel did say, Was to cer-tain poor
2. They looked a-bove, and there saw a star, As it shone in the
3. And by the light of that same bright star There were three wise men
4. The star drew nigh un-to the north-west; O-ver Beth-le-hem
5. Then en-tered in those wise men all three Ver-y rev-er-ent-
6. Then let us all with one . . ac-cord Sing prais-es un-

shep-herds in fields as they lay— In fields where they lay keep-ing their
east but be-yond them a-far; And to the earth it gave forth great
came from the east coun-try far; To seek the King it was their in-
paus-ed, and there it did rest; And there did shine most bright,and did
ly up-on bend-ed knee, And of-fered there in His pres-
to . . our heav-en-ly Lord, That made the heav-ens and earth of

sheep, On a cold win-ter's night, that was so deep.
light, And con-tin-u-ed so both day and night.
tent, And to fol-low the star wher-ev-er it went.
stay O-ver where the young Child and His moth-er lay.
ence Gifts of gold and of myrrh and of frank-in-cense.
naught, And with His blood man-kind hath bought.

CHORUS f

Now-ell, Now-ell, Now-ell, Now-ell, Born is the King of Is-ra-el.

## 'Tis Midnight Hour

*Moderato scherzando simplice*

1. 'Tis midnight hour, the moon shines bright, The dew-drops blaze beneath her ray, The
2. 'Tis midnight hour, from flow'r to flow'r The way-ward ze - phyr floats a - long, Or

twink-ling stars their trembling light Like beau-ty's eyes dis-play; Then
lin - gers in the shad-ed bow'r To hear the night - bird's song; Then

sleep no more, tho' round thy heart Some ten - der dream may i - dly play, For

*ritard.* *ad lib.*

mid - night song with mag - ic art Shall chase that dream a - way.

# The Lost Chord

Adelaide A. Proctor

Arthur Sullivan

Seat- ed one day at the or - gan, I was wea - ry and ill at ease, And my fin - gers wander'd i - dly O - ver the noi -sy keys; I know not what I was play- ing, Or what I was dreaming then, But I struck one chord of mu - sic, Like the

sound of a great A - men, Like the sound of a great A - men.

It flood - ed the crim-son twi-light, Like the close of an An-gel's

Psalm, And it lay on my fev-er'd spir - it, With a touch of in - fi-nite calm, It

qui - et -ed pain and sor-row, Like love o - ver-com-ing strife, It seem'd the har-mo-nious

# The Lost Chord

ech - o From our dis-cord-ant life, It link'd all per-plex-ed mean-ings In-to

one per-fect peace, And trembled a-way in-to si-lence, As if it were loth to

cease; I have sought but I seek it vain-ly, That one lost chord di-

vine, Which came from the soul of the Or-gan, And en-ter'd in-to

298

# Go 'way, Old Man!

Song of Louisiana Negroes

Arranged by A. M. KEITH

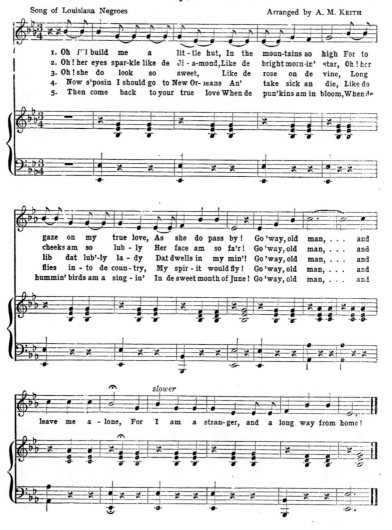

# Lilly Dale

H. S. Thompson

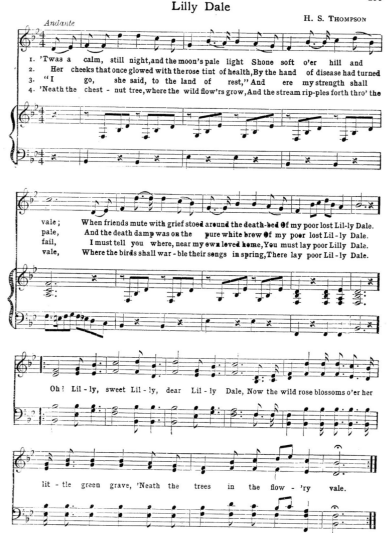

1. 'Twas a calm, still night, and the moon's pale light Shone soft o'er hill and
2. Her cheeks that once glowed with the rose tint of health, By the hand of disease had turned
3. "I go, she said, to the land of rest," And ere my strength shall
4. 'Neath the chest-nut tree, where the wild flow'rs grow, And the stream rip-ples forth thro' the

vale ; When friends mute with grief stood around the death-bed Of my poor lost Lil-ly Dale.
pale, And the death damp was on the pure white brow Of my poor lost Lil-ly Dale.
fail, I must tell you where, near my own loved home, You must lay poor Lilly Dale.
vale, Where the birds shall war-ble their songs in spring, There lay poor Lil-ly Dale.

Oh! Lil-ly, sweet Lil-ly, dear Lil-ly Dale, Now the wild rose blossoms o'er her

lit-tle green grave, 'Neath the trees in the flow-'ry vale.

# In the Gloaming

META ORRED

ANNIE FORTESCUE HARRISON

1. In the gloam-ing O my dar-ling! when the lights are dim and low—
2. In the gloam-ing O my dar-ling! think not bit-ter-ly of me!

And the qui-et shad-ows fall-ing, soft-ly come and soft-ly go,—
Tho' I passed a-way in si-lence, left you lone-ly, set you free,

When the winds are sob-bing faint-ly with a gen-tle, un-known woe,—
F my heart was crushed with long-ing, what had been could nev-er be.

Will you think of me and love me, As you did once long a-go?
It was best to leave you thus, dear, Best for you and best for (Omit.)

me,— It was best to leave you thus, . . . Best for you and best for me. . .

## Annie Laurie

Lady JOHN SCOTT

*Tenderly*

1. Max - wel - ton's braes are bon - nie, Where ear - ly fa's the dew, And 'twas there that
2. Her brow is like the snaw-drift, Her throat is like the swan, Her face it
3. Like dew on th' gow - an ly - ing Is th' fa' o' her fair - y feet, And like winds in

An - nie Lau - rie Gave me her prom - ise true. Gave me her prom - ise true, Which
is the fair - est That e'er the sun shone on. That e'er the sun shone on, And
sum - mer sigh-ing, Her voice is low and sweet. Her voice is low and sweet, And she's

ne'er for-got will be, And for bon-nie An - nie Lau - rie I'd lay me doon and dee.
dark blue is her e'e, And for bon-nie An - nie Lau - rie I'd lay me doon and dee.
a' the world to me, And for bon-nie An - nie Lau - rie I'd lay me doon and dee.

# My Grandma's Advice

Anonymous

1. My Grand-ma lives on yon-der lit-tle green, Fine old la - dy as
2. These false young men they flat-ter and de-ceive, So, my love, you must
3. The first came a court - ing was lit - tle Johny Green, Fine young man as
4. The next came a court - ing was young El-lis Grove,'Twas then we met with a
5. Thinks I to my-self, there's some mis - take: What a fuss these

ev - er was seen; She of - ten cau - tioned me with care, Of
not be - lieve; They'll flat-ter, they'll coax, till you are in their snare, And a -
ev - er was seen; But the words of my Grand - ma ran in my head, And I
joy - ous love; With a joy - ous love I couldn't be a - fraid, You'd
old folks make! If the boys and the girls had all been so a - fraid, Then

all false young men to be - ware. Tim - e - i tim - e - um tum
way goes poor old grand - ma's care. Tim - e - i tim - e - um tum
could not hear one word he said. Tim - e - i tim - e - um tum
bet - ter get mar - ried than die an old maid. Tim - e - i tim - e - um tum
Grand-ma her - self would have died an old maid. Tim - e - i tim - e - um tum

tim - e - um pa ta, . . . Of all false young men to be - ware.
tim - e - um pa ta, . . And a - way goes poor old Grand - ma's care.
tim - e - um pa ta, And I could not hear one word he said.
tim - e - um pa ta, . . . You'd bet - ter get mar - ried than die an old maid.
tim - e - um pa ta, . . . Then Grandma her - self would have died an old maid.

## O Come, Come Away

1. Oh come, come a - way, from la - bor now re - pos - ing, Let bu - sy care a -
2. From toil, and the cares, with which the day is clos - ing, The hour of eve brings
3. While sweet Phil o - mel the wea - ry trav - 'ler cheer - ing, With eve - ning songs her
4. The bright day is gone, the moon and stars ap - pear - ing, With sil - ver light il -

while for - bear, Oh, come, come a - way. Come, come our so - cial joys re - new,
sweet re - prieve, Oh, come, come a - way. Oh, come, where love will smile on thee,
note pro - longs, Oh, come, come a - way. In an - sw'ring songs of sym - pa - thy,
lume the night, Oh, come, come a - way. We'll join in grate - ful songs of praise,

And there, where love and friendship grew, Let true hearts welcome you, Oh, come, come a - way.
And round its hearth will gladness be, And time fly mer - ri - ly, Oh, come, come a - way.
We'll sing in tune-ful har - mo - ny, Of hope, joy, lib - er - ty, Oh, come, come a - way.
To Him who crowns our peaceful days, With health, hope, happiness, Oh, come, come a - way.

# Embarrassment

F. ABT

1. I fain   a winning tale would tell thee, And know my-self scarce what it   is !   And
2. I fain would sing in plain-tive mea-sure   A lay   that to thy heart should go,   But
3. I fain would write a lov-ing let - ter That might to me thy heart   in-cline,   But

if   the question thou shouldst ask me,   My an - swer should be on-ly this :   'Tis
when   I seek the tuneful trea - sure,   A voice   within me an-swers so :   'Tis
here   a-gain I fare no bet - ter   For all   my tho'ts in this com-bine :   I

thee I   love with all   my heart, 'Tis thee   a - lone, yes, thee, . .   I
thee I   love with all   my heart, 'Tis thee   a - lone, yes, thee, . .   I
love but thee   with all   my heart, But thee   a - lone, yes, thee, . .   I

love but thee with all my heart, But thee a - lone, yes, thee! . . . .

## The Son of God Goes Forth to War

Bishop HEBER

H., S. CUTLER

1. The Son of God goes forth to war, A king-ly crown to gain; His blood-red ban-ner
2. The mar-ty: first, whose ea - gle eye Could pierce beyond the grave, Who saw his Mas-ter
3. A glo-rious band, the cho-sen few On whom the Spir-it came, Twelve valiant saints, their
4. A no - ble ar - my, men and boys, The ma-tron and the maid, A - round the Saviour's

streams a - far: Who fol - lows in His train? Who best can drink His cup of woe,
in the sky, And called on Him to save: Like Him, with par - don on his tongue
hope they knew, And mocked the cross and flame: They met the ty - rant's brandished steel,
throne re-joice, In robes of light ar-rayed: They climbed the steep as - cent of heav'n

Tri-umphant o - ver pain, Who patient bears his cross below, He fol-lows in His train.
In midst of mor-tal pain, He pray'd for them that did the wrong: Who follows in his train?
The li - on's go - ry mane; They bowed their necks the death to feel: Who follows in their train?
Thro' per-il, toil, and pain: O God, to us may grace be giv'n To fol-low in their train. A-men.

# In Old Madrid

CLIFTON BINGHAM

H. TROTÈRE

Tempo di Bolero

1. Long years a-
2. Far, far a-

go,    in old Ma-drid, Where soft-ly sighs of love the light gui-tar, Two sparkling
way    from old Ma-drid, Her lov-er fell, long years a-go, for Spain;—A con-vent

eyes    a lat-tice hid, Two eyes as dark-ly bright as love's own star!   There
veil    those sweet eyes hid, And all the vows that love had sigh'd were vain!   But

on the casement ledge, when day was o'er, A ti-ny hand was light-ly laid; A
still, between the dusk and night, 'tis said, Her white hand opes the lat-tice wide, The

face looked out, as from the riv - er shore There stole a ten - der ser - e -
faint sweet ech - o of that ser - e - nade Floats wierd - ly o'er the mist - y

nade! . . . Rang the lov - er's hap - py song, Light and low from
tide! . . . Still she lists her lov - er's song, Still he sings up -

shore to shore, But ah! the riv - er flow'd a - long Be -
on the shore, Though flows a stream than all more strong Be -

tween them ev - er - more. . . .

# In Old Madrid

con tenerezza

"Come, my love, the stars are shin - ing, Time is fly - ing, Love is sigh - ing;

a tempo

Come, for thee a heart is pin - ing, Here a - lone I wait for thee!

*1*  D.C.

*2*

thee, a - lone I wait, . . I wait for thee, my love, . . I wait for

a tempo

thee; O come, my love, . . I wait for thee, I wait for

rall.

colla voce

## In Old Madrid

## Sweet and Low

ALFRED TENNYSON

JOSEPH BARNBY

*pp Larghetto*

1. Sweet and low, sweet and low, Wind of the west - ern sea; Low, low,
2. Sleep and rest, sleep and rest, Fa - ther will come to thee soon; Rest, rest on

breathe and blow, Wind of the west - ern sea; O - ver the roll - ing
moth - er's breast, Fa - ther will come to thee soon; Fa - ther will come to his

wa - ters go, Come from the dy - ing moon and blow, Blow him a - gain to
babe in the nest, Sil - ver sails all out of the west, Un - der the sil - ver

me, While my lit - tle one, while my pret - ty one sleeps.
moon, Sleep, my lit - tle one, sleep my pret - ty one, sleep.

## Marching Through Georgia

HENRY C. WORK

1. Bring the good old bu - gle, boys! we'll sing an - oth - er song —
2. How the dar - keys shout - ed when they heard the joy - ful sound!
3. Yes, and there were Un - ion men who wept with joy - ful tears,
4. "Sher - man's dash - ing Yan - kee boys will nev - er reach the coast!"
5. So we made a thor - ough - fare for Free - dom and her train,

Sing it with a spir - it that will start the world a - long—Sing it as we used to sing it,
How the turkeys gobbled which our com - mis - sa - ry found! How the sweet po - ta - toes e - ven
When they saw the honor'd flag they had not seen for years; Hardly could they be restrained from
So the sau - cy reb - els said, and 'twas a handsome boast, Had they not for- got, a - las! to
Six - ty miles in la - ti - tude—three hundred to the main; Treason fled be- fore us, for re-

fif - ty thou - sand strong, While we were march - ing through Geor - gia.
start - ed from the ground, While we were march - ing through Geor - gia.
break - ing forth in cheers, While we were march - ing through Geor - gia.
reck - on with the host, While we were march - ing through Geor - gia.
sis - tance was in vain, While we were march - ing through Geor - gia.

**Stars of the Summer Night**

MALE VOICES

I. B. WOODBURY

*p dolce*

1. Stars of the sum-mer night, Far in yon az - ure deeps, Hide, hide your
2. Moon of the sum-mer night, Far down yon west - ern steeps, Sink, sink in
3. Wind of the sum-mer night, Where yon - der wood-bine creeps, Fold, fold thy
4. Dreams of the sum-mer night, Tell her, her lov - er keeps Watch, while in

gold - en light, She sleeps, my la - dy sleeps, She sleeps, she sleeps, my la - dy sleeps.
sil - ver light, She sleeps, my la - dy sleeps, She sleeps, she sleeps, my la - dy sleeps.
pin-ions light, She sleeps, my la - dy sleeps, She sleeps, she sleeps, my la - dy sleeps.
slumbers light She sleeps, my la - dy sleeps, She sleeps, she sleeps, my la - dy sleeps.

*rall. pp*

312

# Battle Hymn of the Republic

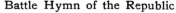

JULIA WARD HOWE                                    Old Plantation Melody

1. Mine eyes have seen the glo - ry of the com-ing of the Lord; He is
2. I have seen him in the watch-fires of a hun-dred cir - cling camps; They have
3. I have read a fier - y gos - pel, writ in bur-nished rows of steel, "As ye
4. He has sound - ed forth the trum - pet that shall nev - er call re - treat; He is
5. In the beau - ty of the lil - ies Christ was born a - cross the sea, With a

tramp - ing out the vin - tage where the grapes of wrath are stored; He hath
build - ed Him an al - tar in the eve - ning dews and damps; I have
deal with my con - tem - ners, so with you my grace shall deal; Let the
sift - ing out the hearts of men be - fore his judg-ment - seat; O, be
glo - ry in His bo - som that trans - fig - ures you and me; As He

loosed the fateful lightning of his ter - ri - ble quick sword : His truth is march - ing on.
read his righteous sentence by the dim and flar - ing lamps : His day is march - ing on.
He - ro, born of wo-man, crush the ser-pent with his heel, Since God is march - ing on.
swift, my soul, to an-swer Him! be ju - bi - lant, my feet : Our God is march - ing on.
died to make men ho - ly, let us die to make men free, While God is march - ing on.

**CHORUS**

Glo - ry, glo - ry, hal - le - lu - jah! Glo - ry, glo - ry, hal - le - lu - jah!

Glo - ry, glo - ry, hal - le - lu - jah! His truth is march - ing on.

# John Brown's Body

**1** John Brown's body lies a-mould'ring in the grave,
John Brown's body lies a-mould'ring in the grave,
John Brown's body lies a-mould'ring in the grave,
His soul is marching on!
Glory, glory, hallelujah!
Glory, glory, hallelujah!
Glory, glory, hallelujah!
His soul is marching on!

**2** The stars of heaven are looking kindly down,
On the grave of old John Brown! Cho. — Glory, etc.

**3** He's gone to be a soldier in the army of the Lord!
His soul is marching on. Cho. — Glory, etc.

**4** John Brown's knapsack is strapped upon his back!
His soul is marching on. Cho. — Glory, etc.

## JOHN BROWN'S BODY (Another Version)

**1** Old John Brown lies a-mouldering in the grave,
Old John Brown lies slumbering in his grave —
But John Brown's soul is marching with the brave,
His soul is marching on.
Glory, glory, hallelujah!
Glory, glory, hallelujah!
Glory, glory, hallelujah!
His soul is marching on.

**2** He has gone to be a soldier in the army of the Lord,
He is sworn as a private in the ranks of the Lord —
He shall stand at Armageddon with his brave old sword,
When Heaven is marching on.
Glory, glory, hallelujah, etc.
For Heaven is marching on.

**3** He shall file in front where the lines of battle form —
He shall face to front when the squares of battle form —
Time with the column, and charge with the storm,
Where men are marching on.
Glory, glory, hallelujah, etc.
True men are marching on.

**4** Ah, foul tyrants! do ye hear him where he comes?
Ah, black traitors! do ye know him as he comes?
In thunder of the cannon and roll of the drums,
As we go marching on.
Glory, glory, hallelujah, etc.
We all go marching on.

**5** Men may die, and moulder in the dust —
Men may die, and arise again from dust,
Shoulder to shoulder, in the ranks of the Just,
When Heaven is marching on.
Glory, glory, hallelujah, etc.
The Lord is marching on.

H. H. BROWNELL

# The Old Sexton

PARK BENJAMIN

HENRY RUSSELL

1. Nigh to a grave that was new - ly made, Lean'd a sex - ton old, on his
2. "I gath - er them in; for, man and boy, Year af - ter year of
3. "Ma - ny are with me, but still I'm a - lone; I'm king of the dead—and I
4. "I gath - er them in and their fi - nal rest is here, down here, in the

earth - worn spade; His work was done, and he paused to wait The
grief and joy, I've build - ed the hous - es that lie a - round, In
make my throne On a mon - u-ment slab of mar - ble cold, And my
earth's dark breast!" And the Sex - ton ceased—for the fu - n'ral train Wound

staccato colla voce

fu - n'ral train thro' the o - pen gate: A rel - ic of by - gone
ev - 'ry nook of this bu - rial ground. Moth - er and daugh - ter,
scep - tre of rule is the spade I hold; Come they from cot - age or
mute - ly o'er that sol - emn plain; And I said to my heart—when

days was he, And his locks were white as the foam - y sea; And
fa - ther and son, Come to my sol -i - tude, one by one,— But
come they from hall, Man - kind are my sub - jects— all, all, all! Let them
time is told, A might - ier voice than that sex - ton's old Will

these words came from his lips so thin, "I gath-er them in, I gath-er them in,
come they stran-gers or come they kin— I gath-er them in, I gath-er them in,
loi - ter in pleas - ure, or toil -ful-ly spin— I gath-er them in, I gath-er them in,
sound o'er the last trump's dread-ful din—"I gath-er them in, I gath-er them in,

gath-er, gath-er, gath-er, I gath-er them in."

# The Sword of Bunker Hill

W. R. WALLACE

B. COVERT

*Allegretto*

1. He lay up - on his dy - ing bed; His eye was grow - ing dim, When
2. The sword was bro't, the sol-dier's eye Lit with a sud - den flame; And
3. "'Twas on that dread, im - mor-tal day, I dared the Brit-on's band, A
4. "Oh, keep the sword!"—his ac-cents broke— A smile— and he was dead! His

with a fee - ble voice he call'd His weep-ing son to him: "Weep
as he grasp'd the an-cient blade, He murmured War - ren's name: Then
cap - tain raised this blade on me— I tore it from his hand; And
wrin - kled hand still grasped the blade Up - on that dy - ing bed. The

not, my boy!" the vet-'ran said, "I bow to Heav'n's high will,— But
said, "My boy, I leave you gold.— But what is rich - er still, I
while the glo - rious bat - tle raged, It light - ened free-dom's will— For
son re-mains; the sword re-mains— Its glo - ry grow-ing still— And

quick - ly from yon ant - lers bring The Sword of Bun - ker Hill; But
leave you, mark me, mark me now — The Sword of Bun - ker Hill; I
boy, the God of free - dom blessed The Sword of Bun - ker Hill; For,
twen - ty mil - lions bless the sire, And Sword of Bun - ker Hill; And

quick - ly from yon ant - lers bring The Sword of Bun - ker Hill."
leave you, mark me, mark me now — The Sword of Bun - ker Hill.
boy, the God of free - dom blessed The Sword of Bun - ker Hill.
twen - ty mil - lions bless the sire, And Sword of Bun - ker Hill.

## The Spring
### ROUND

Dr. HAYES

The Spring is come, I hear the birds that sing from bush to bush.

Hark! hark! I hear them sing.

The lin - net and the lit - tle wren, the black-bird and the thrush.

318

## The Field of Monterey

M. DIX SULLIVAN

1. The sweet church bells are peal-ing out A cho-rus wild and free, And
2. When spring was here with op-'ning flow'rs And I the proud May queen, And
3. The per-sim-mon is blush-ing now, The paw-paw's fruit is red, But
4. The bu-gles swell their wild-est notes And loud the can-non roar, And

ev - 'ry thing re - joic - ing For the glo - rious vic - to - ry; But
all the young and gay were met To dance up - on the green; The
he, the loved and man - ly one, Lies low a - mong the dead. And
mad - ly peal the sweet church bells For ho - ly rest no more; But

bit - ter tears are gush - ing For the gal - lant and the gay. Who
no - blest and the man - li - est Was by my side that day, Who
bit - ter tears are fall - ing For the gal - lant and the gay Who
lone - ly hearts are bleed - ing Up - on this glo - ri - ous day, For the

now in death are sleep-ing On the field of Mon-te-rey; On the
now in death is sleep-ing On the field of Mon-te-rey; On the
now in death are sleep-ing On the field of Mon-te-rey; On the
loved in death are sleep-ing On the field of Mon-te-rey; On the

field of Mon-te-rey, Who now in death are sleep-ing On the field of Mon-te-rey.
field of Mon-te-rey, Who now in death is sleep-ing On the field of Mon-te-rey.
field of Mon-te-rey, Who new in death are sleep-ing On the field of Mon-te-rey.
field of Mon-te-rey, For the lov'd in death are sleep-ing On the field of Mon-te-rey

## Our Native Song

METHFESSEL

1. O sing with voi-ces clear and strong, The song of songs up-rais-ing; Our
2. Thou old-en, bard-ic fa-ther-land, Thou land of truth and beau-ty, Thou
3. With thee for aye we cast our lot; To home and vir-tue tru-ly We

own, our fa-thers' na-tive song, Set wood-land ech-oes prais-ing.
dear, thou well-be-lov-ed land, Thy praise is joy and du-ty.
ded-i-cate our hand, and heart, And soul, and spir-it new-ly.

# Gaudeamus Igitur

*Andante*

1. Let us now in youth re-joice, None can just-ly blame us;
2. Where have all our fa-thers gone? Here we'll see them nev-er:
3. Raise we, then, the joy-ous shout: Life to Al - ma Ma - ter!

For, when gold - en youth has fled, And in age our joys are dead,
Seek the gods' se - rene a - bode  Cross the dol - 'rous Sty-gian flood;
Life to each Pro - fes - sor here, Life to all our com-rades dear,

*cres.*  *f*

Then the dust doth claim us, Then the dust doth claim us.
There they dwell for - ev - er, There they dwell for - ev - er.
May they leave us nev - er, May they leave us nev - er.

## Gaudeamus Igitur

Gaudeamus igitur,
  Juvenes dum sumus;
Gaudeamus igitur,
  Juvenes dum sumus;
Post jucundam juventutem,
Post molestam senectutem,
  Nos habebit humus,
  Nos habebit humus.

Ubi sunt, qui ante nos
  In mundo fuere?
Ubi sunt, qui ante nos
  In mundo fuere?

Transeas ad superos,
Abeas ad inferos,
  Quos si vis videre,
  Quos si vis videre.

Vivat academia,
  Vivant professores,
Vivat academia,
  Vivant professores,
Vivat membrum quodlibet,
Vivant membra quælibet,
  Semper sint in flore,
  Semper sint in flore.

# The Dutch Company

MALE VOICES

1. Oh! when you hear the roll of the big bass drum, Then you may know that the
2. When Greek meets Greek, then comes the tug of war, When Deitch meets Deitch, then comes the

Deitch have come; For the Deitch com-pa-ny is the best com-pa-ny That
la - ger beer; For the Deitch com-pa-ny is the best com-pa-ny That

ev - er came o - ver from Old Ger - ma-ny. Ho - ra ho - ra

ho - ra la la la la, Ho - ra, Ho - ra, ho - ra la la la la,

Tra la la la la, Tra la la la la, He is my oys - ter raw.

# Love's Young Dream

THOMAS MOORE

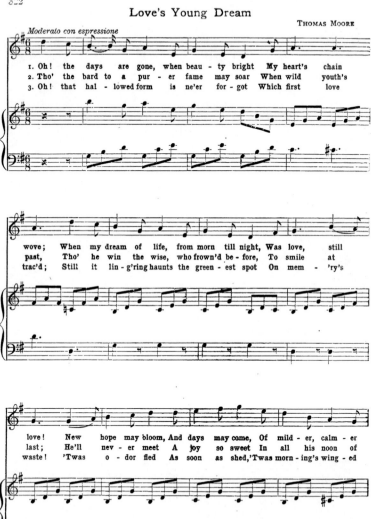

*Moderato con espressione*

1. Oh! the days are gone, when beau - ty bright My heart's chain
2. Tho' the bard to a pur - er fame may soar When wild youth's
3. Oh! that hal - lowed form is ne'er for - got Which first love

wove; When my dream of life, from morn till night, Was love, still
past, Tho' he win the wise, who frown'd be - fore, To smile at
trac'd; Still it lin - g'ring haunts the green - est spot On mem - 'ry's

love! New hope may bloom, And days may come, Of mild - er, calm - er
last; He'll nev - er meet A joy so sweet In all his noon of
waste! 'Twas o - dor fled As soon as shed,'Twas morn - ing's wing - ed

beam, But there's nothing half so sweet in life, As love's young
fame, As when first he sung to wo - man's ear His soul - felt
dream, 'Twas a light that ne'er can shine a - gain On life's dull

dream! Oh! there's noth-ing half so sweet in life, As love's young dream!
flame, And, at ev - 'ry close, she blush'd to hear The one lov'd name!
stream! Oh! 'twas light that ne'er can shine a - gain On life's dull stream.

## Cradle Song

1. Sleep, ba - by, sleep! Thy fa - ther guards the sheep, Thy moth - er shakes the
2. Sleep, ba - by, sleep! The large stars are the sheep, The lit - tle ones the
3. Sleep, ba - by, sleep! Our Sav - iour loves His sheep, He is the Lamb of

dreamland-tree, And from it fall sweet dreams for thee; Sleep, ba - by, sleep! Sleep, ba - by, sleep!
lambs, I guess, The gen-tle moon the shep-herd-ess; Sleep, ba - by, sleep! Sleep, ba - by, sleep!
God on high, Who for our sakes came down to die; Sleep, ba - by, sleep! Sleep, ba - by, sleep!

# Jerusalem

NELLA

HENRY PARKER

1. From out their peace-ful vil-lage A-long the sun-lit
2. He rides as Is-rael's rul-ers Once rode in king-ly

way, The Prince of Peace leads on-ward A pil-grim band this day. Then
state, The palm-leaves wave a-round Him, The peo-ple throng the gate. Re-

lo! with shout tri-umph-ant They hear the hill-side ring, With shouts of crowds that
joice, O Gold-en Ci-ty! Let loud Ho-san-nas ring, While thro' thy streets He

has-ten To greet their pro-phet King. Ho-san-na! Ho-
rid-eth, Thy Sav-iour and thy King. Ho-san-na! Ho-

## Jerusalem

King!.. King!.. Ho - san - - - - - - - - na,

Ho - san - - na!

## Farewell Song

From the German, by H. ZICK

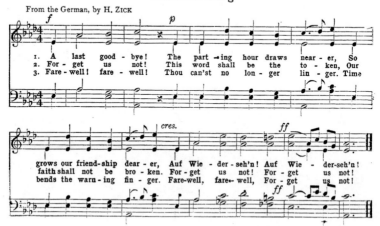

1. A  last  good - bye!  The  part - ing  hour  draws  near - er,  So
2. For - get  us  not!  This  word  shall  be  the  to - ken,  Our
3. Fare - well!  fare - well!  Thou  can'st  no  lon - ger  lin - ger. Time

grows our friend-ship dear - er, Auf Wie - der - seh'n! Auf Wie - der-seh'n!
faith shall not be bro - ken. For - get us not! For - get us not!
bends the warn - ing fin - ger. Fare-well, fare - well, For - get us not!

# Home Again

MARSHALL S. PIKE

1. Home a-gain, home a-gain From a for-eign shore! And oh, it
2. Hap-py hearts, hap-py hearts, With mine have laughed in glee, But oh, the
3. Mu-sic sweet, mu-sic soft, Lin-gers round the place, And oh, I

fills my soul with joy To meet my friends once more. Here I dropped the
friends I loved in youth Seem hap-pi-er to me; And if my guide should
feel the child-hood charm That time can-not ef-face. Then give me but my

part-ing tear, To cross the o-cean's foam, But now I'm once a-gain with those
be the fate Which bids me long-er roam, But death a-lone can break the tie
homestead roof, I'll ask no pal-ace dome, For I can live a hap-py life

CHORUS

Who kind-ly greet me home. Home a-gain, home a-gain, From a for-eign shore!
That binds my heart to home.
With those I love at home.

And oh, it fills my soul with joy To meet my friends once more.

# Belle Mahone

J. H. McNaughton

*With simplicity*

1. Soon be-yond the har-bor bar, Shall my bark be sail-ing far,— O'er the world I
2. Lone-ly like a withered tree, What is all the world to me? Life and light were
3. Calm-ly, sweet-ly slumber on, (On-ly one I call my own!) While in tears I

wan-der lone, Sweet Belle Ma - hone. . . O'er thy grave I weep good-bye,
all in thee, Sweet Belle Ma - hone. . . Dai - sies pale are grow-ing o'er
wan-der lone, Sweet Belle Ma - hone. . . Fa - ded now seems ev - 'ry-thing,

Hear, O hear my lone-ly cry, O without thee what am I, Sweet Belle Ma - hone?
All my heart can e'er a-dore, Shall I meet thee nev-er-more, Sweet Belle Ma - hone?
But when comes e - ter-nal spring, With thee I'll be wan-der-ing, Sweet Belle Ma - hone?

## Belle Mahone

CHORUS

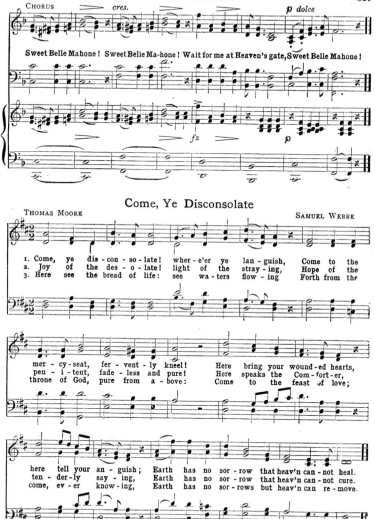

Sweet Belle Mahone! Sweet Belle Ma-hone! Wait for me at Heaven's gate, Sweet Belle Mahone!

## Come, Ye Disconsolate

THOMAS MOORE

SAMUEL WEBBE

1. Come, ye dis-con-so-late! wher-e'er ye lan-guish, Come to the
2. Joy of the des-o-late! light of the stray-ing, Hope of the
3. Here see the bread of life: see wa-ters flow-ing Forth from the

mer-cy-seat, fer-vent-ly kneel! Here bring your wound-ed hearts,
pen-i-tent, fade-less and pure! Here speaks the Com-fort-er,
throne of God, pure from a-bove: Come to the feast of love;

here tell your an-guish; Earth has no sor-row that heav'n can-not heal.
ten-der-ly say-ing, Earth has no sor-row that heav'n can-not cure.
come, ev-er know-ing, Earth has no sor-rows but heav'n can re-move.

# Would I Were with Thee

Mrs. Norton

Carlo Bosetti

1. Would I were with thee ev - 'ry day and hour, Which now I
2. Would I were with thee when, the world for - get - ting, Thy wea - ry
3. Would I were with thee when, no lon - ger feign - ing The hur - ried
4. Would I were with thee when the day is break - ing, And when tho

pass so sad - ly far from thee; Would that my form pos-sess'd the ma - gic
limbs up - on the turf are thrown, While bright and red our eve - ning sun is
laugh that sti - fles back a sigh, When thy young lip pours forth its sweet com -
moon has lit the lone - ly sea, Or when in crowds some care - less note a -

power To follow where my heavy heart would be; What-e'er thy lot
set - ting, And all thy tho'ts be - long to heav'n a - lone; While hap - py dreams
plaining, And tears have quench'd the light within thine eye; When all seems dark
waking Speaks to thy heart in mem - o - ry of me! In joy or pain,

o'er land or sea, Would I were with thee e - ter-nal-ly !
thy thoughts em-ploy, Would I were with thee in . . . thy joy !
and sad be-low, Would I were with thee in . . . thy woe !
by sea or shore, Would I were with thee ev - - er-more !

## Lutzow's Wild Hunt

WEBER

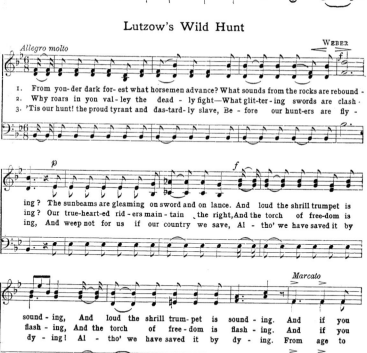

*Allegro molto*

1. From yon-der dark for-est what horsemen advance? What sounds from the rocks are rebound -
2. Why roars in yon val-ley the dead-ly fight—What glit-ter-ing swords are clash ·
3. 'Tis our hunt! the proud tyrant and das-tard-ly slave, Be - fore our hunt-ers are fly -

ing? The sunbeams are gleaming on sword and on lance. And loud the shrill trumpet is
ing? Our true-heart-ed rid-ers main-tain the right, And the torch of free-dom is
ing, And weep not for us if our country we save, Al-tho' we have saved it by

sound-ing, And loud the shrill trum-pet is sound-ing. And if you
flash-ing, And the torch of free-dom is flash-ing. And if you
dy-ing! Al-tho' we have saved it by dy-ing. From age to

Marcato

## Lutzow's Wild Hunt

1 & 2. ask what you there be-hold— 'Tis the hunt, 'Tis the hunt.
3. age it shall still be told— 'Twas the hunt, 'Twas the hunt.

1 & 2. 'Tis the hunt of Lut-zow the free and the bold, the bold;
3. 'Twas the hunt of Lut-zow the free and the bold, the bold;

'Tis the hunt of Lut-zow, the free and the bold.
'Twas the hunt of Lut-zow, the free and the bold.

## Lovely Night

### MALE VOICES

F. X. CHWATAL

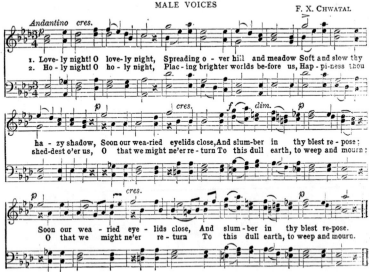

1. Love-ly night! O love-ly night, Spreading o-ver hill and meadow Soft and slow thy
2. Ho-ly night! O ho-ly night, Plac-ing brighter worlds be-fore us, Hap-pi-ness thou

ha-zy shadow, Soon our wea-ried eyelids close, And slumber in thy blest re-pose;
shed-dest o'er us, O that we might ne'er re-turn To this dull earth, to weep and mourn;

Soon our wea-ried eye-lids close, And slum-ber in thy blest re-pose.
O that we might ne'er re-turn To this dull earth, to weep and mourn.

# Santa Lucia

Neapolitan Boat Song

1. O, moon, whose mys - tic veil, From the skies fall - ing, Gilds sigh - ing
2. Zeph - yrs are ne'er at rest O'er the sea bring - ing Cool - ness to
3. What great - er joy can be In our love - dream - ing, Than thus to

wave - lets pale, To our hearts call - ing; Glo - rious the sum - mer night,
brow and breast, Far a - way sing - ing. Still waits my bark for thee,
drift with thee, O'er wave - lets gleam - ing? Bride borne o'er sum - mer sea,

Sea - strand and billows white, San - ta Lu - ci - a, San - ta Lu - ci - a!
Come, dream and drift with me, San - ta Lu - ci - a, San - ta Lu - ci - a!
Na - ples, thy pride to be, San - ta Lu - ci - a, San - ta Lu - ci - a!

# Robin Ruff

HENRY RUSSELL

1. If I had but a thou - sand a year, Gaf - fer Green! If I
2. The best wish you could have, take my word, Rob - in Ruff, Would scarce
3. I'd do I . . scarce - ly know what, Gaf - fer Green, I'd
4. But when you are a - ged and grey, Rob - in Ruff, And the
5. I scarce - ly can tell what you mean, Gaf - fer Green, For your
6. There's a place that is bet - ter than this, Rob - in Ruff, And I

had but a thou-sand a year, . . What a man would I be, and what
find you in bread or in beer; . . But be hon - est and true, and say
go, faith! I hard - ly know where; . I'd scat - ter the chink and leave
day of your death it draws near, . . Say what with your pains would you
ques - tions are al - ways so queer, . But as oth - er folks die, I sup -
hope in my heart you'll go there, . . Where the poor man's as great though he

sights would I see, If I had but a thou - sand a
what would you do If you had but a thou - sand a
oth - ers to think, If I had but a thou - sand a
do with your gains, If you then had a thou - sand a
pose so must I.— What, and give up your thou - sand a
hath no es - tate, Aye, as if he'd a thou - sand a

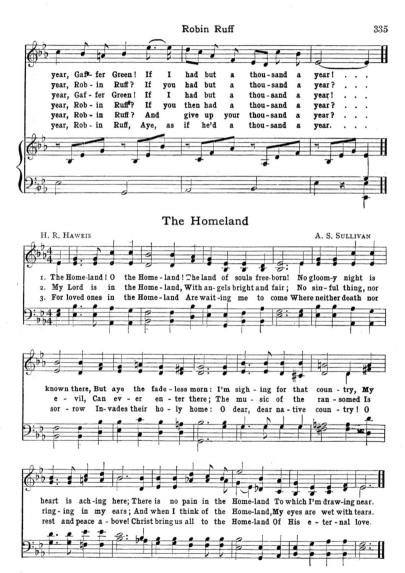

year, Gaf-fer Green! If I had but a thou-sand a year! . . .
year, Rob-in Ruff? If you had but a thou-sand a year? . . .
year, Gaf-fer Green! If I had but a thou-sand a year! . . .
year, Rob-in Ruff? If you then had a thou-sand a year? . . .
year, Rob-in Ruff? And give up your thou-sand a year? . . .
year, Rob-in Ruff, Aye, as if he'd a thou-sand a year. . . .

## The Homeland

H. R. HAWEIS

A. S. SULLIVAN

1. The Home-land! O the Home-land! The land of souls free-born! No gloom-y night is
2. My Lord is in the Home-land, With an-gels bright and fair; No sin-ful thing, nor
3. For loved ones in the Home-land Are wait-ing me to come Where neither death nor

known there, But aye the fade-less morn: I'm sigh-ing for that coun-try, My
e - vil, Can ev - er en - ter there; The mu - sic of the ran-somed Is
sor - row In-vades their ho - ly home: O dear, dear na-tive coun-try! O

heart is ach-ing here; There is no pain in the Home-land To which I'm draw-ing near.
ring-ing in my ears; And when I think of the Home-land, My eyes are wet with tears.
rest and peace a - bove! Christ bring us all to the Home-land Of His e - ter-nal love.

# When the Lights are Low

GERALD M. LANE

1. When twi-light falls on the dim old walls, And day is past and done; As we sit and dream in the fad-ing gleam, Come mem-'ries one by one. . . . Old friends known in the years long gone, In fan-cy greet us still, And voi-ces dear, that we long to hear, The si-lence seem to fill.

2. With dis-tant sounds in the streets a-round, The throng goes surg-ing by; But far a-way in dreams we stray, Where ver-dant mead-ows lie. . . . There once more, as in days of yore, To roam each well-known way, Till o-ver all night's shad-ows fall, And dreamland fades a-way.

Just when the day is o - ver, Just when the lights are low, . . .

Back to the heart re - turn - eth Life's gold - en long a - go; . . .

Far, far a - way we wan - der, Watch-ing the fire - light gleams; . .

Far, far a - way from the world's shadows grey, In - to the land of dreams.

HENRY C. WATSON

# O Loving Heart, Trust On

L. M. GOTTSCHALK

*Andante moderato*

1. There are
2. That happy

tho'ts which seem to come from heav'n . . To calm all pain, all pain and strife ; As dew falls
tho't . . shed o'er my life . . . A bright, a bright and joy - ful ray, As sun-light

on the parch-ed flower To nur-ture it, to nourish it to
gilds the night's dim clouds Ere breaks, ere breaks the glo-rious

*cres.*

*f espress.*

life. . . . . There came to me a hap - py thought, One morn when hope seem'd
day. . . . . My soul is bath'd in sun - shine, All gloom - y dreams are

*dim.*

## O Give Me a Home by the Sea

E. A. HOSMER

*Con spirito*

1. Oh! give me    a home by    the sea,    Where wild waves are crest - ed    with
2. At  morn when the sun from   the east    Comes man - tled  in    crim - son  and
3. At  eve  when the moon in  her pride    Rides queen  of  the    soft  sum - mer

foam,    Where shrill  winds  are car - ol - ing    free,    As
gold,    Whose hues    on    the bil-lows  are    cast,    Which
[night,    And gleams    on    the mur-mur -ing    tide,    With

o'er  the blue  wa-ters they    come;    For I'd list  to  the ocean's loud
spar - kle with splendor  un - told,—    Oh!    then  by the  shore  would I
floods of her    sil - ver - y    light,—    Oh    earth has  no beau-ty  so

roar, And joy in its stormi - est glee, Nor ask in this wide world for
stray, And roam as the hal - cy - on free, From en — vy and care far a -
rare, No place that is dear - er to me. Then give me so free and so

more, . . . Than a home by the deep heav-ing sea, A home, a
way, . . . At my home by the deep heav-ing sea! home, my
fair, . . . A home by the deep heav-ing sea! A home, a

home, A home by the heav - ing sea, A
home, My home by the heav - ing sea, My
home, A home by the heav - ing sea, A

## O Give Me a Home by the Sea

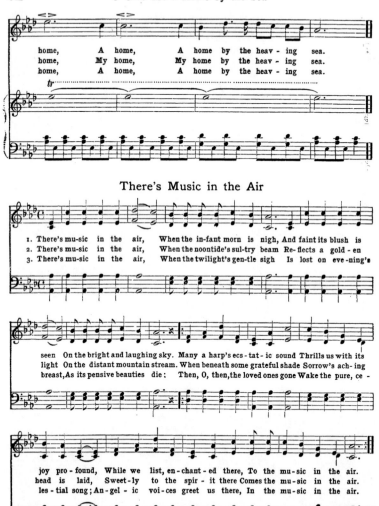

home,    A    home,      A    home    by    the    heav - ing    sea.
home,    My    home,      My    home    by    the    heav - ing    sea.
home,    A    home,      A    home    by    the    heav - ing    sea.

## There's Music in the Air

1. There's mu-sic in the air,    When the in-fant morn is nigh, And faint its blush is
2. There's mu-sic in the air,    When the noontide's sul-try beam Re- flects a gold - en
3. There's mu-sic in the air,    When the twilight's gen-tle sigh Is lost on eve -ning's

seen On the bright and laughing sky. Many a harp's ecs-tat-ic sound Thrills us with its
light On the distant mountain stream. When beneath some grateful shade Sorrow's ach- ing
breast, As its pensive beauties die:   Then, O, then, the loved ones gone Wake the pure, ce -

joy pro - found, While we list, en - chant - ed there, To the mu-sic in the air.
head is laid,   Sweet-ly to the spir - it there Comes the mu-sic in the air.
les - tial song; An - gel - ic voi-ces greet us there, In the mu-sic in the air.

# Rig-a-jig

### (MALE VOICES)

*Presto*

1. As I was walk - ing down the street, Heigh - o, heigh - o, heigh -
2. Said I to her, "What is your trade?" Heigh - o, heigh - o, heigh -

o, heigh- o, A pret - ty girl I chanced to meet, Heigh-o, heigh-o, heigh-o.
o, heigh- o, Said she to me, "I'm a weav-er's maid," Heigh-o, heigh-o, heigh-o.

CHORUS

Rig - a - jig - jig, and a - way we go, a - way we go, a - way we go;

Rig - a - jig - jig, and a - way we go, Heigh-o, heigh-o, heigh - o.

FINE

D.S.

heigh - o, heigh - o, heigh - o, heigh - o, heigh - o, heigh - o, heigh - o, heigh - o.

# What Fairy-like Music

Mrs. C. B. Wilson

J. De-Pinna

Solo *Grazioso*

1. What fai - ry - like mu-sic steals o-ver the sea, En-trancing the sen-ses with
2. The winds are all hush'd and the wa-ters at rest; They sleep like the passions in

*p*

**Duet**

charm'd mel - o - dy? What fairy-like mu-sic steals o-ver the sea, En-trancing the
in - fan-cy's breast! The winds are all hush'd and the waters at rest; They sleep like the

sen - ses with charm'd mel-o-dy? 'Tis the voice of the mer-maid, that floats o'er the
pas - sions in in - fan-cy's breast. Till storms shall un-chain them from out their dark

main, As she mingles her song with the gon-do-lier's strain! 'Tis the voice of the
cave, And break the re-pose of the soul and the wave, 'Till storms shall un-

*poco cres.*

mermaid that floats o'er the main, As she mingles her song with the gon-do-lier's strain:
chain them from out their dark cave, And break the re-pose of the soul and the wave.

*p*

## Mary Had a Little Lamb

1. Ma-ry had a lit-tle lamb, lit-tle lamb, lit-tle lamb, Ma-ry had a
2. And ev-'rywhere that Ma-ry went, Ma-ry went, Ma-ry went, And ev-'rywhere that

lit-tle lamb, Its fleece was white as snow.
Ma-ry went, The lamb was sure to go.

3 It followed her to school one day,
  Which was against the rule.

4 It made the children laugh and play
  To see a lamb at school.

5 And so the teacher turned him out,
  But still he lingered near.

6 And waited patiently about
  Till Mary did appear.

# Over the Garden Wall

HARRY HUNTER

G. D. FOX

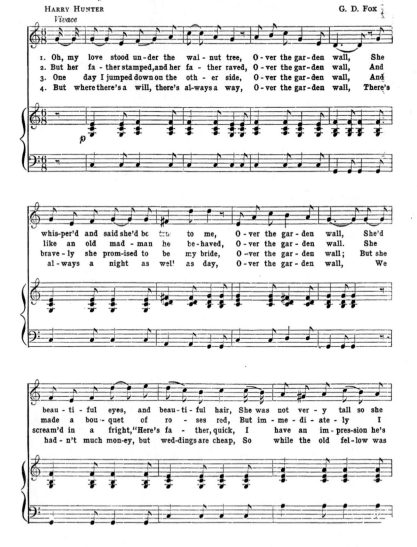

1. Oh, my love stood un-der the wal-nut tree, O-ver the gar-den wall, She whis-per'd and said she'd be true to me, O-ver the gar-den wall, She'd beau-ti-ful eyes, and beau-ti-ful hair, She was not ver-y tall so she

2. But her fa-ther stamped, and her fa-ther raved, O-ver the gar-den wall, And like an old mad-man he be-haved, O-ver the gar-den wall. She made a bou-quet of ro-ses red, But im-me-di-ate-ly I

3. One day I jumped down on the oth-er side, O-ver the gar-den wall, And brave-ly she prom-ised to be my bride, O-ver the gar-den wall; But she scream'd in a fright, "Here's fa-ther, quick, I have an im-pres-sion he's

4. But where there's a will, there's al-ways a way, O-ver the gar-den wall, There's al-ways a night as well as day, O-ver the gar-den wall, We had-n't much mon-ey, but wed-dings are cheap, So while the old fel-low was

stood on a chair, And ma-ny a time have I kissed her there, O-ver the gar-den wall.
popped up my head, He gave me a buck-et of wa-ter instead, O-ver the gar-den wall.
bring-ing a brick;" But I got the im-pression of one good kick, O-ver the gar-den wall.
snor-ing a-sleep, With a lad and a lad-der she managed to creep O-ver the gar-den wall.

CHORUS

O - ver the gar - den wall, . . The sweet-est girl of all, . . There

nev - er were yet such eyes of jet, And you may bet, I'll nev - er for - get The

night our lips in kiss - es met, O - ver the gar - den wall. . .

# Simon the Cellarer

W. H. Bellamy

J. L. Hatton

1. Old Si-mon the Cell-ar - er keeps a rare store, Of Malm-sey and Mal - voi- sie . . And
2. Dame Mar- ger-y sits in her own still room, And a ma - tron sage is she. . . From
3. Old Si -mon reclines in his high-back'd chair, And talks about tak-ing a wife; . And

Cyp-rus,and who can say how man-y more! For a char-y old soul is he. . . A
thence oft at cur-few is waft-ed a fume; She says it is Rose-ma - rie, . . She
Mar-ger-y of - ten is heard to de-clare She ought to be settled in life, . . She

char-y old soul is he. . . Of Sack and Ca- na - ry he nev - er doth fail, And
says it is Rose-ma - rie. . . But there's a small cupboard behind the back stair, And the
ought to be set-tled in life. . But Mar-ger-y has (so the maids say) a tongue And she's

all the year round there is brew-ing of ale, Yet he nev-er ail-eth, he
maids say they of-ten see Mar-ger - y there, Now Mar-ger-y says that she
not ver - y hand-some, and not ver - y young, So somehow it ends with a

quaint - ly doth say, While he keeps to his so - ber six flag-ons a day;
grows ver - y old And must take a some-thing to keep out the cold!
shake of the head, And Si - mon he brews him a tank-ard in-stead,

But ho! ho! ho! His nose doth show How oft the black Jack to his lips doth go.
But ho! ho! ho! Old Si-mon doth know, Where many a flask of his best doth go.
While ho! ho! ho! He will chuckle and crow, What! marry old Mar-ger-y no, no, no!

## Massa's in de Cold Ground

STEPHEN C. FOSTER.

1. Round de mea-dows am a - ring - ing De dark - ey's mourn - ful song, While de
2. When de au-tumn leaves were fall-ing, When de days were cold, 'Twas hard to
3. Mas - sa make de dark-eys love him, Cayse he was so kind; Now, dey

mock-ing-bird am sing - ing, Hap - py as de day am long. Where de i - vy am a -
hear old mas-sa call-ing, Cayse he was so weak and old. Now de or-ange-trees am
sad - ly weep a - bove him, Mourn-ing cayse he leave dem be-hind. I can-not work be-fore to -

creep - ing O'er de grass - y mound, Dare old mas-sa am a - sleep - ing,
bloom - ing, On de sand - y shore, Now de sum-mer days am com -ing,
mor - row, Cayse de tear - drop flow; I try to drive a - way my sor - row,

CHORUS

Sleep-ing in de cold, cold ground. Down in de corn - field Hear dat mourn-ful
Mas - sa ne - ber calls no more.
Pick - in' on de old ban - jo.

sound; All de dark-eys am a - weep - ing, Mas-sa's in de cold, cold ground.

JOHANNA GADSKI

One of Germany's most popular opera singers. She was born in Anclam, Prussia,
1871, received her musical training in her own country, and first appeared in grand
opera in New York. She created many Wagnerian parts, and made a remarkable
concert tour through America in 1898–99. Her popular encore is "Drink to Me
Only with Thine Eyes"—Heart Songs, p. 105.

**LOUISE HOMER**

A noted American contralto, in private life the wife of Sidney Homer, the composer. She was born in Pittsburgh, and made her debut as an opera singer in Paris, 1898. She has sung at Covent Garden, London, and for ten successive seasons at the Metropolitan Opera House, New York. Her popular encore is "Abide With Me"—Heart Songs, p. 447.

# Annie Lisle

H. S. Thompson

*Andante moderato*

1. Down where the wav-ing wil-lows 'Neath the sunbeams smile, Shad-ow'd o'er the
2. Sweet came the hal-low'd chiming Of the Sabbath bell, Borne on the
3. "Raise me in your arms, dear mother, Let me once more look On the green and

murm'ring wa-ters Dwelt sweet Annie Lisle; Pure as the for-est lil-y,
morn-ing breez-es Down the wood-y dell. On a bed of pain and an-guish
wav-ing wil-lows, And the flow-ing brook; Hark! those strains of an-gel mu-sic,

Nev-er thought of guile Had its home within the bo-som of sweet Annie Lisle.
Lay dear An-nie Lisle, Chang'd were the lovely fea-tures, Gone the hap-py smile.
From the choirs a-bove, Dear-est moth-er, I am go-ing; Tru-ly 'God is Love.'"

# Annie Lisle

SOLO, *then* CHORUS

Wave wil-lows, mur-mur wa-ters, Gold - en sun-beams, smile!

*mf*

*Repeat pp*

Earth - ly mu - sic can-not wa - ken Love- ly An - nie Lisle.

# Camptown Races

S. C. FOSTER

*Allegro vivace*

1. De Camptown la - dies sing dis song, Doo-dah! doo-dah! De Camptown race -track
2. De long-tail'd fil - ly, and de big black hoss, Doo-dah! doo-dah! Dey fly de track, and dey
3. Old mu - ley cow came on to de track, Doo-dah! doo-dah! De bob-tail fling her
4. See dem fly - in' on a ten-mile heat, Doo-dah! doo-dah! Round de race - track,

*mp*

nine miles long, Oh! doo-dah day! I came down dar wid my hat cav'd in, Doo-dah!
both cut a-cross, Oh! doo-dah day! De blind hoss stick'n in a big mud-hole, Doo-dah!
o-ber his back, Oh! doo-dah day. Den fly a-long like a rail-road car, Doo-dah!
den re-peat— Oh! doo-dah day! I win my money on de bob-tail nag, Doo-dah!

doo-dah! I go back home wid a pock-et full of tin, Oh! doo-dah day!
doo-dah! Can't touch de bottom wid a ten-feet pole, Oh! doo-dah day.
doo-dah! Run-nin a race wid a shoot-in' star, Oh! doo-dah day!
doo-dah! I keep my mon-ey in an old tow bag, Oh! doo-dah day!

SOLO; *then* CHORUS

Gwine to run all night, . Gwine to run all day, . . I'll

# Camptown Races

bet my mon-ey on de bob-tail nag, Some-bo-dy bet on de bay. . .

# Gentle Annie

S. C. FOSTER

*Andante con moto*

1. Thou wilt come no more, gen-tle An-nie,    Like a flow'r thy spir-it did de-
2. We have roam'd and lov'd 'mid the bow-ers,    When thy down - y cheeks were in their
3. Ah! the hours grow sad while I pon-der    Near the si - lent spot where thou art

part;    Thou art gone, a - las! like the man-y    That have
bloom;    Now I stand a - lone 'mid the flow-ers,    While they
laid,    And my heart bows down when I wan-der    By the

bloom'd in the sum-mer of the heart. Shall we nev - er more be -
min - gle their perfumes o'er thy tomb. Shall we nev - er more be -
streams and the meadows where we stray'd. Shall we nev - er more be -

hold thee, Nev-er hear thy winning voice a-gain? When the Spring-time comes, gen-tle

An - nie, When the wild flow'rs are scat-ter'd o'er the plain?

# Baby Mine

CHARLES MACKEY

ARCHIBALD JOHNSTON

1. I've a let-ter from thy sire, Ba-by mine, Ba-by mine; I could read and nev-er tire, Ba-by mine, Ba-by mine; He is sail-ing o'er the sea, He is com-ing home to me, He is com-ing back to thee! Ba-by

2. Oh, I long to see his face, Ba-by mine, Ba-by mine; In his old ac-cus-tom'd place, Ba-by mine, Ba-by mine; Like the rose of May in bloom, Like a star a-mid the gloom, Like the sun-shine in the room, Ba-by

3. I'm so glad, I can-not sleep, Ba-by mine, Ba-by mine; I'm so hap-py, I could weep, Ba-by mine, Ba-by mine; He is sail-ing o'er the sea, He is com-ing home to me, He is com-ing back to thee! Ba-by

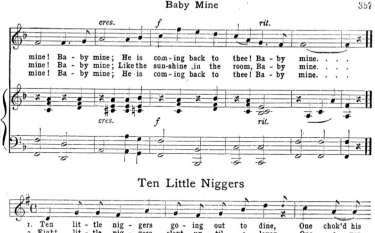

## Ten Little Niggers

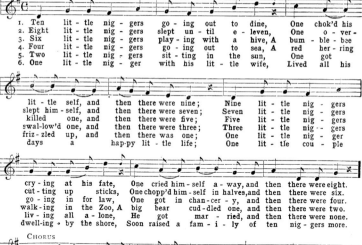

# Hark! I Hear a Voice

roll, we roll, O'er . . the deep blue sea. . .

## Peter Gray

(MALE VOICES)

*Andante*

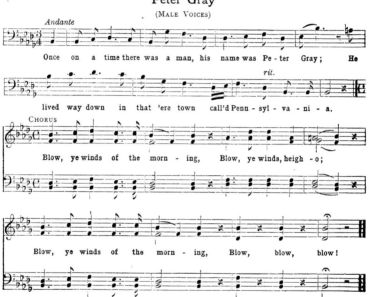

Once on a time there was a man, his name was Pe-ter Gray; He lived way down in that 'ere town call'd Penn-syl-va-ni-a.

CHORUS

Blow, ye winds of the morn-ing, Blow, ye winds, heigh-o;

Blow, ye winds of the morn-ing, Blow, blow, blow!

2 Now Peter Gray he fell in love, all with a nice young girl;
The first three letters of her name were L-U-C, Anna Quirl. Cho.

3 But just as they were going to wed, her papa he said "No!"
And consequently she was sent way off to Ohio. Cho.

4 And Peter Gray he went to trade for furs and other skins,
Till he was caught and scalp-y-ed, by the bloody Inji-ins. Cho.

5 When Lucy Anna heard the news, she straightway took to bed,
And never did get up again until she di-i-ed. Cho.

# The Mermaid

*Moderato*

1. 'Twas Fri - day morn . when we . . set . . sail, And we
2. Then up spake the cap - tain . . of our gal - lant ship, And a
3. Then up spake the cook of our gal - lant ship, And a
4. Then three times a - round went our gal - lant ship, And

were not far from the land, When the cap - tain spied a
well - spok - en man was he; "I have mar - ried a wife in
red hot cook was he; "I care much more for my
three times a - round went she; Then three times a - round went our

love - ly mer - maid, With a comb and a glass in her hand. O, the
Sa - lem town, And to - night she a wid - ow will be." O, the
ket - tles and my pots, Than I do for the depths of the sea." O, the
gal - lant ship, And she sank to the depths of the sea. O, the

o - cean waves may roll, And the storm - y winds may blow, While

we poor sail - ors go skip - ping to the tops, And the land - lub - bers lie down be -

low, be-low, be-low, And the land-lub-bers lie down be-low.

## Forsaken

(MALE VOICES)    KOSCHAT

*Slow*

1. For - sak - en, for - sak - en, for - sak - en am I; Like a
2. A mound in the church - yard, that blos - soms hang o'er; It is

stone in the cause-way, my bur - ied hopes lie; I go to the
there my love sleep-eth, to wak - en no more; 'Tis there all my

church-yard, my eyes fill with tears; And kneel-ing I weep there, Oh, my
foot-steps, my pas-sions all lead; And there my heart turn - eth; I'm for-

love, loved for years; And kneel-ing I weep there; Oh, my love, loved for years.
sak - en in - deed; And there my heart turn - eth; I'm for - sak - en in-deed.

# Beautiful Bells

### DUET AND CHORUS

GEORGE COOPER

Arr. by W. F. WELLMAN, jr.

1. Beau-ti-ful bells! O beau-ti-ful bells! Ring-ing so sweetly a-gain and a-gain!
2. Voice of the morn And voice of the night, Wak-en, O wak-en the mem'ries of old!

Welcomes of joy and wea-ry fare-wells, Chim...g in sunlight and rain.
Bring to my heart your dreams of delight, Vis-ions of beauty un-told!

Long, long a-go, so dear un-to me, O hap-py and pure was the

mes-sage you bore, Loud o'er the vale, and soft o'er the sea, O could I but

hear you once more! Beau-ti-ful bells! or mer-ry or sad,

Tell - ing your mes - sage of good - ness to all; Whis - per of

mo - ments hopeful and glad, Van-ished be-yond our re - call!

**CHORUS**

Beau - ti - ful bells! O beau-ti - ful bells! Ring-ing so sweet-ly a-gain and a-gain

Beau-ti - ful, beau-ti-ful, beau-ti - ful bells! Beau - ti - ful, beau - ti - ful, beau- ti- ful bells!

*rall.*

Welcomes of joy and wea-ry farewells, Beau-ti - ful, beau-ti-ful, beau-ti - ful bells!

Beau - ti - ful, beau-ti-ful, beau-ti - ful bells! Beau-ti - ful, beau-ti - ful, beau - ti - ful bells!

*8va.*

# Lullaby

From JAKOBOWSKI's "Erminie"

1. Dear moth-er, in dreams I see her, . . With lov'd face sweet and calm, . . And
2. Ah! e'en when her life was ebb-ing, . . Her words were all to me, . . My

hear her voice With love re-joice When nest-ling on her arm. . . . I
fu-ture years Were all her fears, Her fate 'twas not to see. . . . My

think how she soft-ly press'd me, Of the tears in each glist'-ning eye, . . As her
fa-ther, I heard him weep-ing, As in sor-row he hov-er'd nigh, . . And my

watch she'd keep, When she rock'd to sleep Her child with this lul-la-by, Bye,
moth-er's plaint, In her ac-cent faint, Was ev-er this lul-la-by, Bye,

bye, bye, bye, bye, bye, bye, bye, bye, bye, bye, bye, bye.

*mf First* SOLO, *then with* CHORUS.

Bye, bye, drowsiness o'er-taking, Pret-ty lit-tle eye-lids sleep. Bye, bye,

*p* (*Only second time*)

Bye, bye, bye, bye, bye, bye, bye, bye, bye, bye,

I'll await thy waking. Darling, be thy slumbers deep! deep, bye, bye, bye, bye.

bye, bye, bye, bye, bye, bye, bye, bye, bye.

## Buffalo Gals

1. As I went lum-brin' down de street,
2. I ax'd her if she'd hab some talk,
3. I'd like to make dat gal my wife,

down de street,down de street, A lub-ly gal I chanc'd to meet, Oh!
hab some talk, hab some talk, Her feet cov-er'd up de whole side walk, As
gal my wife, gal my wife; I would be hap-py all my life, If I

she was fair to view. Oh! Buf-fa-lo gals, will ye come out to-night,will ye
she stood side by me. Oh! Buf-fa-lo gals, will ye come out to-night,will ye
had her by my side. Oh! Buf-fa-lo gals, will ye come out to-night,will ye

come out to-night, will ye come out to-night, Buf-fa-lo gals, will ye

MARIA GAY

A particularly vivacious mezzo-soprano, whose greatest success has
been "Carmen." She is Spanish by birth, a native of Catalonia, and
her principal following is in the United States. Her popular encore is
"Castanets are Sounding"—Heart Songs, p. 178.

ERNESTINE SCHUMANN-HEINK

The famous Austrian prima donna. She was born near Prague, Austria, 1861, and at the age of seventeen was leading contralto at the Dresden Court Opera. She has been most popular in Germany and in America, and has appeared in nearly all the leading cities of the United States. Her popular encore is "Home to Our Mountains"—Heart Songs, p. 452.

## Buffalo Gals

come out to-night, And dance by de light ob de moon?

## Keller's American Hymn

M. KELLER

*f Maestoso*

1. Speed our Re-pub-lic, O Fa-ther on high, Lead us in path-ways of
2. Fore-most in bat-tle, for Free-dom to stand, We rush to arms when a-
3. Rise up, proud ea-gle, rise up to the clouds, Spread thy broad wing o'er this

*p* *cres.*

jus-tice and right; Rul-ers as well as the ruled, one and all,
roused by its call; Still as of yore when George Wash-ing-ton led,
fair west-ern world! Fling from thy beak our dear ban-ner of old!

*8: mf* *f*

Gir-dle with vir-tue, the ar-mor of might! Hail! three times hail to our
Thunders our war-cry, "We con-quer or fall!" Hail! three times hail to our
Show that it still is for free-dom un-furled! Hail! three times hail to our

FINE *mf* D.S.

coun-try and flag! Rul-ers as well as the ruled, one and all,
coun-try and flag! Still as of yore when George Wash-ing-ton led,
coun-try and flag! Fling from thy beak our dear ban-ner of old!

# 'Tis but a Little Faded Flower

J. R. THOMAS

fad - ed flow'r. 'Tis but a lit - tle fad - ed flow'r, But oh, how fond - ly
gold - en hair? 'Tis but a lit - tle fad - ed flow'r, But oh, how fond - ly

dear! 'Twill bring me back one gold-en hour, Through ma-ny, thro' ma-ny a wea-ry year.

## Old Hundred

Rev. Isaac Watts

Goudimel

1. From all that dwell be - low the skies, Let the Cre - a - tor's praise a - rise;
2. E - ter - nal are Thy mer - cies, Lord; E - ter - nal truth at - tends Thy word;

Let the Re - deem - er's name be sung Through ev-'ry land, by ev - 'ry tongue.
Thy praise shall sound from shore to shore, Till suns shall rise and set no more.

# Just Before the Battle, Mother

G. F. Root

G. F. Root

1. Just be - fore the bat - tle, moth-er, I am think - ing most of you,
2. Hark! I hear the bu - gles sounding, 'Tis the sig - nal for the fight;

While up - on the field we're watch-ing, With the en - e - my in view.
Now may God pro - tect us, moth-er, As He ev - er does the right.

Com - rades brave are round me ly - ing, Filled with tho'ts of home and God; .. For
Hear the "Bat - tle Cry of Free-dom," How it swells up - on the air; .. Oh,

well they know that on the mor-row Some will sleep be- neath the sod. ..
yes, we'll ral - ly round the standard, Or we'll per - ish no - bly there. .

CHORUS

Fare-well, moth-er, you may nev-er, you may never, mother, Press me to your heart a-gain; .. But

*rit.* *Repeat pp.*

oh, you'll not for-get me, Moth-er, you will not forget me If I'm numbered with the slain.

## Juanita

*mf Andante*

1. Soft o'er the foun-tain, Ling 'ring falls the south-ern moon; Far o'er the mountain,
2. When in thy dreaming, Moons like these shall shine a-gain, And day-light beam-ing

*mf*

Breaks the day too soon! In thy dark eye's splendor, Where the warm light loves to dwell,
Prove thy dreams are vain, Wilt thou not, re-lent-ing, For thy ab-sent lov-er sigh,

*p slower*     *mf a tempo*

Wea-ry looks, yet ten-der, Speak their fond fare-well! Ni - ta! Jua - ni - ta!
In thy heart con sent-ing To a pray'r gone by! Ni - ta! Jua - ni - ta!

*p*    *mf*

*p tenderly. rit.*

Ask thy soul if we should part: Ni - ta! Jua - ni - ta! Lean thou on my heart.
Let me lin-ger by thy side! Ni - ta! Jua - ni - ta! Be my own fair bride!

*p*

# A Little More Cider

A. Hart

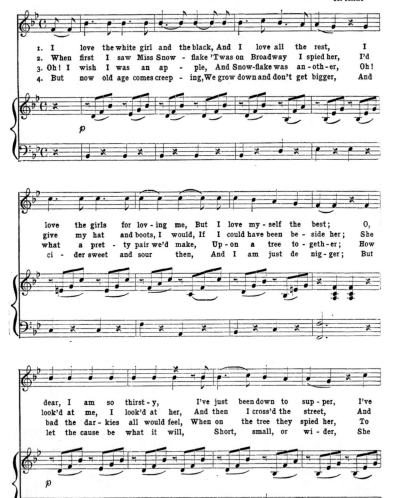

1. I love the white girl and the black, And I love all the rest, I
2. When first I saw Miss Snow - flake 'Twas on Broadway I spied her, I'd
3. Oh! I wish I was an ap - ple, And Snow-flake was an - oth - er, Oh!
4. But now old age comes creep - ing, We grow down and don't get bigger, And

love the girls for lov - ing me, But I love my - self the best; O,
give my hat and boots, I would, If I could have been be - side her; She
what a pret - ty pair we'd make, Up - on a tree to - geth - er; How
ci - der sweet and sour then, And I am just de nig - ger; But

dear, I am so thirst - y, I've just been down to sup - per, I've
look'd at me, I look'd at her, And then I cross'd the street, And
bad the dar - kies all would feel, When on the tree they spied her, To
let the cause be what it will, Short, small, or wi - der, She

drank three pails of ap - ple jack, And a tub of ap - ple but - ter.
then she smil - ing said to me, "A lit - tle more ci - der sweet."
think how lus - cious we would be, When we're made in - to ci - der.
am de ap - ple of my soul, And I'm bound to be be - side her.

CHORUS

A lit - tle more ci - der too, A lit - tle more ci - der too, A

lit - tle more ci - der for Miss Di - nah, A lit - tle more ci - der too.

# Home, Sweet Home

John Howard Payne

Henry R. Bishop

1. 'Mid pleas - ures and pal - a - ces, though we may roam, Be it
2. An ex - ile from home, splendor daz - zles in vain; Oh!
3. How sweet 'tis to sit 'neath a fond fa - ther's smile, And the
4. To thee I'll re - turn, o - ver - bur - den'd with care, The

ev - er so hum - ble, there's no place like home! A
give me my low - ly thatch'd cot - tage a - gain; The
cares of a moth - er to soothe and be - guile; Let
heart's dear - est so - lace will smile on me there; No

charm from the skies seems to hal - low us there, Which,
birds sing - ing gai - ly, that come at my call; Give me
oth - ers de - light 'mid new pleas - ures to roam, But
more from that cot - tage a - gain will I roam, Be it

# Kathleen Mavourneen

Mrs. Crawford

F. Nicholls Crouch

1. Kath - leen Ma - vour - neen! the grey dawn is break-ing, ... The
2. Kath - leen Ma - vour - neen! a - wake from thy slum - bers; .. The

horn of the hun - ter is heard on the hill; The lark from her
blue mountains glow in the sun's gold-en light; Ah! where is the

light wing the bright dew is shak - ing, Kathleen .. Mavour-neen! what,
spell that once hung on my num - bers? A - rise in ... thy beau-ty, thou

slum - b'ring still! Oh, hast thou for - got-ten how soon we must sev-er? Oh,
star of my night. Ma-vour - neen, Ma-vourneen, my sad tears are falling, To

*Espressivo e legato*

hast thou for - got-ten this day we must part? It may be for
think that from E - rin and thee I must part; It may be for

years, and it may be for - ev - er; Oh, why . . art thou si - lent, thou
years, and it may be for - ev - er; Then why . . art thou si - lent, thou

voice of     my heart?   It  may . . . be for years, and   it may be    for -

ev - er;    Then   why . . . . art thou si - lent,  Kath-leen   Ma-vour-neen?

## John Anderson, My Jo

ROBERT BURNS

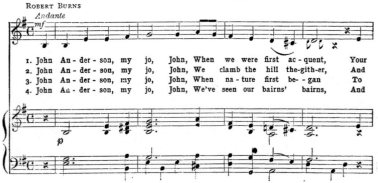

1. John An - der - son, my   jo,   John,  When   we were first ac - quent,   Your
2. John An - der - son, my   jo,   John,  We    clamb the   hill the-gith-er,   And
3. John An - der - son, my   jo,   John,  When   na - ture first be - - gan    To
4. John An - der - son, my   jo,   John,  We've   seen our bairns'   bairns,   And

locks were like the ra - ven, Your bon - ny brow was brent; But
mon-y a can - ty day, John, We've had wi' ane an - ith - er; Now
try her can - ny hand, John, Her mas - ter-wark was man; And
yet, my dear John An - der-son, I'm hap - py in your arms, And

now your brow is beld, John, Your locks are like the snaw; Yet
we maun tot - ter down, John, But hand in hand we'll go; And we'll
you a - mang the lave, John, Sae trig frae tap to toe— She
sae are ye in mine, John; I'w sure ye'll ne'er say no, Tho' the

bless - ings on your frost - y pow, John An - der-son, my jo!
sleep the - gith - er at the foot, John An - der-son, my jo.
proved her - sel' nae jour - ney - wark, John An - der-son, my jo.
days are gane that we ha'e seen, John An - der-son, my jo.

# Her Bright Smile Haunts Me Still

W. T. WRIGHTON

1. 'Tis years since last we met, And we may not meet a-gain; I have strug - gled to for - get, But the strug - gle was in vain; For her voice lives on the breeze, And her spir - it comes at will; In the

2. At the first sweet dawn of light, When I gaze up - on the deep, Her form still greets my sight, While the stars their vig - ils keep; When I close mine ach - ing eyes, Sweet dreams my sen - ses fill; And from

3. I've sail'd 'neath a - lien skies, I have trod the des - ert path, I have seen the storm a - rise, Like a gi - ant in his wrath; Ev - 'ry dan - ger I have known, That a reck-less life can fill; Yet her

mid - night, on the seas,    Her bright smile haunts me still.    For her
sleep   when I   a - rise,    Her bright smile haunts me still.    When I
pres - ence is not flown,    Her bright smile haunts me still.    Ev - 'ry

voice   lives on the breeze,    And her spir - it comes at will ;    In the
close   mine ach - ing eyes,    Sweet dreams   my sens - es   fill,    And from
dan - ger I have known,    That a reck - less life can fill ;    Yet her

mid - night, on   the seas,    Her bright smile haunts me still.
sleep   when I   a - rise,    Her bright smile haunts me still.
pres - ence is   not flown,    Her bright smile haunts me still.

# Yankee Doodle

1. Fath'r and I went down to camp A - long with Cap - tain Good - win, And
2. And there was Cap - tain Wash - ing - ton Up - on a slap - ping stal - lion, A
3. And then the feath - ers on his hat, They look'd so tar - nal fin - ey, I
4. And there they had as wamp - ing gun, As big as a log of ma - ple,
5. And ev - 'ry time they fired it off It took a horn of pow - der; It
6. I went as near to it my - self, As Ja - cob's un - der - pin - in', And

there we saw the men and boys, As thick as has - ty pud - ding.
giv - ing or - ders to his men, I guess there was a mil - lion.
want - ed pes - ki - ly to get, To give to my Je - mi - ma.
On a deu - ced lit - tle cart,—A load for fa - ther's cat - tle.
made a noise like fa - ther's gun, On - ly a na - tion loud - er.
fa - ther went as near a - gain,—I tho't the deuce was in him.

**Chorus**

Yan - kee doo - dle keep it up, Yan - kee doo - dle dan - dy,

Mind the mu - sic and the step, And with the girls be hand - y.

7 It scared me so, I ran the streets,
  Nor stopped, as I remember,
  Till I got home, and safely locked
  In granny's little chamber.  Cho.

8 And there I see a little keg,
  Its heads were made of leather,
  They knocked upon't with little sticks,
  To call the folks together.  Cho.

9 And there they'd fife away like fun,
  And play on corn-stalk fiddles,
  And some had ribbons red as blood,
  All bound around their middles.  Cho.

10 The troopers too, would gallop up,
   And fire right in our faces;
   It scared me almost half to death
   To see them run such races.  Cho.

11 Uncle Sam came there to change
   Some pancakes and some onions,
   For 'lasses cakes to carry home
   To give his wife and young ones.  Cho.

12 But I can't tell you half I see,
   They kept up such a smother;
   So I took my hat off, made a bow,
   And scampered home to mother.  Cho.

## Bohunkus

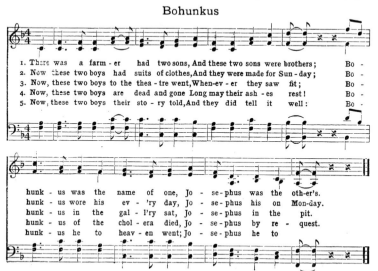

1. There was a farm - er had two sons, And these two sons were brothers; Bo -
2. Now these two boys had suits of clothes, And they were made for Sun - day; Bo -
3. Now, these two boys to the thea - tre went, When-ev - er they saw fit; Bo -
4. Now, these two boys are dead and gone Long may their ash - es rest! Bo -
5. Now, these two boys their sto - ry told, And they did tell it well: Bo -

hunk - us was the name of one, Jo - se-phus was the oth-er's.
hunk - us wore his ev - 'ry day, Jo - se-phus his on Mon-day.
hunk - us in the gal - l'ry sat, Jo - se-phus in the pit.
hunk - us of the chol - era died, Jo - se-phus by re - quest.
hunk - us he to heav - en went; Jo - se-phus he to

# Listen to the Mocking Bird

ALICE HAWTHORNE

val - ley, . . . the val - ley, . . . She's sleep - ing in the
tem- ber, . . . Sep - tem- ber, . . . 'Twas in the mild Sep -
sa - ken, . . . for - sa - ken, . . . I feel like one for -

val - ley, . . . . And the mock-ing bird is sing-ing where she lies.
tem- ber, . . . . And the mock-ing bird was sing-ing far and wide.
sa - ken, . . . . Since my Hal - ly is no lon - ger with me now.

*First*, SOLO: *then* CHORUS

Lis - ten to the mock-ing bird, Lis-ten to the mock-ing bird, The

## Listen to the Mocking Bird

mock-ing bird still sing-ing o'er her grave, Lis-ten to the mock-ing bird,

Lis-ten to the mocking bird, Still sing-ing where the weeping willows wave.

## O Music
ROUND

O mu - sic sweet mu - sic, your prais - es we'll sing, We

will tell of the pleas - ure and glad - ness you bring.

# The Blue Bells of Scotland

Mrs. James Grant

Folksong

*Andante moderato*

1. Oh! where, tell me where is your Highland lad-die gone? Oh! where, tell me where is your
2. Oh! where, tell me where did your Highland lad-die dwell? Oh! where, tell me where did your
3. Oh! what, tell me what if your Highland lad be slain? Oh! what, tell me what if your

High - land lad - die gone? He's gone with streaming ban - ners where
High - land lad - die dwell? He dwelt in bon - nie Scot - land, where
High - land lad be slain? Oh, no! true love will be his guard and

no - ble deeds are done, And it's oh, . . in my heart I wish him safe at home.
blooms the sweet blue bell, And it's oh, . . in my heart I lo'e my lad - die well.
bring him safe a - gain, For it's oh, my heart would break if my Highland lad were slain

# We'd Better Bide a Wee

CLARIBEL

1. The puir auld folk at hame, ye mind, Are frail and fail-ing sair, And weel I ken they'd
2. When first we told our sto-ry, lad, Their blessing fell sae free, They gave no tho't to
3. I fear me sair, they're failing baith, For when I sit a-part, They'll talk o' Heav'n sae

miss me, lad, Gin I came hame nae mair; The grist is out, the
self at all, They did but think of me; But, lad-die, that's a
earn-est-ly, It well nigh breaks my heart; So, lad-die, din-na

times are hard, The kin are on-ly three, I can-na leave the auld folk now, We'd
time a-wa, And mith-er's like to dee, I can-na leave the auld folk now, We'd
urge me mair, It sure-ly win-na be, I can-na leave the auld folk now, We'd

bet-ter bide a - wee,    I can -na leave the auld folk now, We'd bet-ter bide a - wee. . .

## He Leadeth Me

Rev. JOSEPH H. GILMORE                                    W. B. BRADBURY

1. He   lead - eth me!   O   bless - ed thought! O   words with heav'n'ly   com - fort fraught!
2. Lord,  I    would clasp Thy hand   in mine, Nor   ev - er mur - mur   nor   re - pine;
3. And when   my task   on earth   is done, When   by   Thy grace, the   vic-t'ry's won,

What - e'er   I   do, wher - e'er   I   be,   Still 'tis God's hand   that lead - eth me.   He
Con - tent, what-ev - er   lot   I   see,   Since 'tis   my   God   that lead - eth me.   He
E'en death's cold wave I   will not   flee,   Since 'tis   my   God   that lead - eth me.   He

lead-eth me, He lead - eth me!  By His own hand He   lead-eth me. He lead - eth me.

# Sailing

GODFREY MARKS

1. Y'heave ho! my lads, the wind blows free; A pleas - ant gale is on our lee, And

2. The sai - lor's life is bold and free; His home is on the roll-ing sea, And

3. The tide is flow - ing with the gale; Y'heave ho! my lads, set ev - 'ry sail. The

soon a - cross the o - cean clear Our gal - lant barque shall brav - ly steer; But ere we

nev - er heart more true or brave Than he who launch-es on . . the wave. A-far he

har - bor bar we soon shall clear, Fare-well once more to home so dear; For when the

part from England's shores tonight A song we'll sing for home and beau-ty bright.

speeds in dis-tant climes to roam; With jo - cund song he rides the sparkling foam.

temp - est ra - ges loud and long, That home shall be our guid - ing star a - mong.

Then here's to the sail - or and here's to the hearts so true Who will think of him up -

on the wa-ters blue. Sail - ing, sail - ing o - ver the bound-ing main; For

ma-ny a storm - y wind shall blow ere Jack comes home a - gain. Sail - ing, sail-ing

o-ver the bounding main; For ma-ny a stormy wind shall blow ere Jack comes home a - gain.

# Those Evening Bells

THOMAS MOORE

Attributed to BEETHOVEN

1. Those eve - ning bells, those eve - ning bells, How ma - ny a
2. Those joy - ous hours are past a - way, And, ma - ny a
3. And so 'twill be when I am gone, That tune - ful

tale . their mu - sic tells, Of youth and home and that sweet time, When
heart, that then was gay, With - in . the tomb now dark - ly dwells, And
peal will still ring on, While oth - er bards shall walk these dells, And

last I heard their sooth - ing chime! Of sooth - ing chime!
hears no more those eve - ning bells! With - eve - ning bells!
sing your praise, sweet eve - ning bells. While eve - ning bells.

# The Bull-Dog

*Moderato*

1. Oh! the bull-dog on the bank! And the bull-frog in the pool; Oh! the bull-dog on the
2. Oh! the bull-dog stoop'd to catch him, And the snapper caught his paw; Oh! the bull-dog stoop'd to
3. Says the mon-key to the owl, "O what'll you have to drink?" Says the mon-key to the
4. Pharaoh's daughter on the bank; Lit-tle Mo-ses in the pool; Pharaoh's daughter on the

*Più allegro*

bank! And the bull-frog in the pool; Oh! the bull-dog on the bank, And the
catch him, And the snap-per caught his paw; Oh! the bull-dog stoop'd to catch him, And the
owl, "O what'll you have to drink?" Says the mon-key to the owl, "O
bank; Lit-tle Mo-ses in the pool; Pha-raoh's daugh-ter on the bank; Lit-tle

*ritard.*

bull-frog in the pool. The bull-dog call'd the bull-frog A green old wa-ter fool.
snap-per caught his paw; The pol-ly-wog died a-laughing To see him wag his jaw.
what'll you have to drink?" "Since you are so ver-y kind, I'll take a bottle of ink."
Mo-ses in the pool; She fish'd him out with a ten-foot pole, And sent him off to school.

**CHORUS**

Sing-ing tra, la, la, la, la, la, Sing-ing tra la, la, la, la, la, la, Sing-ing

tra, la, la, Sing-ing tra, la, la, tra, la, la, la, tra, la, la, la, tra la, la, la, la.

*Repeat pp*

tra, la, la.

# Nancy Lee

FRED E. WEATHERLY

STEPHEN ADAMS

*With spirit*

1. Of all . . the wives as e'er you know, . . . . Yeo ho ! . . lads !
2. The har - bor's past, the breez - es blow, . . . . Yeo ho ! . . lads !
3. The boa' - s'n pipes the watch be - low ; . . . . Yeo ho ! . . lads !

ho ! Yeo ho ! . . yeo ho ! There's none like Nan -cy Lee I trow, . .
ho ! Yeo ho ! . . yeo ho ! 'Tis long e'er we come back I know,
ho ! Yeo ho ! . . yeo ho ! Then here's a health be - fore we go, . . .

. . Yeo ho ! . . yeo ho ! . . yeo ho ! See there she stands an'
. . Yeo ho ! . . yeo ho ! . . yeo ho ! But true an' bright from
. . Yeo ho ! . . yeo ho ! . . yeo ho ! A long, long life to

## Nancy Lee

star . shall be, Yeo ho! . we go a - cross the sea! The sail-or's

wife, the sail-or's star shall be, The sail - or's wife his star shall be. . . .

*colla voce*

## Out on the Deep

SAMUEL K. COWAN

*mf Allegro moderato*

FREDERIC N. LOHR

1. Out . . on the deep, when the sun is low, . . And the sea with splen - dor
2. Out . . on the deep, when the sun is dead, . . And the first sweet star doth

*mf*

*marcato*      *cres.*

burns, . . . With his sca - ly spoil from his eve - ning toil, The
gleam, . . . Of a day that is dead and a love is fled, The

*cres.*

fish - er home - ward turns, . . And his oars flash bright, in the
fish - er oft will dream, . . And he thinks, though far, . . like that

o - cean light, . . And he knows that eyes on shore . . . Look
first bright star, . . She is still . . be-yond, as of yore, . . . And his

out . . . on the deep . . for his bright . . oar sweep; . And he
oars . . . gleam bright . . in its sweet . . pale light, . . And he

sings as he swings his oar: . . . . "A long sweep, lads, and a strong sweep,
sings as he plies his oar: . . . . "A long sweep, lads, and a low sweep,

boys,     And a    song    as a - way    we     go ! . . . .     For the hearts   that
boys,     And a    song    as a - way    we     go ! . . . .     For the star     of

yearn     for our home    re - turn, When the eve - ning sun   is   low, . . .
Love,     that is bright,   a - bove, And   its gleam   in the wave   be - low, . . .

When the eve - ning    sun . .   is   low. . . . . . . . . . . . . . . . . . . .
And   its gleam in the wave . .   be - low. . . . . . . . . . . . . . . . . . . . .

Aura Lee

1. As the black-bird in the spring, 'Neath the wil-low tree
2. On her cheek the rose was born; 'Twas mu-sic when she spake;

Sat and pip'd, I heard him sing, Sing of Au - ra Lee.
In her eyes the rays of morn, With sud - den splen-dor break.

Au - ra Lee! Au - ra Lee! Maid of gold - en hair!

Sun - shine came a - long with thee, And swal-lows in the air.

# Let Me Dream Again

B. C. STEPHENSON

ARTHUR SULLIVAN

1. The sun is set - ting and the hour is late, Once more I
2. The clock is strik - ing in the bel - fry tower, And warns us

stand be - side the wick - et gate, The bells are ring-ing out the
of the ev - er - fleet - ing hour, But neith - er heeds the time which

dy - ing day, The chil - dren sing-ing on their home - ward way, And
on - ward glides, For time may pass a - way, but love a - bides! I

he is whisp'ring words of sweet in - tent, While I, half doubting,
feel his kiss - es on my fev - 'red brow, If we must part,

# Sally in Our Alley

Henry Carey

Old English Air

Andante

1. Of all the girls that are so smart, There's none like pret-ty
2. Of all the days with-in the week, I dear-ly love but
3. My mas-ter, and the neigh-bors all, .. Make game of me and

*pp*

Sal-ly; She is the dar-ling of my heart, And lives in our. .
one day; And that's the day that comes be-twixt The Sat-ur-day and
Sal-ly; And but for her I'd rath-er be A slave, and row a

al-ley: There is no la-dy in the land That's half so sweet as
Mon-day: Oh, then I'm dress'd all in my best, To walk a-broad with
gal-ley. But when my seven long years are out, Oh, then I'll mar-ry

*p*

Sal-ly; She is the dar-ling of my heart, And lives in our al-ley.
Sal-ly; She is the dar-ling of my heart, And lives in our al-ley.
Sal-ly, And then how hap-pi-ly we'll live! But not in our al-ley.

## The Quilting Party

*Andante*

1. In the sky the bright stars glit-tered, On the bank the pale moon shone; And 'twas
2. On my arm a soft hand rest-ed, Rest-ed light as o-cean foam; And 'twas
3. On my lips a whis-per trem-bled, Trem-bled till it dared to come; And 'twas
4. On my life new hopes were dawn-ing, And those hopes have liv'd and grown; And 'twas

*cres.*                                   *dim.*

from Aunt Di-nah's quilt-ing par-ty, I was see-ing Nel-lie home.

*p* REFRAIN                               *cres.*

I was see-ing Nel-lie home, I was see-ing Nel-lie home; And 'twas

*dim. e rit.*

from Aunt Di-nah's quilt-ing par-ty, I was see-ing Nel-lie home.

# The Star-Spangled Banner

Francis Scott Key

Samuel Arnold

1. Oh! say, can you see, by the dawn's ear - ly light, What so proud-ly we
2. On the shore, dim - ly seen thro' the mists of the deep, Where the foe's haughty
3. Oh! thus be it ev - er when free-men shall stand Be - tween their loved

hailed at the twilight's last gleam - ing, Whose broad stripes and bright stars thro' the
host in dread si - lence re - po - ses, What is that which the breeze, o'er the
homes and wild war's des - o - la - tion; Blest with vic-t'ry and peace, may the

per - il - ous fight, O'er the ram-parts we watch'd, were so gal-lant - ly streaming? And the
tow - er - ing steep, As it fit - ful - ly blows, half conceals, half dis - clos - es? Now it
heav'n-res - cued land Praise the pow'r that hath made and pre-served us a na - tion. Then

rock-et's red glare, the bombs bursting in air, Gave proof thro' the night that our
catch -es the gleam of the morn-ing's first beam In full glo - ry re - flect - ed, now
con - quer we must, when our cause it is just, And this be our mot-to,—"In

poco ritard.

flag was still there. Oh, say, does that star - span - gled ban - ner yet
shines on the stream; 'Tis the star-span - gled ban - ner: Oh, long may it
God is our trust!" And the star-span - gled ban - ner In tri - umph shall

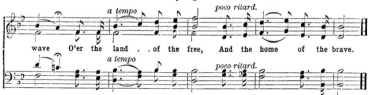

wave   O'er the   land . . of the   free,   And the   home   of   the brave.

## Too Late! Too Late

Miss M. LINDSAY

1. Late, late, so late! and dark the night, and chill! Late, late, so late! But
2. No light had we: for that we do re-pent, And, learn - ing this, the

we can en -ter still! Too   late!   too   late,   ye can-not   en-ter
bride-groom will re -•lent. Too   late!   too   late,   ye can-not   en-ter

now,   Too   late!   too   late,   ye cannot   en-ter   now.

# Loch Lomond

Scotch Folksong

*Andante con moto*

1. By yon bon - nie banks, and by yon bon - nie braes, Where the sun shines bright on Loch
2. 'Twas there that we part - ed in yon sha-dy glen, On the steep, steep side o' Ben
3. The wee bir - dies sing and the wild flow-ers spring, And in sun-shine the wa - ters are

Lo - mon', Where me and my true love Were ev - er wont to gae, On the
Lo - mon', Where in pur - ple hue The Hie - land hills we view, And the
sleep - in', But the bro-ken heart it kens Nae sec-ond Spring a - gain, Tho' the

*Faster*

bon-nie, bon-nie banks of Loch Lo - mon' Oh! ye'll tak' the high - road and
moon com-ing out in the gloam - ing. Oh! ye'll tak' the high - road and
wae-fu' may cease frae their greet - in'. Oh! ye'll tak' the high - road and

# Loch Lomond

*cres.* *rall.*

I'll tak' the low-road, And I'll be in Scot-land a - fore ye, But me and my true love will

*cres.* *rit.*

nev - er meet a - gain On the bon-nie, bon-nie banks of Loch Lo - mond. . .

*a tempo* *rit.*

## Silent Night

Anonymous                                                    German Folksong

1. Si-lent night, peace-ful night! All things sleep, shepherds keep Watch on Bethlehem's silent hill,
2. Bright the star shines a - far,  Guid-ing trav'lers on their way, Who their gold and incense bring,
3. Light a - round! joyous sound! An - gel voices wake the air; "Glo-ry be to God in heav'n;

And un - seen, while all is still,  An - gels watch a - bove,  An - gels watch a - bove.
Of - f'rings to the prom-ised King, Child of Da - vid's line,  Child of Da - vid's line.
Peace on earth to you  is giv'n, Christ the Sav-iour's come,  Christ the Saviour's come."

# Michael Roy

**Allegretto** *mf*

1. In Brook-lyn cit-y there lived a maid, And she was known to fame; Her
2. She fell in love with a char-coal man, Mc-Clos-key, was his name; His
3. Mc-Clos-key shout-ed and hol-lered in vain, For the don-key would-n't stop, And he

*mf*

moth-er's name was Ma-ri Ann, And hers was Ma-ri Jane;— And
fight-ing weight was sev-en stone ten, And he loved sweet Ma-ri Jane; He
threw Ma-ri Jane right o-ver his head, Right in-to a pol-i-cy shop; When Mc-

ev-'ry Sat-ur-day morn-ing She used to go o-ver the riv-er, And
took her to ride in his char-coal cart, On a fine St. Pat-rick's day, But the
Clos-key saw that ter-ri-ble sight, His heart it was moved with pi-ty, So he

*p*

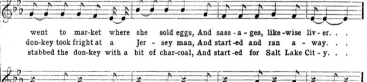

went to mar-ket where she sold eggs, And sass - a - ges, like -wise liv - er. . .
don-key took fright at a Jer - sey man, And start -ed and ran a - way. . .
stabbed the don-key with a bit of char-coal, And start -ed for Salt Lake Cit - y. . .

CHORUS f                                                              shouted

For oh! . . for oh! . . he was my dar - ling boy, . . FOR

Repeat Chorus pp

he was the lad with the au - burn hair, And his name was Mi - chael Roy. .

# Ah! I Have Sighed to Rest Me

C. JEFFERYS

From VERDI's "Il Trovatore"

*Andante sostenuto*
*dolce*

1. Ah! . . . . I have sigh'd to rest . . . me    Deep . . . . in the qui-et
2. Out . . . . of the love I bear . . thee,    Yield . . . . I my life for

grave,— . . . . sigh'd to rest me,    But    in vain do I
thee;    Wilt    thou not think, . .    Wilt thou not think    of

grave.    O fare    thee well,    my Le-o-no-ra,fare thee well! . .
me?    O think    of me,    my Le-o-no-ra,fare thee well! . .

Ah!    I have sigh'd for rest,    Yet all in vain do I    crave, . .    O

fare . . thee-well, my Le - o - no - ra, fare-thee-well!     well!

*col canto*     *a tempo*

*a tempo*

Out of the love I   bear   thee,     Yield I   my life for thee.   Ah! think of
Tho' I   no more be - hold   thee,     Yet is thy name a spell,     Yet is thy

me,     ah; think of   me, my Le - o - ra,  fare - thee - well!
name,     yet is thy name a   spell,

Cheer-ing my last lone hour, Le - o - no - ra, fare - well! . . .

## The Two Roses

MALE VOICES

WERNER

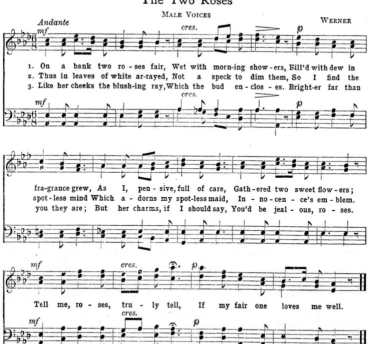

1. On a bank two ro - ses fair, Wet with morn-ing show-ers, Fill'd with dew in
2. Thus in leaves of white ar-rayed, Not a speck to dim them, So I find the
3. Like her cheeks the blush-ing ray, Which the bud en - clos - es. Bright-er far than

fra-grance grew, As I, pen - sive, full of care, Gath-ered two sweet flow-ers,
spot - less mind Which a - dorns my spot-less maid, In - no - cen - ce's em-blem;
you they are; But her charms, if I should say, You'd be jeal - ous, ro - ses.

Tell me, ro - ses, tru - ly tell, If my fair one loves me well.

# Meerschaum Pipe

1. O who will smoke my meerschaum pipe, meerschaum pipe, O who will smoke my meerschaum
2. O who will use my green umbrell', green um-brell', O who will use my green um-
3. O who will wear my cast-off boots, cast-off boots, O who will wear my cast-off
4. O who will go to see my girl, see my girl, O who will go to see my,
5. O who will kiss her ru-by lips, ru-by lips, O who will kiss her ru-by

pipe, meerschaum pipe, O who will smoke my meerschaum pipe, When I am gone a-
brell', green umbrell', O who will use my green um-brell', When I am gone a-
boots, cast-off boots, O who will wear my cast-off boots, When I am gone a-
girl, see my girl, O who will go to see my girl, When I am gone a-
lips, ru-by lips, O who will kiss her ru-by lips, When I am gone a-

way? Al-lie Ba-zan, Pat-sey Mo-ran, Ma-ry Mc-Cann, Cann, Cann!*
way? Some oth-er man, Some oth-er man, Some oth-er man, man, man!
way? Al-lie Ba-zan, Pat-sey Mo-ran, Ma-ry Mc-Cann, Cann, Cann!
way? Al-lie Ba-zan, Pat-sey Mo-ran, Ma-ry Mc-Cann, Cann, Cann!
way? Al-lie Ba-zan, Pat-sey Mo-ran, Ma-ry Mc-Cann, Cann, Cann!

* Or, on last two notes, any stanza, "Bad Man!"

# The Midshipmite

Fred. E. Weatherly

Stephen Adams

1. 'Twas in fif - ty - five, on a win-ter's night, Cheer-i - ly, my lads, yo ho! We'd
2. We launch'd the cut - ter and shoved her out, Cheer-i - ly, my lads, yo ho! The
3. "I'm done for now; good - bye!" says he, Stead-i - ly, my lads, yo ho! "You

got the Roosh - an lines in sight, When up comes a lit - tle
lub - bers might ha' heard us shout, As the Mid - dy cried, "Now, my
make for the boat, nev - er mind for me!" "We'll take 'ee back, sir, or

Mid-ship-mite, Cheer-i - ly, my lads, yo ho! "Who'll go a - shore to-night," says he, "An'
lads, put a-bout; Cheer-i - ly, my lads, yo ho! We made for the guns an' ramm'd 'em tight, But the
die," says we! Cheer-i - ly, my lads, yo ho! So we hoisted him in, in a terrible plight, An' we

spike their guns a - long wi' me?" "Why, bless 'ee, sir, come a-long!" says we,
mus - ket shots came left and right, An' down drops the poor lit - tle Mid - ship-mite,
pull'd ev -'ry man with all his might, An' sav'd the poor lit - tle Mid - ship-mite,

Cheer-i - ly, my lads, yo ho! Cheer-i - ly, my lads, yo ho! . . . With a

long, long pull, An' a strong, strong pull, Gai - ly, boys, make her go? . . . And we'll

drink to-night To the Mid - ship-mite, Singing cheer-i - ly, lads, yo ho! . . . .

# Firmly Stand, My Native Land

### (MALE VOICES)

NÄGELI

*With energy*

1. Firm-ly stand, firm-ly stand, my na - tive land, Firm-ly stand, firm-ly stand, my na - tive land, Free in heart, and true in hand, All that's love - ly cher-ish; Thus shall God re-main thy friend, Then shall heav'n thy walls defend, Free-dom! Free-dom! Freedom shall not per - ish! Firm-ly stand, firm-ly stand, Firm-ly stand, firm-ly stand, my na - tive land, my na - tive land.

2. Safe-ly dwell, safe-ly dwell, my na - tive land, Safe-ly dwell, safe-ly dwell, my na - tive land, May thy sons u - ni-ted stand, Firm and true for-ev - er; God for-bid the day should rise, When 'tis said our free-dom dies! Free-dom! Free-dom! Freedom die? Oh, nev - er! Safe-ly dwell, safe-ly dwell, Safe-ly dwell, safe-ly dwell, my na - tive land, my na - tive land.

3. Sing for joy, sing for joy, my na - tive land, Sing for joy, sing for joy, my na - tive land, In thee dwells a no - ble band, All thy weal to cher-ish; God with might will guard thee round, While thy steps in truth are found, Freedom! Free-dom! Freedom shall not per - ish! Sing for joy, sing for joy, Sing for joy, sing for joy, my na - tive land, my na - tive land.

# Dear Evelina, Sweet Evelina

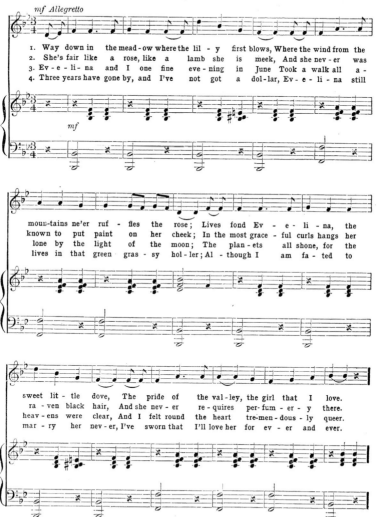

1. Way down in the mead-ow where the lil - y first blows, Where the wind from the
2. She's fair like a rose, like a lamb she is meek, And she nev - er was
3. Ev - e - li - na and I one fine eve - ning in June Took a walk all a -
4. Three years have gone by, and I've not got a dol-lar, Ev - e - li - na still

moun-tains ne'er ruf - fles the rose; Lives fond Ev - e - li - na, the
known to put paint on her cheek; In the most grace - ful curls hangs her
lone by the light of the moon; The plan - ets all shone, for the
lives in that green gras - sy hol - ler; Al - though I am fa - ted to

sweet lit - tle dove, The pride of the val - ley, the girl that I love.
ra - ven black hair, And she nev - er re - quires per - fum - er - y there.
heav - ens were clear, And I felt round the heart tre-men - dous - ly queer.
mar - ry her nev - er, I've sworn that I'll love her for ev - er and ever.

## Dear Evelina, Sweet Evelina

Dear Ev - e - li - na, sweet Ev - e - li - na, My love for

thee shall nev - er, nev - er die; nev - er, nev - er die.

## Hail! Columbia

J. HOPKINSON                                                        PHYLA

1.      Hail! Colum - bia, hap - py land!        Hail! ye he - roes, heav'n-born band, Who
2.  Im - mor - tal pa - triots, rise once more!  De - fend your rights, de - fend your shore; Let
3.      Sound, sound the trump of fame!          Let   Wash - ing-ton's great name Ring
4.  Be - hold the chief who now com - mands, Once more to serve his coun - try stands, The

fought and bled in    free - dom's cause, Who fought and bled in    free - dom's cause, And
no  rude foe, with    im - pious hand, Let   no  rude foe, with    im - pious hand In -
through the world with loud ap - plause! Ring thro' the world with loud ap - plause! Let
rock  on which the    storm will beat! The rock  on which the    storm will beat! But

when the storm of war was gone, En-joyed the peace your val-or won; Let
vade the shrine where sa-cred lies, Of toil and blood, the well-earned prize; While
ev-'ry clime, to free-dom dear, Lis-ten with a joy-ful ear; With
armed in vir-tue, firm and true, His hopes are fixed on Heav'n and you; When

in-de-pen-dence be your boast, Ev-er mind-ful what it cost,
off-'ring peace, sin-cere and just, In heav'n we place a man-ly trust, That
e-qual skill, with stead-y pow'r, He gov-erns in the fear-ful hour Of
hope was sink-ing in dis-may, When gloom ob-scured Co-lum-bia's day, His

Ev-er grate-ful for the prize, Let its al-tar reach the skies.
truth and jus-tice may pre-vail, And ev-'ry scheme of bond-age fail!
hor-rid war, or guides with ease, The hap-pier time of hon-est peace.
stead-y mind, from chang-es free, Re-solved on death or Lib-er-ty.

CHORUS

Firm, u-nit-ed, let us be, Rally-ing round our lib-er-ty,

As a band of broth-ers joined, Peace and safe-ty we shall find.

# Kitty Tyrrell

CHARLES JEFFERYS

C. W. GLOVER

1. You're look-ing as fresh as the morn, dar-ling, You're look-ing as bright as the
2. I've built me a neat lit-tle cot, dar-ling, I've pigs and po-ta-toes in
3. You're smil-ing, and that's a good sign, dar-ling, Say "yes" and you'll nev-er re -

day ; But while on your charms I'm di-lat-ing, You're steal-ing my poor heart a -
store ; I've twen-ty good pounds in the bank, love, And may-be a pouud or two
pent ; Or if you would rath-er be si-lent. Your si-lence I'll take for con-

way : But keep it and wel-come, ma-vour-neen, Its loss I'm not go-ing to
more : It's all ve-ry well to have rich-es, But I'm such a cov-e-tous
sent ; That good-na-tured dim-ple's a tell-tale, Now all that I have is your

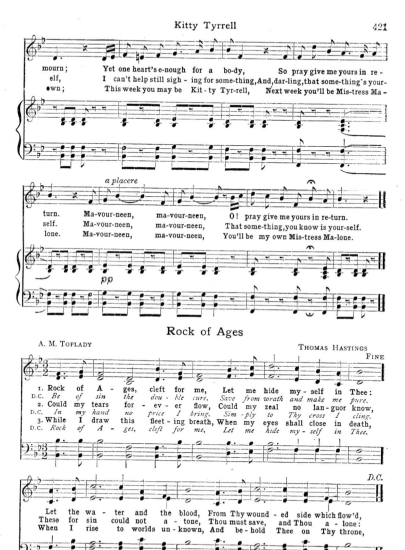

mourn; Yet one heart's e-nough for a bo-dy, So pray give me yours in re-

elf, I can't help still sigh - ing for some-thing, And, dar-ling, that some-thing's your-

own; This week you may be Kit - ty Tyr-rell, Next week you'll be Mis-tress Ma-

*a placere*

turn. Ma-vour-neen, ma-vour-neen, O! pray give me yours in re-turn.

self. Ma-vour-neen, ma-vour-neen, That some-thing, you know is your-self.

lone. Ma-vour-neen, ma-vour-neen, You'll be my own Mis-tress Ma-lone.

*pp*

## Rock of Ages

A. M. TOPLADY

THOMAS HASTINGS

FINE

1. Rock of A - ges, cleft for me, Let me hide my - self in Thee:

D.C. *Be of sin the dou - ble cure, Save from wrath and make me pure.*

2. Could my tears for - ev - er flow, Could my zeal no lan - guor know,

D.C. *In my hand no price I bring, Sim - ply to Thy cross I cling.*

3. While I draw this fleet - ing breath, When my eyes shall close in death,

D.C. *Rock of A - ges, cleft for me, Let me hide my - self in Thee.*

D.C.

Let the wa - ter and the blood, From Thy wound - ed side which flow'd,

These for sin could not a - tone, Thou must save, and Thou a - lone:

When I rise to worlds un - known, And be - hold Thee on Thy throne,

# My Mother's Bible

George P. Morris

Henry Russell

*With great feeling and expression*

1. This book is all that's left me now! Tears will un-bid-den start! . . With
2. Ah, well do I re-mem-ber those Whose names these rec-ords bear! . . Who
3. My fa-ther read this ho-ly book To broth-ers, sis-ters dear! . . How
4. Thou tru-est friend man ev-er knew! Thy con-stan-cy I've tried! . . When

fal-t'ring lip and throb-bing brow, I press it to my heart. For
round the hearth-stone used to close, Af-ter the eve-ning prayer; And
calm was my poor moth-er's look, Who leaned God's word to hear! Her
all were false I found thee true, My coun-sel-lor and guide. The

ma-ny gen-er-a-tions passed Here is our fam-'ly tree! . . My
speak of what this vol-ume said, In tones my heart would thrill: . . Though
an-gel face! I see it yet! What throng-ing mem-'ries come! . . A-
mines of earth no treas-ures give, From me this book could buy; . . For,

My Mother's Bible

moth - er's hands this bi - ble clasped, She dy-ing gave it me. . . .
they are with the si - lent dead, Here are they liv - ing still. . . .
gain that lit - tle group is met With-in the halls of home! . . .
teach - ing me the way to live, It taught me how to die. . . .

## Nearer, My God, to Thee

S. F. ADAMS

L. MASON

1. Near - er, my God, to Thee, Near - er to Thee; E'en tho' it be a cross
2. Though like the wan-der-er, The sun gone down, Dark-ness be o - ver me,
3. There let the way ap-pear Steps un - to heaven; All that Thou send-est me
4. Or if on joy - ful wing, Cleav-ing the sky, Sun, moon, and stars for - got,

That rais - eth me, Still all my song shall be, Near - er, my God, to Thee,
My rest a stone,— Yet in my dreams I'd be Near - er, my God, to Thee,
In mer - cy given; An - gels to beck - on me, Near - er, my God, to Thee,
Up - ward I fly, Still all my song shall be, Near - er, my God, to Thee,

Near - er, my God, to Thee, Near - er to Thee.

## The Flowers that Bloom in the Spring

W. S. GILBERT

From SULLIVAN'S "Mikado"

1. The flow-ers that bloom in the spring, Tra la, Breathe prom-ise of mer-ry sun-shine, As we mer-ri-ly dance and we sing, Tra la, We wel-come the hope that they bring, Tra la, Of a sum-mer of ro-ses and wine, Of a sum-mer of ro-ses and wine, And that's what we mean when we

2. The flow-ers that bloom in the spring, Tra la, Have noth-ing to do with the case. I've got to take un-der my wing, Tra la, A most un-at-trac-tive old thing, Tra la, With a car-i-ca-ture of a face, With a car-i-ca-ture of a face, And that's what I mean when I

say that a thing Is wel-come as flow-ers that bloom in the spring, Tra
say or I sing, "Oh, both - er the flow-ers that bloom in the spring!"Tra

la la la la, Tra la la la la, The flow-ers that bloom in the spring, Tra

la la la la, Tra la la la la, Tra la la la la la.

## Cooper's Song

From Von Suppé's "Boccacio"

*Allegro deciso*

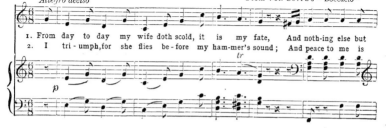

1. From day to day my wife doth scold, it is my fate, And noth-ing else but
2. I tri - umph, for she flies be-fore my ham-mer's sound; And peace to me is

## Cooper's Song

sing-ing, With an-vil loud-ly ring-ing, And jov-ial tra-la-ra-la, .. Can
giv-en, For far a-way she's driv-en, By mer-ry tra-la-ra-la, .. It

bring her down, tra-la. Tra-la-ra la la la la la oi-a
makes her flee, tra-la. Tra-la-ra la la la la la oi-a

he, oi-a-ha, la la ra la la la la la tra-la-ra-

la tra la la la, la! . . . . . . . . . . . . .

# Twinkling Stars are Laughing, Love

J. P. ORDWAY

*Dolce e legato*

1. Twink - ling stars are laugh - ing, love,
2. Gold - en beams are shin - ing, love,

*legato e delicato*

Laugh - ing on you and me ;
Shin - ing on you to bless ;

While your bright eyes look in mine, . .
Like the queen of night you fill . . .

*cres.*

Peep - ing stars they seem to be.
Dark - est space with love - li - ness.

*dim.*

The Bass Staff alone may be used as an Accompaniment for the first eight measures.

Trou - bles come and    go,    love,      Bright-est    scenes   must leave our sight;
Sil - ver stars how bright, love,      Moth- er    moon   in throne - ly   might,

But     the star    of    hope, love,      Shines   with ra - diant beams to-night.
Gaze    on us    to   bless, love,      Pur - est vows   here   made   to - night.

CHORUS

Twink-ling stars are laugh-ing,   love,    Laugh-ing   on   you and    me;

*dolce e legato*

While your bright eyes look in mine, Peep-ing stars they seem to be.

*cres.*        *rall.*

## Bruce's Address

ROBERT BURNS

*Andante maestoso*

Scotch Melody

1. Scots, wha hae wi' Wal-lace bled, Scots, whom Bruce has of-ten led, Wel-come to your
2. Wha will be a trai-tor's knave? Wha will fill a cow-ard's grave? Wha sae base as
3. By op-pres-sion's woes and pains, By your sons in ser-vile chains, We will drain our

go - ry bed, Or to vic - to - ry! Now's the day, and now's the hour!
be a slave, Let him turn and flee! Wha for Scot-land's king and law,
dear - est veins, But they shall be free! Lay the proud u - surp - ers low,

See the front of bat - tle low'r, See approach proud Edward's pow'r, Chains and slavery!
Free-dom's sword will strongly draw, Freeman stand, or free-man fa'? Let him fol-low me!
Ty - rants fall in ev - 'ry foe! Lib - er-ty's in ev - 'ry blow! Let us do and die!

## Do They Think of Me at Home

J. E. CARPENTER

CHAS. W. GLOVER

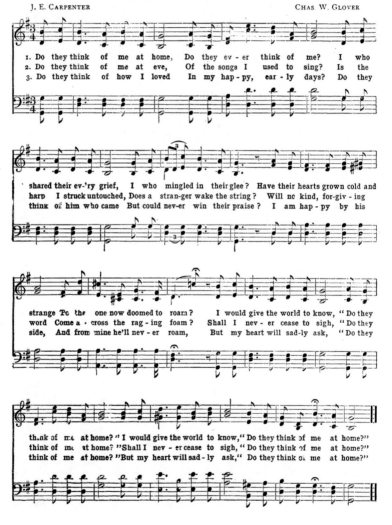

1. Do they think of me at home, Do they ev - er think of me? I who
2. Do they think of me at eve, Of the songs I used to sing? Is the
3. Do they think of how I loved In my hap - py, ear - ly days? Do they

shared their ev-'ry grief, I who mingled in their glee? Have their hearts grown cold and
harp I struck untouched, Does a stran-ger wake the string? Will no kind, for-giv - ing
think of him who came But could nev-er win their praise? I am hap - py by his

strange To the one now doomed to roam? I would give the world to know, "Do they
word Come a - cross the rag - ing foam? Shall I nev - er cease to sigh, "Do they
side, And from mine he'll nev - er roam, But my heart will sad-ly ask, "Do they

think of me at home? "I would give the world to know, "Do they think of me at home?"
think of me at home? "Shall I nev - er cease to sigh, "Do they think of me at home?"
think of me at home? "But my heart will sad - ly ask, "Do they think of me at home?"

# A Life on the Ocean Wave

EPES SARGENT                       HENRY RUSSELL

1. A life on the o - cean wave, A home on the roll - ing deep, Where the
2. Once more on the deck I stand Of my own swift-glid - ing craft, Set
3. The land is no longer in view, The clouds have be - gun to frown, But

scat - tered wa - ters rave, And the winds their rev - els keep:
sail! fare - well to the land, The gale fol-lows far a - baft.
with a stout ves - sel and crew We'll say "Let the storm come down!"

Like an ea - gle caged I pine On this dull, un - chang-ing shore; Oh!
We shoot thro' the sparkling foam, Like an o - cean bird set free: Like the
And the song of our heart shall be, While the winds and the wa - ters rave, A

give me the flash - ing brine, The spray and the tem - pest roar!
o - cean bird, our home We'll find far out on the sea!
life on the heav - ing sea, A home on the bound - ing wave!

# Rock Me to Sleep, Mother

ERNEST LESLIE

With feeling

1. Back-ward, turn back-ward, oh, time in your flight, Make me a child a-gain
2. O - ver my heart, in the days that are flown, No love like moth-er-love
3. Come, let your brown hair, just light - ed with gold, Fall on your shoul-ders a -

just for to - night! Moth-er, come back from the ech - o - less shore,
ev - er has shone; No oth - er wor-ship a - bides and en - dures,
gain as of old; Let it drop o - ver my fore-head to - night,

Take me a - gain to your heart as of yore; Kiss from my fore-head the
Faith - ful, un - self - ish, and pa-tient like yours; None like a moth - er can
Shad - ing my faint eyes a - way from the light; For with its sun - ny - edged

fur - rows of care, Smooth the few sil - ver threads out of my hair, O - ver my
charm a - way pain, From the sick soul and the world-wea-ry brain; Slum-ber's soft
shad - ows once more, Hap - ly will throng the sweet vis - ions of yore, Lov-ing - ly,

ritard.

slum - bers your lov - ing watch keep; Rock me to sleep, moth-er, rock me to sleep.
calms o'er my heav-y lids creep; Rock me to sleep, moth-er, rock me to sleep.
soft - ly, its bright bil-lows sweep; Rock me to sleep, moth-er, rock me to sleep.

# The Lone Fish-ball

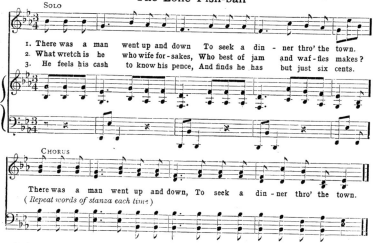

SOLO

1. There was a man   went up and down   To seek a din - ner thro' the town.
2. What wretch is he   who wife for - sakes,   Who best of jam   and waf - fles makes?
3. He feels his cash   to know his pence,   And finds he has   but just six cents.

CHORUS

There was a man went up and down, To seek a din - ner thro' the town.
(*Repeat words of stanza each time.*)

4 He finds at last a right cheap place,
  And enters in with modest face.

5 The bill of fare he searches through,
  To see what his six cents will do.

6 The cheapest viand of them all
  Is "Twelve and a half cents for two Fish-balls."

7 The waiter he to him doth call,
  And gently whispers, — "one Fish-ball."

8 The waiter roars it through the hall,
  The guests they start at "one Fish-ball!"

9 The guest then says, quite ill at ease,
  "A piece of bread, sir, if you please."

10 The waiter roars it through the hall,
  "We don't give bread with one Fish-ball!"

MORAL

11 Who would have bread with his Fish-ball,
  Must get it first, or not at all.

12 Who would Fish-ball with fixin's eat,
  Must get some friend to stand the treat.

# We'll Pay Paddy Doyle

CHANTEY SONG

Way - ay - ay, .. ah! We'll pay Pad - dy Doyle for his boots!

# Go to Sleep, Lena Darling

J. K. EMMET                                                J. K. EMMET

1. Close your eyes, Le - na, my dar-ling, While I sing your lul - la - by; Fear thou no
2. Bright be de morn - ing, my dar-ling, Ven you ope your eyes; Sunbeams glow all

dan-ger, Le - na; Move not, dear Le - na, my dar-ling, For your broo-der watch-es
round you, Le - na, Peace be with thee, love, my dar-ling, Blue and cloudless be the

nigh you, Le - na dear.    An- gels guide thee, Le - na dear, my dar - ling, Noth-ing e - vil
sky for Le - na dear. Birds sing their bright songs for thee, my dar - ling, Full of sweet-est

can come near; Brightest flow - ers blow for thee,    Dar - ling sis - ter, dear to me.
mel - o - dy; An-gels ev - er hov - er near,    Dar - ling sis - ter, dear to me.

CHORUS

Go  to  sleep,  go  to sleep, my  ba - by, my  ba - by, my  ba - by;

## Long, Long Ago

T. H. BAYLY

# Polly-wolly-doodle

1. Oh, I went down south for to see my Sal, Sing Pol-ly-wol-ly-doo-dle all the day;
2. Oh, my Sal, she am a maid-en fair, Sing Pol-ly-wol-ly-doo-dle all the day;
3. Oh, I came to a river, an' I couldn't get across, Sing Pol-ly-wol-ly-doo-dle all the day;

My Sal-ly am a spun-ky gal; Sing Pol-ly-wol-ly-doo-dle all the day.
With cur-ly eyes and laugh-ing hair, Sing Pol-ly-wol-ly-doo-dle all the day.
An I jump'd upon a nigger, an' I tho't he was a hoss, Sing Pol-ly-wol-ly-doo-dle all the day.

Fare thee well, fare thee well, Fare thee well, my fair-y fay, For I'm going to Lou'-si-a-na, For to see my Su-sy-an-na, Sing Pol-ly-wol-ly-doo-dle all the day.

4 Oh, a grass-hopper sittin' on a railroad track,
A-pickin' his teef wid a carpet tack.

5 Oh, I went to bed, but it wasn't no use,
My feet stuck out for a chicken roost.

6 Behind de barn, down on my knees,
I thought I heard that chicken sneeze.

7 He sneezed so hard wid de hoopin'-cough,
He sneezed his head an' his tail right off.
*And so on, ad infin.*

# Speed Away! Speed Away

I. B. Woodbury

1. Speed a-way! Speed a-way! on thine er - rand of light! There's a young heart a -
2. Wilt thou tell her, bright song-ster, the old chief is lone; That he sits all the
3. And oh! wilt thou tell her, blest bird on the wing, That her moth - er hath
4. Go, bird of the sil - ver wing! fet - ter - less now; Stoop not thy bright

wait - ing thy com - ing to-night; She will fon - dle thee close, she will ask for the
day by his cheer-less hearth-stone; That his tom - a-hawk lies all un - no - ted the
ev - er a sad song to sing; That she stand-eth a - lone, in the still qui - et
pin - ions on yon moun-tain's brow; But hie thee a - way o'er rock, riv - er and

loved, Who pine up - on earth since the "Day Star" has roved; She will ask if we
while, And his thin lips wreathe ev - er in one sun - less smile; That the old chief-tain
night, And her fond heart goes forth for the be - ing of light, Who had slept in her
glen, And find our young "Day Star" ere night close a - gain. Up! on - ward! let

miss her, so long is her s'ay. Speed a - way! Speed a - way! Speed a - way!
mourns her, and why will she stay? Speed a - way! Speed a - way! Speed a - way!
bo - som, but who would not stay? Speed a - way! Speed a - way! Speed a - way!
noth - ing thy mis - sion de - lay. Speed a - way! Speed a - way! Speed a - way!

# Come Back to Erin

CLARIBEL

1 & D.C. Come back to E - rin, Ma-vour - neen, Ma-vour - neen, Come back, A-roon, to the
2. O - ver the green sea, Ma-vour - neen, Ma-vour - neen, Long shone the white sail that
3. Oh, may the an - gels while wak - in' or sleep - in', Watch o'er my bird in the

land of thy birth; . . Come with the sham-rocks and spring-time, Ma-vour - neen,
bore thee a - way; . . Rid - ing the white waves that fair sum - mer morn - in',
land far a - way, . . And it's my pray'rs will con-sign to their keep - in',

And its Kil-lar - ney shall ring with our mirth. Sure, when you left us, our
Just like a May-flower a - float on the bay. Oh, but my heart sank when
Care o' my jew - el by night and by day. When by the fire - side I

beau - ti - ful dar - ling, Lit - tle we thought of the lone win - ter days,
clouds came be-tween us, Like a grey cur - tain the rain fall - ing down;
watch the bright em - bers, Then all my heart flies a - way o'er the sea,

Lit - tle we tho't of the hush of the star - shine, O - ver the moun - tain, the
Hid from my sad eyes the path o'er the o - cean, Far, far a - way, where my
Cra - vin' to know if my dar - lin' re-mem - bers, Or if her thot's may be

bluffs and the brays! Then And its Kil - lar - ney shall ring with our mirth.
Col - leen had flown. Then
cross - in' to me. Then

*D.C.* | 2

*colla voce.*

## Three Little Kittens

### CHANT

TENORS

1, 2, 3. Once upon a time there were three little kittens who lay in a basket of saw - aw - dust;

BASSES

*After last stanza*

Said the { first / second / third } little kitten un-to the { other two / little cats, } { If you don't get / out of this, then } I must! *That's all.*

# Hail to the Chief

Sir Walter Scott

James Sanderson

1. Hail to the Chief who in tri-umph ad-van-ces! Hon-or'd and bless'd be the ev-er-green Pine! . . Long may the tree, in his ban-ner that glan-ces, Flour-ish, the shel-ter and grace of our line! Hail to the Chief who in tri-umph ad-van-ces, Hon-or'd and bless'd be the ev-er-green Pine! . . Long may the tree, in his ban-ner that glan-ces, Flour-ish, the shel-ter and

2. Ours is no sap-ling, chance-sown by the foun-tain, Bloom-ing at Bel-tane, in win-ter to fade; When the whirlwind has stripp'd ev-'ry leaf on the moun-tain, The more shall Clan-Al-pine ex-ult in her shade. Ours is no sap-ling, chance-sown by the foun-tain, Bloom-ing at Bel-tane, in win-ter to fade, When the whirl-wind has stripp'd ev-'ry leaf on the moun-tain, The more shall Clan-Al-pine ex-

3. Row, vas-sals, row for the pride of the High-lands! Stretch to your oars, for the ev-er-green Pine! . . O, that the rose-bud that gra-ces yon is-lands, Were wreath'd in a gar-land a-round him to twine! Row, vas-sals, row, for the pride of the High-lands! Stretch to your oars for the ev-er-green Pine! . . O, that the rose-bud that gra-ces yon is-lands, Were wreath'd in a gar-land a-

*f Allegro*

grace of our line! Heav'n send it hap-py dew, Earth lend its sap a-new;
ult in her shade. Moor'd in the rift-ed rock, Proof to the tem-pest shock,
round him to twine! O, that some seed-ling gem, Wor-thy such no-ble stem,

Gai-ly to bour-geon and broadly to grow; While ev-'ry High-land glen,
Firm-er he roots him, the ru-der it blow; Mentieth and Bread-al-bane, then,
Hon-or'd and bless'd in their sha-dow might grow! Loud should Clan-Al-pine then

Sends our shout back a-gain, "Rod-er-igh Vich Al-pine dhu, ho! i-e-roe!"
Ech-o his praise a-gain, "Rod-er-igh Vich Al-pine dhu, ho! i-e-roe!"
Ring from the deepmost glen, "Rod-er-igh Vich Al-pine dhu, ho! i-e-roe!"

## Come, Thou Almighty King

C. WESLEY                                        F. GIARDINI

1. Come, Thou Al-might-y King, Help us Thy name to sing, Help us to praise; Fa-ther! all-
2. Come, Thou In-car-nate Word, Gird on Thy might-y sword; Our pray'r at-tend; Come, and Thy
3. Come, Ho-ly Com-fort-er! Thy sa-cred wit-ness bear, In this glad hour: Thou, who al-

glo-ri-ous, O'er all vic-to-ri-ous, Come, and reign o-ver us, An-cient of days.
peo-ple bless, And give Thy word suc-cess, Spir-it of ho-li-ness! On us de-scend.
might-y art, Now rule in ev-'ry heart, And ne'er from us de-part, Spir-it of pow'r!

# The Low-Backed Car

Samuel Lover

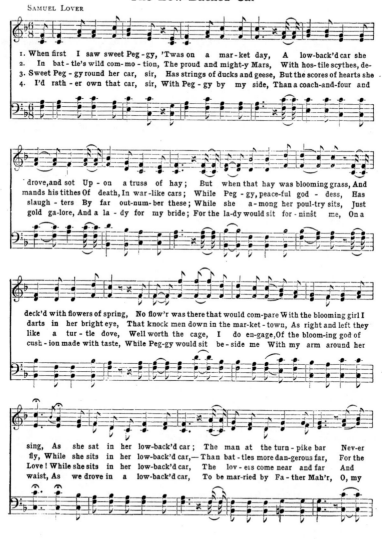

1. When first I saw sweet Peg-gy, 'Twas on a mar-ket day, A low-back'd car she
2. In bat-tle's wild com-mo-tion, The proud and might-y Mars, With hos-tile scythes, de-
3. Sweet Peg-gy round her car, sir, Has strings of ducks and geese, But the scores of hearts she
4. I'd rath-er own that car, sir, With Peg-gy by my side, Than a coach-and-four and

drove, and sot Up-on a truss of hay; But when that hay was blooming grass, And
mands his tithes Of death, In war-like cars; While Peg-gy, peace-ful god-dess, Has
slaugh-ters By far out-num-ber these; While she a-mong her poul-try sits, Just
gold ga-lore, And a la-dy for my bride; For the la-dy would sit for-ninst me, On a

deck'd with flowers of spring, No flow'r was there that would com-pare With the blooming girl I
darts in her bright eyes, That knock men down in the mar-ket-town, As right and left they
like a tur-tle dove, Well worth the cage, I do en-gage, Of the bloom-ing god of
cush-ion made with taste, While Peg-gy would sit be-side me With my arm around her

sing, As she sat in her low-back'd car; The man at the turn-pike bar Nev-er
fly, While she sits in her low-back'd car,— Than bat-tles more dan-gerous far, For the
Love! While she sits in her low-back'd car, The lov-ers come near and far And
waist, As we drove in a low-back'd car, To be mar-ried by Fa-ther Mah'r, O, my

*rall.* *a tempo* *rall. ad lib.*

ask'd for the toll, But just rubbed his auld poll, And look'd af-ter the low-back'd car.
doc - tor's art Can-not cure the heart That is hit from the low-back'd car.
en - vy the chick-en That Peg-gy is pick-in', As she sits in the low-back'd car.
heart would beat high At her glance and her sigh, Tho' it beat in a low-back'd car.

## The Miller of the Dee

CHARLES MACKAY

1. There dwelt a mil - ler, hale and bold, Be-side the riv - er Dee; He wrought and sang from
2. "Thou'rt wrong, my friend!" said old King Hal, "As wrong as wrong can be; For could my heart be
3. The mil - ler smiled and doff'd his cap: "I earn my bread" quoth he; "I love my wife, I
4. "Good friend," said Hal, and sigh'd the while, "Farewell! and happy be; But say no more, if

morn till night, No lark more blithe than he; And this the bur - den of his song For -
light as thine, I'd glad - ly change with thee. And tell me now what makes thee sing With
love my friend, I love my chil-dren three. I owe no debt I can - not pay, I
thou'dst be true, That no one en - vies thee; Thy meal - y cap is worth my crown; Thy

ev - er used to be, "I en - vy no one, no, not I! And no one en - vies me!"
voice so loud and free, While I am sad, tho' I'm the King, Be-side the riv - er Dee?"
thank the riv - er Dee, That turns the mill that grinds the corn To feed my babes and me!"
mill my king-dom's fee! Such men as thou are Eng-land's boast, O mil-ler of the Dee!"

# Farewell

From the German, by H. ZICK

SILCHER

1. Love! so beau - ti - ful and true! I must leave to - mor - row,
2. In true friend-ship heart to heart Close - ly clings for - ev - er,
3. When soft breez - es kiss your cheek, Touch your hands ca - ress - ing,

Can no lon - ger be with you, Part - ing caus - es sor - row.
Sun and moon on high may part, But true friends will nev - er.
Sighs they are and thee may seek, Send by me with bless - ing;

Ah! I love thee faith - ful - ly, More than words can tell to thee;
Who the depths of woe can tell, When two lov - ers say fare-well,
Thou - sands send I day by day, And with thee I bid them stay,

Yet from thee must wan - der, Yet from thee must wan - der.
Say fare-well for - ev - er, Say fare-well for - ev - er.
To re - call me to thee, To re - call me to thee!

# Auld Robin Gray

Lady ANN LINDSAY

Old Melody

1. Young Ja - mie lo'ed me weel, and he sought me for his bride, But
2. He had na been gone a week but on - ly twa, When my
3. My fa - ther urged me sair, my mith - er did - na speak, But she

sav - ing a crown he had naeth-ing else be-side; To make that crown a pound, my
fa-ther brake his arm, and our cow was stown a-wa'; My mith-er she fell sick, and my
look'd in my face till my heart was like to break; They gied him my hand tho' my

Ja - mie gaed to sea, And the crown and the pound were baith for me.
Ja - mie at the sea, And auld Rob - in Gray cam' a - court - ing me.
heart was at the sea; And auld Rob - in Gray is gude - man to me.

# Rosalie

*Tempo di valse*

1. I'm Pierre de Bon - ton de Pa - ree, de Pa - ree, I drink my di -
2. I'm Pierre de Bon - ton de Pa - ree, de Pa - ree, I'm called by les
3. I go to the fete de Mar-quise, de Mar-quise, I go and make

vine eau - de - vie, eau - de - vie. As I ride out each day in my lit - tle cou -
dames très jo - li; très jo - li; When I ride out each day in my lit - tle cou -
love at my ease, at my ease. I go to her père and de-mand for my

pé, I tell you I'm some-thing to see. . . . . But I care not what
pé, I tell you I'm some-thing to see. . . . . But I care not what
own The hand of my sweet Ro - sa - lie. . . . . But I care not what

## Rosalie

oth - ers may say, . . . I'm in love with Ro - sa - lie.   Charm-ing

Rose,   pret-ty Rose, . . I'm in love with my Ro - sa - lie. . . .

## Abide with Me

H. F. LYTE

W. H. MONK

1. A - bide with  me! Fast  falls the  ev - en - tide, The  dark-ness
2. Swift  to  its  close  ebbs  out life's lit - tle  day;  Earth's  joys grow
3. Hold  Thou Thy  cross  be - fore my clos - ing  eyes;  Shine  thro' the

deep - ens— Lord, with  me  a - bide! When  oth - er help - ers  fail, and
dim,  its  glo - ries pass a - way; Change and de - cay  in  all a -
gloom and  point me  to  the  skies; Heav'n's morn-ing breaks, and earth's vain

com - forts  flee, Help  of  the help - less, O  a - bide  with  me!
round I  see;  O  Thou who chang-est not, a - bide  with  me!
shad - ows  flee;  In  life, in death, O  Lord, a - bide  with  me!

# The Laird o' Cockpen

1. The Laird o' Cockpen he's proud an' he's great, His
2. Doun by the dyke-side a la-dy did dwell, At his
3. His wig was weel-pouth-er'd, as good as when new, His

mind is ta'en up wi' the things o' the state; He want-ed a wife his
ta-ble-head he thocht she'd look well; M'-Cle-ish's ae doch-ter a'
waist-coat was white, his coat it was blue; He put on a ring, a

braw house to keep, But fa-vour wi' woo-in' was fash-ious to seek.
Clav-ers'-ha' Lee, A pen-ni-less lass wi' a lang ped-i-gree.
sword, and cock'd hat; And wha could re-fuse the Laird wi' a' that?

4 He mounted his mare, and rade cannilie :
An' rapped at the yett o' Clavers'-ha' Lee.
"Gae tell Mistress Jean to come speedily ben :
She's wanted to speak wi' the Laird o' Cockpen."

5 Mistress Jean she was makin' the elder-flower wine—
"What brings the Laird here at sic a like time ?"
She put aff her apron, an' on her silk goun,
Her mutch wi' red ribbons, an' gaed awa' doun.

6 An' when she came ben, he bowed fu' low ;
An' what was his errand he soon let her know.
Amazed was the Laird when the lady said—"Na."
An' wi' a laigh curtsie she turned awa'.

7 Dumbfoundered was he—but nae sigh did he gie';
He mounted his mare, and rade cannilie ;
An' aften he thocht, as he gaed through the glen,
"She's daft to refuse the Laird o' Cockpen."

# Tramp! Tramp! Tramp

GEORGE F. ROOT

1. In the pris - on cell I sit, Think - ing, Moth - er dear, of you, And our
2. In the bat - tle front we stood When their fierc - est charge they made, And they
3. So, with - in the pris - on cell, We are wait - ing for the day That shall

bright and hap - py home so far a - way; And the tears they fill my eyes Spite of
swept us off a hun - dred men or more; But be - fore we reached their lines They were
come to o - pen wide the i - ron door; And the hol - low eye grows bright, And the

D.S. *neath the star - ry flag We shall*

FINE

all that I can do, Though I try to cheer my com - rades and be gay.
beat - en back, dis - mayed, And we heard the cry of vic - t'ry o'er and o'er.
poor heart al - most gay, As we think of see - ing home and friends once more.

*breathe the air a - gain Of the free land in our own be - lov - ed home.*

CHORUS

D.S.

Tramp! tramp! tramp! the boys are march-ing. Cheer up, com-rades, they will come, And be -
march - ing on. O cheer up, com - rades, they will come,

# Rosa Lee

*Allegretto*

1. When I lib'd in Ten-nes-see, U - li - a - li o - la - e, I went court-in'
2. I said "You lub-by gal,dat's plain, U - li - a - li o - la - e, Breff as sweet as

Ro - sa Lee, U - li - a - li o - la - e. Eyes as dark as win-ter night,
su - gar-cane, U - li - a - li o - la - e. Feet so large and come-ly too,Might

Lips as red as ber-ry bright,When first I did her woo-ing go, She
make a cra - dle ob each shoe. Ro - sa, take me for your beau, She

said "Now don't be fool-ish,Joe." U - li - a - li o - la - e, Court-in' down in

Ten - nes - see, U - li - a - li o - la - e, 'Neath de wild Ba - na - na - tree.

## Were You Ever in Rio Grand
### (A "HEAVE THE ANCHOR" CHANTEY-SONG)

1. Were you ev - er in Ri - o Grand? Way, Ri - o, O were you ev - er on that strand? We're
2. Where the Portugee girls can be found, Way, Ri - o, And they are the girls to waltz around, We're

bound for the Ri - o Grand? Way, .. Ri - o, Way, .. Ri - o, Then

fare you well, my pret - ty young girl, we're bound for the Ri - o .. Grand.

# Home to Our Mountains

C. JEFFERYS

From VERDI'S "Il Trovatore"

Home to our moun-tains Let us re - turn, love, There in its young days

Peace had its reign; There shall thy sweet song fall on my slum - bers,

MANRICO

There shall thy lute make me joy - ous a - gain. Rest thee, my moth - er,

kneel - ing be - side thee, I will pour forth my

trou - ba - dour lay. Oh, sing and wake now thy sweet lute's soft

num - bers, Lull me to rest, charm my sor - rows a - way, Oh, way.

Yes, I will pour forth. . my trou - ba - dour lay. lay.

## Now the Day is Over

S. BARING-GOULD · J. BARNBY

1. Now the day is o - ver, Night is draw - ing nigh,
2. Je - sus, give the wea - ry Calm and sweet re - pose,
3. When the morn - ing wak - ens, Then may we a - rise

Shad - ows of the eve - ning Steal a - cross the sky.
With Thy ten - d'rest bless - ing, May our eye - lids close.
Pure and fresh and sin - less In Thy ho - ly eyes.

eve - ning Steal a - cross the sky.

# The Rainy Day

H. W. Longfellow

William R. Dempster

1. The day is cold, and dark, and drear-y; It rains, and the
2. My life is cold, and dark, and drear-y; It rains, and the
3. Be still, sad heart! and cease re - pin-ing; Be - hind the

wind is nev - er wea - ry; The vine still clings to the
wind is nev - er wea - ry; My thoughts still cling to the
clouds is the sun still shin - ing; Thy fate is the com - mon

moul - der - ing wall, But at ev - 'ry gust the dead leaves fall, And the
moul - der - ing past, But the hopes of youth fall thick in the blast, And the
fate of all, In - to each life some rain must fall, Some

day is dark and drear-y, . . . . And the day is
days are dark and drear-y, . . . . And the days are
days must be dark and drear-y, . . . . Some days must be

*pp*

dark and drear-y, . . . . And the day is dark and drear - y.
dark and drear-y, . . . . And the days are dark and drear - y.
dark and drear-y, . . . . Some days must be dark and drear - y.

*p*

## Jesus! the Very Thought of Thee

E. CASWALL                                     J. B. DYKES

1. Je - sus! the ver - y thought of Thee With sweet-ness fills my breast;
2. Nor voice can sing, nor heart can frame, Nor can the mem - 'ry find
3. O hope of ev - 'ry con - trite heart! O joy of all the meek!

But sweet - er far Thy face to see, And in Thy pres - ence rest.
A sweet - er sound than Thy blest name, O Sav - iour of man - kind!
To those who fall, how kind Thou art! How good to those who seek!

# Maryland! My Maryland

J. R. RANDALL, adapted

1. Thou wilt not cow - er in the dust, Ma - ry - land! my Ma - ry - land!
2. Thou wilt not yield the Van - dal toll, Ma - ry - land i my Ma - ry - land!
3. I see no blush up - on thy cheek, Ma - ry - land! my Ma - ry - land!
4. I hear the dis - tant thun - der hum, Ma - ry - land! my Ma - ry - land!

Thy gleam - ing sword shall nev - er rust, Ma - ry - land! my Ma - ry - land!
Thou wilt not crook to his con - trol, Ma - ry - land! my Ma - ry - land!
Tho' thou wast ev - er brave - ly meek, Ma - ry - land! my Ma - ry - land!
The Old Line bu - gle, fife and drum, Ma - ry - land! my Ma - ry - land!

Re - mem - ber Car - roll's sa - cred trust, Re - mem - ber How - ard's war - like thrust,
Bet - ter the fire up - on thee roll, Bet - ter the shot, the blade, the bowl,
For life and death, for woe and weal, Thy peer - less chiv - al - ry re - veal,
Come to thine own he - ro - ic throng, That stalks with Lib - er - ty a - long,

And all thy slum - b'rers with the just, Ma - ry - land! my Ma - ry - land!
Than cru - ci - fix - ion of the soul, Ma - ry - land! my Ma - ry - land!
And gird thy beau - teous limbs with steel, Ma - ry - land! my Ma - ry - land!
And ring thy daunt - less slo - gan song, Ma - ry - land! my Ma - ry - land!

## The Old Cabin Home

# Looking Back

Louisa Gray

Arthur Sullivan

1. I heard a voice long years a-go, A voice so wondrous sweet and low, That
2. But ere our sum-mer pass'd a-way, That gen-tle voice was hush'd for aye; I

trem-bling tears un-bid-den rose From the depths of love's re-pose. . . . It
watch'd my love's last smile and knew, How well the angel's lov'd her too. . . . Then

float-ed thro' my dreams at night, And made the dark-est day seem
si-lent but with blind-ing tears, I gath-er'd all the joy of

bright, It whis-per'd to my heart, "My love," And nest-ling there for-got to
years And laid it with my dreams of old, . . Where all I lov'd slept white and

## Haul on the Bowlin'
### (A SHORT-HAUL CHANTEY-SONG)

1. Haul on the bow-lin', Our bul-ly ship's a - roll - in'! Haul on the bow-lin', the bow-lin', haul!
2. Haul on the bow-lin', Our cap-tain he's a - growl-in'! Haul on the bow-lin', the bow-lin', haul!
3. Haul on the bow-lin', O Kit - ty, you're my darl-in'! Haul on the bow-lin', the bow-lin', haul!

# For You

ARTHUR CHAPMAN

SYDNEY SMITH

*Andante espressivo*

1. They say the years have swallow's wings, But mine have leaden feet, Since last we stood and
2. They told me if we linked our lives, That you would rue the day, And when the sor-rows

*Bass with octaves*

said "good-bye," That eve in June-tide sweet; I read the an-guish in your eyes, As
gath-ered round, Your love would pass a-way; But had I known what life would be When

*f con dolore* — *dim. e ritard.* — *p*

sad you turn'd a-way, But oh! you guessed not what I bore, The tears I could not stay. For
ev-'ry hope had fled, Those cru-el words I spoke that night, Had ne'er by me been said. For

*dim. e ritard*

REFRAIN *Lento, e con moto espressivo*

you! for you! my dar - ling, I spoke those words un - true. . . I

left you, tho' I loved you, And broke my heart for you! . .

. . For you! for you! my dar - ling, I spoke those words un - true, I

left you, tho' I loved you, And broke my heart for you.

# Alice, Where art Thou

J. Ascher

*Andante con espressione*

1. The birds sleep - ing gen - tly, Sweet Ly - ra gleam-eth bright, Her
2. The sil - ver rain fall - ing Just as it fall - eth now; And

*Bass with octaves*

rays tinge the for - est, And all seems glad to-night. The
all things sleep gen - tly! Ah! Al - ice, where art thou? I've

wind sigh - ing by me, Cool - ing my fev - er'd brow; The
sought thee by lake - let, I've sought thee on the hill, . . And

stream flows as ev - er, Yet, Al - ice, where art thou? One
in the pleas-ant wild - wood, When winds blew cold and chill; I've

year back    this e - ven,    And thou  wert by my  side,
sought thee   in  for - est;   I'm look - ing heav'nward now,

And        thou  wert by my side,    Vow - - ing . . . .    to
I'm        look - ing heav'nward now;   Oh!    there . . .   'mid

love me; One year  past    this e - ven,    And thou  wert by my side,
star-shine,—I've sought thee   in  for - est,    I'm look-ing heav'nward now.

Vow - ing  to love   me, Al - ice, what - e'er might    be - tide.
Oh! . . . there a - mid    the star-shine, Al - ice, I know,    art thou.

# No One to Love

A. H. G. RICHARDSON

Arranged by C. EVEREST

1. No one to love, none to ca-ress, Roam-ing a-lone through this world's wil-der-ness; Sad is my heart, joy is un-known, For in my sor-row I'm weep-ing a-lone; No gen-tle voice,

2. In dreams a-lone, loved ones I see, And well-known voi-ces then whis-per to me; Sigh-ing I wake, wak-ing I weep; Soon with the loved and the lost I shall sleep. Oh, bliss-ful rest!

3. No one to love, none to ca-ress, None to re-spond to this heart's ten-der-ness! Trust-ing I wait; God in His love Prom-is-es rest in His man-sions a-bove; Oh, bliss in store,

(For D.C. sing words of first stanza)

no    ten - der smile      Makes me    re - joice,      or cares be - guile. . .
what heart would stay,     Un - loved, un-bless'd,     from heaven a - way ? . .
oh,   joy   mine own,      There nev - er - more        to weep a - lone !  . .

## Blow, Boys, Blow

### (A HOISTING CHANTEY-SONG)

1. Blow,  my  bul - lies,  I  long  to  hear  you,  Blow,  boys,  blow !
2. A  Yan - kee  ship's  gone down  the  riv - er,  Blow,  boys,  blow !  And
3. Dan - dy - funk  and  don - key's  liv - er,  Blow,  boys,  blow !  Then

Blow,  my  bul - lies,  I  come  to  cheer  you,  Blow,  my  bul - ly  boys,  blow !
what do you  think  they got  for  din - ner ? Blow,  my  bul - ly  boys,  blow !
blow,  my  boys,  for  bet - ter  wea - ther,  Blow,  my  bul - ly  boys,  blow !

## One Sweetly Solemn Thought

Phœbe Carey

R. S. Ambrose

One sweet-ly sol-emn thought Comes to me o'er and o'er,

I am near-er home to-day Than I've ev-er been be-fore.

Near-er my Fa-ther's house, Where the man-y man-sions be,

Near-er the great white throne, .. Near-er the crys-tal sea.

Near - er the bounds of life, Where we lay our bur-dens down,

Near - er leav - ing the cross, . . Near - er gain - ing the crown.

but ly-ing darkly be - tween, . . Wind-ing a-down thro' the night, . .

Is the si - lent, un - known stream, That leads at last to the light.

cres.   rall.

## One Sweetly Solemn Thought

Fa - ther, be near when my feet    Are slip - ping o'er the brink,    For it

may be    I    am near - er home,    Near - er    now    than I think.

## Blow the Man Down

### (A HOISTING CHANTEY-SONG)

SOLO                              CHORUS                              SOLO

1. As   I was a - walking down Para-dise Street,  (Way !   Hey !   Blow the man down!) A
2. Says she   to me, "Will you stand treat ?" (Way !   Hey !   Blow the man down!) "De-

CHORUS

pret - ty young dam-sel I chanced for to meet.  ( Give me some time to blow the man down.)
lighted," says I, "for a charm-er so sweet." ( Give me some time to blow the man down.)

# The Red, White and Blue

D. T. Shaw

Thomas A Becket

1. O Co-lum-bia, the gem of the o-cean, The home of the brave and the
2. When war wing'd its wide des-o-la-tion, And threat-en'd the land to de-
3. The star-span-gled ban-ner bring hith-er, O'er Co-lum-bia's true sons let it

tree, The shrine of each pa-triot's de-vo-tion, A world of-fers hom-age to
form, The ark then of free-dom's foun-da-tion, Co-lum-bia, rode safe thro' the
wave ; May the wreaths they have won nev-er with-er, Nor its stars cease to shine on the

thee ; Thy man-dates make he-roes as-sem-ble, When lib-er-ty's form stands in
storm ; With the gar-lands of vic-t'ry a-round her, When so proud-ly she bore her brave
brave ; May the ser-vice u-nit-ed ne'er sev-er, But hold to their col-ors so

*FINE*

view ; Thy ban-ners make tyr-an-ny trem-ble, When borne by the red, white and blue,
crew, With her flag proud-ly float-ing be-fore her, The boast of the red, white and blue,
true ; The ar-my and na-vy for-ev-er, Three cheers for the red, white and blue,

*D.S.*

When borne by the red, white and blue, When borne by the red, white and blue, Thy
The boast of the red, white and blue, The boast of the red, white and blue, With her
Three cheers for the red, white and blue, Three cheers for the red, white and blue, The

## Nora O'Neal

WILL S. HAYS

1. Oh! I'm lone - ly to - night, love, with - out you, And I sigh for one glance of your
2. Oh! the night - in - gale sings in the wild - wood, As if ev - er - y note that he
3. Oh! why should I weep tears of sor - row? Or why does my hope lose its

eye; For sure there's a charm, love, a - bout you, When
knew Was learned from your sweet voice in child - hood, To re -
place? Won't I meet you, my dar - ling, to - mor - row, And

ev - er I know you are nigh. Like the beam of the star when 'tis
mind me, sweet No - ra, of you. But I think, love, so of - ten a -
smile on your beau - ti - ful face? Will you meet me? Oh, say, will you

smil - ing, Is the glance which your eye can't con - ceal, And your
bout you, And you don't know how hap - py I feel, But I'm
meet me With a kiss, at the foot of the lane? And I'll

voice is so sweet and be - guil-ing That I love you, sweet No - ra O'-Neal. Oh !
lone - ly to-night, love, without you, My dar -ling, sweet No - ra O'-Neal. Oh !
prom-ise when-ev - er you greet me, That I'll nev - er be lone - ly a - gain. Oh !

don't think that ev - er I'll doubt you, My love I will nev - er con-ceal; Oh! I'm

lone - ly to-night, love, with-out you, My dar-ling, sweet No - ra O' Neal.

## Kind Words are Dear to All

NELLY E. ELWELL

P. E. VAN NOORDEN

*Andante con moto*

1. Speak gen - tly, there's e-nough of care! Be-neath the bright-est smile, . . . The
2. Speak gen - tly, kind words bless the lips From whence they sweet-ly fall . . . . Like

lips may ut - ter mer - ry words, The heart be sad the while, . . . . The
dew - drops to the droop-ing flow'rs, Kind words are dear to all, . . . . . Kind

heart be sad the while. A kind word is a lit - tle thing, But
words are dear to all. The heart grows strong be - neath their light, Dark

oh! how great its pow'r To light us on to no - ble deeds, In
vis - ions fade a - way, We wake as from a trou - bled dream, To

some sad, si - lent hour, In some sad, si - lent hour, To
wel - come hope's bright ray, To wel - come hope's bright ray, We

*pp*

light us on to no - ble deeds, In some sad, si - lent hour.
wake as from a trou - bled dream, To wel - come hope's bright ray.

*rall.*

## The Promised Land

1. I have a Fa-ther in the prom-ised land, I have a Fa-ther in the prom-ised land,
2. I have a Sav-iour in the prom-ised land, I have a Sav-iour in the prom-ised land,
3. I have a crown in the prom-ised land, I have a crown in the prom-ised land,
4. I hope to meet you in the prom-ised land, I hope to meet you in the prom-ised land,

D.C. *I'll a-way, I'll a - way to the prom-ised land, I'll a-way, I'll a - way to the prom-ised land,*

D.C.

My Fa - ther calls me, I must go To meet Him in the prom- ised land.
My Sav-iour calls me, I must go To meet Him in the prom- ised land.
When Je - sus calls me, I must go To wear it in the prom- ised land.
At Je - sus' feet a joy - ous band; We'll praise Him in the prom- ised land.
*My Fa - ther calls me I must go To meet Him in the prom - ised land.*

# The Soldier's Tear

ALEXANDER LEE

T. H. BAYLY

*Larghetto*

1. Up - on the hill he turned To take a last fond look Of the val - ley and the village church, And the cot-tage by the brook. He list-ened to the sounds so fa - mil - iar to his ear, And the sol - dier leant up - on his sword, And

2. Be - side that cot-tage porch A girl had knelt in pray'r: She held a - loft a snow - y scarf Which flut-tered in the air; She breathed a sigh for him, A pray'r he could not hear, But he paused to bless her as she knelt, And

3. He turn'd and left the spot, Oh, do not think him weak, For dauntless was the sol-dier's heart, Tho' tears were on his cheek. Go watch the foremost ranks In dan - ger's dark ca - reer, Be sure the hand most dar - ing there Has

wiped . . a - way   a   tear.

## When to Thy Vision

From GOUNOD'S " Faust "

1. When to thy vis - ion life ap - pears sweet - ly smil - ing, Then all a -
2. As two fond flow'r - ets on one stem u - nit - ed, So link'd by

bout me seems to smile on me, But if sad tears come and naught seems life be -
des - ti - ny our hearts are bound, Should ev - er sor - rows come, or hopes be

guil - ing, Then, O my lov'd one, then, O my lov'd one, then I will weep for thee, will weep for thee.
blight - ed, Then ev - er faith - ful, then ev - er faith - ful, I shall be faithful, ev - er faithful found.

# Sweet Spirit, Hear My Prayer

LURLINE

*Largamente*

WM. VINCENT WALLACE

1. Oh! Thou, to whom this heart ne'er yet   Turned in an-guish or re-gret,   The
2. Oh! Thou, to whom my thot's are known,   Calm, oh! calm these trembling fears;   Ah!

*dolente*

past for-give, the fu-ture spare;   Sweet Spir-it, hear my pray'r!   Oh!
turn a-way the world's cold frown,   And dry my fall-ing tears!   Oh!

*dolcissimo*

leave me not a-lone in grief,   Send this blight-ed heart re-lief!   **Send this**

*dolcissimo*

blight-ed heart re-lief! . . . Make Thou my life thy fu-ture care,   Sweet

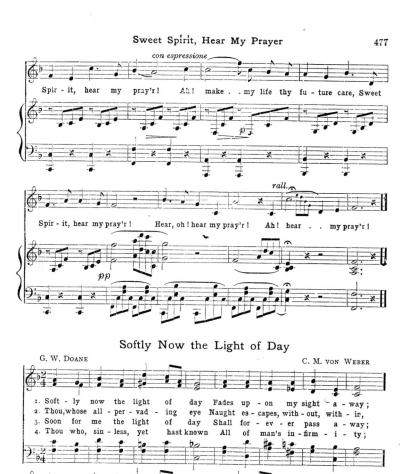

## Sweet Spirit, Hear My Prayer

*con espressione*

Spir - it, hear my pray'r! Ah! make . . my life thy fu - ture care, Sweet

*p*

*rall.*

Spir - it, hear my pray'r! Hear, oh! hear my pray'r! Ah! hear . . my pray'r!

*pp*

## Softly Now the Light of Day

G. W. DOANE

C. M. VON WEBER

1. Soft - ly now the light of day Fades up - on my sight a - way;
2. Thou, whose all - per - vad - ing eye Naught es - capes, with - out, with - in,
3. Soon for me the light of day Shall for - ev - er pass a - way;
4. Thou who, sin - less, yet hast known All of man's in - firm - i - ty;

Free from care, from la - bor free, Lord, I would com - mune with Thee.
Par - don each in - firm - i - ty, O - pen fault and se - cret sin.
Then, from sin and sor - row free, Take me, Lord, to dwell with Thee.
Then, from Thine e - ter - nal throne, Je - sus, look with pit - ying eye.

# When You and I Were Young

Geo. W. Johnson

J. A. Butterfield

1. I wan- dered to-day to the hill, Mag-gie, To watch the scene be -
2. A ci - ty so si - lent and lone, Mag-gie, Where the young and the gay and the
3. They say I am fee - ble with age, Mag-gie, My steps are less spright-ly than

low; The creek and the creak - ing old mill, Mag-gie, As
best, In pol - ished white man - sions of stone, Mag-gie, Have
then, My face is a well - writ-ten page, Mag-gie, But

we used to long a - go. The green grove is gone from the
each found a place of rest, Is built where the birds used to
time a - lone was the pen. They say we are a - ged and

hill,  Mag-gie,  Where first  the  dai - sies sprung;  The
play,  Mag-gie,  And join  in  the  songs that were sung:  For we
gray,  Mag-gie,  As sprays  by  the  white break-ers flung;  But to

creak-ing old mill is  still,  Mag-gie, Since you and  I  were young.
sang as  gay as  they,  Mag-gie, When you and  I  were young.
me you're as fair  as you were,  Mag-gie, When you and  I  were young.

## God is Love, His Mercy Brightens

JOHN BOWRING                                    ITHAMAR CONKEY

1. God  is  love; His mer - cy  brightens  All  the  path  in  which  we  rove;
2. Chance and change are bu - sy  ev - er;  Man  de - cays, and a - ges  move;
3. E'en  the  hour that dark - est seem-eth  Will  His changeless good - ness prove;
4. He  with earth- ly  cares  en - twin-eth  Hope  and com - fort from  a - bove;

Bliss He wakes and  woe  He  light-ens:  God  is  wis - dom, God  is  love.
But  His  mer - cy  wan - eth  nev - er:  God  is  wis - dom, God  is  love.
From  the  gloom His  bright - ness streameth:  God  is  wis - dom, God  is  love.
Ev - 'ry -where His  glo - ry  shin-eth:  God  is  wis - dom, God  is  love.

# Oh, Hush Thee, My Baby

*Andantino*

1. Oh, hush thee, my ba-by! thy sire was a knight, Thy moth - er a la - dy so
2. Oh, rest thee, my dar-ling, the time soon will come, When sleep shall be brok-en by
3. Oh, fear not the bu-gle tho' loud - ly it blows, It calls but the ward-ers that

love - ly and bright; The woods and the glens from these tow'rs which we see, They
trum - pet and drum; Then rest thee, my dar - ling, oh sleep while you may, For
guard thy re - pose; Their bows would be bend - ed, their blades would be red, Ere the

*lento a tempo*

all are be - long - ing, dear ba - by, to thee. Oh, rest thee, babe, rest thee, babe,
strife comes with man-hood, as light comes with day. Oh, rest thee, babe, rest thee, babe,
step of a foe - man drew near to thy bed. Oh, rest thee, babe, rest thee, babe,

sleep on till day! Oh, rest thee, babe, rest thee, babe, sleep while you may!

## The Three Little Pigs

A. S. GATTY

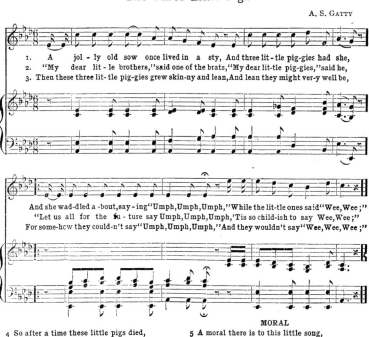

1. A   jol - ly old sow once lived in a sty, And three lit - tle pig-gies had she,
2. "My   dear lit - le brothers," said one of the brats, "My dear lit-tle pig-gies," said he,
3. Then these three lit- tle pig-gies grew skin-ny and lean, And lean they might ver-y well be,

And she wad-dled a -bout, say - ing "Umph, Umph, Umph," While the lit-tle ones said "Wee, Wee ;"
"Let us all for the fu - ture say Umph, Umph, Umph, 'Tis so child-ish to say Wee, Wee ;"
For some-how they could-n't say "Umph, Umph, Umph," And they wouldn't say "Wee, Wee, Wee ;"

4 So after a time these little pigs died,
They all died of *felo de se*,
From trying too hard to say "Umph, **Umph,**
**Umph,**"
When they only could say "Wee, Wee."

MORAL

5 A moral there is to this little song,
A moral that's easy to see,
Don't try when you're young to say "Umph,
Umph, Umph,"
For you only can say "Wee, Wee."

## Mary of Argyle

*Allegretto con delicatezza*

1. I have heard the ma - vis sing-ing His love song to the morn, I have
2. Though thy voice may lose its sweet-ness, And thine eye its bright-ness too, Though thy

seen the dew-drop cling-ing, To the rose just new-ly born; But a
step may lack its fleet-ness, And thy hair its sun - ny hue, Still to

sweet - er song has cheer'd me At the eve-ning's gen - tle close, And I've
me wilt thou be dear - er Than all the world shall own; I have

*cres.*

seen an eye still bright-er Than the dew-drop on the rose; 'Twas thy
loved thee for thy beau - ty, But not for that a - lone; I have

*mf*

## Mary of Argyle

*a tempo*

voice, my gen - tle Ma - ry, And thine art - less win - ning smile, That
watch'd thy heart, dear Ma - ry, And its good - ness was the wile That has

*a tempo*

made this world an E - den, Bon - ny Ma - ry of Ar - gyle.
made thee mine for ev - er, Bon - ny Ma - ry of Ar - gyle.

*ad lib.*

## My Faith Looks Up to Thee

Rev. RAY PALMER

LOWELL MASON

1. My faith looks up to Thee, Thou Lamb of Cal - va - ry, Sav - iour di - vine! Now hear me
2. May Thy rich grace im - part Strength to my faint - ing heart, My zeal in - spire! As Thou hast
3. While life's dark maze I tread, And griefs a - round me spread, Be Thou my Guide; Bid darkness
4. When ends life's transient dream, When death's cold, sullen stream Shall o'er me roll, Blest Saviour,

while I pray; Take all my guilt a - way; Oh, let me from this day Be whol - ly Thine!
died for me, Oh, may my love to Thee Pure, warm, and changeless be, A liv - ing fire!
turn to day, Wipe sor - row's tears a - way, Nor let me ev - er stray, From Thee a - side.
then, in love, Fear and dis - trust re - move; Oh, bear me safe a - bove, A ran - somed soul.

# When Johnny Comes Marching Home

*With spirit*

LOUIS LAMBERT

SOLO / CHORUS / SOLO

1. When Johnny comes marching home a-gain, Hur-rah, hur-rah! We'll give him a heart-y
2. The old church bell will peal with joy, Hur-rah, hur-rah! To wel-come home our
3. Get rea - dy for the Ju - bi - lee, Hur-rah, hur-rah! We'll give the he - ro

CHORUS / SOLO

wel-come then, Hur-rah, hur-rah! The men will cheer, the boys will shout, The
dar - ling boy, Hur-rah, hur-rah! The vil - lage lads and las - sies say, With
three times three; Hur-rah, hur-rah! The lau - rel wreath is rea - dy now To

CHORUS *Repeat ad lib.*

la -dies, they will all turn out, And we'll all feel gay, When Johnny comes marching home.
ro - ses they will strew the way, And we'll all feel gay, When Johnny comes marching home.
place up-on his loy-al brow; And we'll all feel gay, When Johnny comes marching home.

## There Were Three Crows

(TUNE: " WHEN JOHNNY COMES MARCHING HOME")

1 ‖: There were three crows sat on a tree,
O Billy McGee, McGaw :‖
There were three crows sat on a tree,
And they were black as crows could be,
Ref.   And they all flapped their wings and cried
( *Spoken* : Caw ! Caw ! Caw!) Billy McGee, McGaw.

( *Repeat last two lines without "Caw."* )

2 ‖:Said one old crow unto his mate, etc.:‖
" What shall we do for grub to eat ?"   **Ref.**

3 ‖:"There lies a horse on yonder plain, etc.:‖
Who's by some cruel butcher slain.   Ref.

4 ‖:We'll perch upon his bare back-bone, etc.:‖
And pick his eyes out, one by one."   Ref.

## Sweet By-and-By

JOSEPH P. WEBSTER

1. There's a land that is fair-er than day, And by faith we can see it a-far;
2. We shall sing on that beau-ti-ful shore, The me-lo-di-ous songs of the blest,
3. To our boun-ti-ful Fa-ther a-bove, We will of-fer our trib-ute of praise,

For the Fa-ther waits o-ver the way, To pre-pare us a dwell-ing-place there.
And our spir-its shall sor-row no more, Not a sigh for the bless-ing of rest.
For the glo-ri-ous gift of His love, And the bless-ings that hal-low our days.

CHORUS

In the sweet by-and-by, We shall meet on that beau-ti-ful shore,

In the sweet by-and-by, by-and-by,

In the sweet by-and-by, We shall meet on that beau-ti-ful shore.

by-and-by, by-and-by, by-and-by,

# The Carrier Dove

DANIEL JOHNSON

1. Fly a-way to my na - tive land, sweet dove, Fly a-way to my na - tive
2. Oh! fly to her bower, and say, the chain Of the ty - rant is o'er me
3. I shall miss thy vis - it at dawn, sweet dove, I shall miss thy vis - it at

land, . . . And bear these lines to my la - dy love, That I've
now, . . . That I nev - er shall mount my steed a - gain, With
eve, . . . But bring me a line from my la - dy love, And

trac'd with a fee - ble hand. . . . She mar-vels much at my long de -lay, A
hel - met up - on my brow. . . . No friend to my lat - tice a sol - ace brings, Ex-
then I shall cease to grieve! . . . I can bear in a dun-geon to waste away youth, I can

ru - mor of death she has heard, Or she thinks per-haps I
cept when your voice is heard, When you beat the bars with your
fall by the con-quer - or's sword, But I can-not en - dure she should

false - ly stray,— Then fly to her bower, sweet dove.
snow - y wings,— Then fly to her bower, sweet dove.
doubt my truth,— Then fly to her bower, sweet dove.

## Sun of My Soul

J. KEBLE                                    W. H. MONK

1. Sun of my soul, Thou Sav - iour dear, It is not night if Thou be near;
2. When the soft dews of kind - ly sleep My wea-ried eye - lids gen - tly steep,
3. A - bide with me from morn till eve, For with-out Thee I can - not live;
4. Come near and bless us when we wake, Ere thro' the world our way we take,

Oh, may no earth-born cloud a - rise To hide Thee from Thy ser-vant's eyes.
Be my last thought, how sweet to rest For - ev - er on my Sav - iour's breast!
A - bide with me when night is nigh, For with-out Thee I dare not die.
Till in the o - cean of Thy love We lose our - selves in heav'n a - bove.

# Be Kind to the Loved Ones at Home

ISAAC B. WOODBURY

*Andante espressivo*

1. Be kind to thy fa-ther, for when thou wert young, Who lov'd thee so fond-ly as
2. Be kind to thy mother, for lo! on her brow May tra - ces of sor - row be
3. Be kind to thy brother, his heart will have dearth, If the smile of thy joy be with-
4. Be kind to thy sis-ter, not man - y may know The depth of true sis - ter -ly

he?    He caught the first ac-cents that fell from thy tongue, And
seen;    Oh, well may'st thou cherish and com - fort her now, For
drawn;    The flow - ers of feel-ing will fade at their birth, If the
love;    The wealth of the o - cean lies fa - thoms be - low    The

joined in thy . - no-cent glee.    Be kind to thy fa-ther, for
lov - ing and . . . aath she been.    Re - mem - ber thy mother, for
dew of af - . . tion be gone.    Be kind to thy brother, wher-
sur - face that spark - les a - bove.    Be kind to thy fa-ther, once

now    he    is  old,      His  locks  in - ter-min - gled with gray;      His
thee   will  she pray,     As   long   as God giv - eth  her breath;        With
ev - er you are,           The  love   of  a broth - er  shall be           An
fear - less and bold,      Be   kind   to thy moth - er  so near;           Be

foot - steps are fee-ble,  once fear - less and bold,  Thy  fa - ther is pass-ing a - way.
ac - cents of kindness then cheer  her lone way,  E'en  to the dark val-ley of death.
or - na-ment purer  and rich - er by far  Than pearls from the depth of the sea.
kind  to thy broth-er, nor show  thy heart cold, Be  kind to thy sis - ter so dear.

## Holy Ghost, with Light Divine

ANDREW REED

L. M. GOTTSCHALK

1. Ho - ly  Ghost, with light di - vine,  Shine up - on  this heart  of   mine;
2. Ho - ly  Ghost, with pow'r di - vine,  Cleanse this guilt - y heart  of   mine;
3. Ho - ly  Ghost, with joy  di - vine,  Cheer this sad - dened heart  of   mine;
4. Ho - ly  Spir - it all  di - vine,  Dwell with - in  this heart  of   mine;

Chase the  shades of night   a - way,   Turn my  dark-ness in - to  day.
Long hath sin, with - out  con - trol,   Held do - min - ion o'er my  soul.
Bid  my  ma - ny  woes  de - part,  Heal my  wound-ed, bleed-ing heart.
Cast down ev - 'ry  i - dol  throne, Reign su - preme and reign a - lone.

# By the Sad Sea Waves

J. Benedict

1. By the sad sea waves I lis - ten while they moan A la - ment o'er graves of
2. From my care last night, by ho - ly sleep be-guil'd, In the fair dream-light, my

hope and pleas - ure gone; I was young, I was fair, I had
home up - on me smil'd. O how sweet 'mid the dew, Ev - 'ry

once not a care, From the ris - ing of the morn to the set - ting of the sun; Yet I
flow'r that I knew Breath'd a gen-tle wel-come back to the worn and wea - ry child. I a-

pine like a slave, by the sad sea wave. Come a - gain, bright days of
wake in my grave by the sad sea wave. Come a - gain, dear dream, so

hope and pleasure gone, Come a-gain, bright days, Come a-gain, come a-gain.
peace-ful-ly that smil'd, Come a-gain, dear dream, Come a-gain, come a-gain.

## The Glorious Fourth

Old Colonial Melody

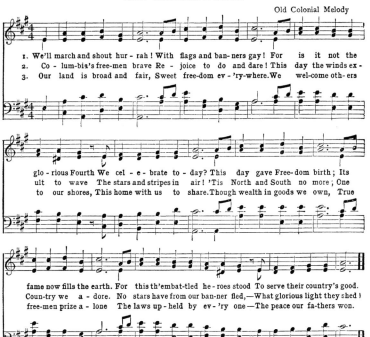

1. We'll march and shout hur - rah! With flags and ban-ners gay! For is it not the
2. Co - lum-bia's free-men brave Re - joice to do and dare! This day the winds ex-
3. Our land is broad and fair, Sweet free-dom ev - 'ry-where. We wel-come oth-ers

glo - rious Fourth We cel - e - brate to - day? This day gave Free-dom birth; Its
ult to wave The stars and stripes in air! 'Tis North and South no more; One
to our shores, This home with us to share. Though wealth in goods we own, True

fame now fills the earth. For this th'embat-tled he - roes stood To serve their country's good.
Coun-try we a - dore. No stars have from our ban-ner fled,—What glorious light they shed!
free-men prize a - lone The laws up-held by ev - 'ry one—The peace our fa-thers won.

## Afterwards

MARY MARK LEMON

JOHN MULLEN

1. Af - ter the day has sung its song of sor - row, And one by one the
2. Some - times my heart grows wea-ry of its sad - ness, Some-times my life grows

gold - en stars appear, I lin - ger yet, where once we met, be - lov - ed, the
wea - ry of its pain, Then, love, I wait and lis-ten for your whis - per,

And seem to feel thy spir- it still is near. The flow'rs have fled that
Till fears de-part and sunshine comes again. It can - not be that

blossom'd in that spring - tide, The birds are mute that sang their songs a-bove,
we should part for - ev - er, That love's sweet song is hush'd for us al - way;

And tho' the years have drifted us asun - der,   Time can-not break the golden chain of love.
I hear it yet, al-tho' its theme be al- ter'd,'Twill reach thy heart and bring thee back some day.

Still   we   can love   al - tho' the shad - ows gath - er,   Still   we can hope,   un -
Love,   we   can love   al - tho' the shad - ows gath - er,   Still   we can hope,   un -

til the clouds be past :  Come to my heart and whisper thro' the silence, "Hope on, dear heart, our

lives shall meet at last." lives shall meet at last. Hope on, dear heart, our lives shall meet at last!"

# Marseillaise Hymn

ROUGET DE LISLE

1. Ye sons of France, a - wake to glo - ry! Hark, hark! what myr-iads bid you
2. O, lib - er - ty! can man re - sign thee, Once hav - ing felt thy gen - 'rous

rise! Your chil-dren, wives, and grand-sires hoa - ry: Be - hold their tears, and hear their
flame? Can dun-geons, bolts, and bars con - fine thee? Or whips thy no - ble spir - it

cries, Be - hold their tears, and hear their cries! Shall hate-ful ty - rants, mis - chief
tame? Or whips thy no - ble spir - it tame? Too long the world has wept be -

breed - ing, With hire-ling hosts, a ruf - fian band, Af - fright and des - o - late the
wail - ing That falsehood's dag - ger ty - rants wield; But free - dom is our sword and

land, While peace and lib - er - ty lie bleeding? To arms, to arms, ye brave! Th'a-
shield, And all their arts are un - a - vail-ing; To arms, to arms, ye brave! Th'a-

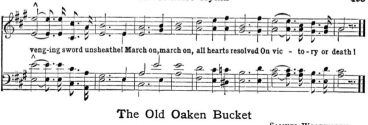

veng-ing sword unsheathe! March on, march on, all hearts resolved On vic - to - ry or death!

## The Old Oaken Bucket

SAMUEL WOODWORTH

1. { How dear to this heart are the scenes of my child-hood, When fond rec - ol -
{ The or - chard, the mead - ow, the deep tan-gled wild-wood, And ev - 'ry loved
D.C. *The old oak - en buck - et, the i - ron-bound buck - et, The moss - cov - ered*

FINE

lec-tion pre - sents them to view! } { The wide - spread-ing pond, and the
spot which my in - fan - cy knew; } { The cot of my fa - ther, the
*buck - et that hung in the well.*

D.C.

mill that stood by it, The bridge and the rock where the cat - a - ract fell; }
dai - ry-house nigh it, And e'en the rude buck - et that hung in the well. }

2 The moss-covered bucket I hailed as a treasure,
  For often at noon, when returned from the field,
I found . the source of an exquisite pleasure,
  The purest and sweetest that nature can yield.
How ardent I seized it, with hands that were
  glowing,
And quick to the white-pebbled bottom it fell,
Then soon, with the emblem of truth overflow-
  ing,                                  [well.
And dripping with coolness, it rose from the
The old oaken bucket, the iron-bound bucket
  The moss-covered bucket arose from the well.

3 How sweet from the green, mossy brim to receive
  it,
  As, poised on the curb, it inclined to my lips!
Not a full-blushing goblet could tempt me to leave
  it,
  Tho' filled with the nectar that Jupiter sips.
And now, far removed from the loved habitation,
  The tear of regret will intrusively swell,
As fancy reverts to my father's plantation,
  And sighs for the bucket that hung in the well.
The old oaken bucket, the iron-bound bucket,
  The moss-covered bucket which hangs in the
  well.

496

# Toyland

GLEN MACDONOUGH

VICTOR HERBERT

*Very slow and dreamily*

1. When you've grown up, my dears, And are as old as I, . . . You'll oft-en pon-der
2. When you've grown up, my dears, There comes a drear-y day . . When 'mid the locks of

on the years That roll so swift-ly by, My dears, that roll so swift-ly
black ap-pears The first pale gleam of gray. My dears, the first pale gleam of

by. . . . And of the man-y lands You will have jour-neyed through, You'll
gray. . . Then of the past you'll dream As gray-haired grown-ups do, . . And

oft re-call The best of all The land your child-hood knew! Your
seek once more Its phan-tom shore, The land your child-hood knew! Your

child - hood knew. Toy - land! Toy - land! Lit - tle girl and

boy - land, While you dwell with - in it, You are ev - er hap - py

then. Child - hood's joy - land, Mys - tic mer - ry Toy - land!

Once you pass its bor-ders you can ne'er re-turn a - gain. . gain.

# Because You're You

REFRAIN.

Not that you are fair, dear, Not that you are true. Not your gold-en

GOVERNOR.

Not that I am fair, dear, Not that I am true.

*Slower.*

hair, dear, Not your eyes of blue. When we ask the rea - son,

i... my gold-en hair dear, Not my eyes of blue. . . When we ask the

Words are all too few! So I know I love you, dear, be - cause you're you.

rea - son, W... are all too few! I love you, dear, because you're you.

*rit.*

# All is Quiet

*Andante*

A. H. Rosewig

1. All is qui - et, all is still, Sleep, my child, and fear not ill,
2. Let thy lit - tle eye - lids close, Like the pet - als of the rose;

Win - try winds blow chill and drear, Lul - la - by, my ba - by dear,
When the morn - ing sun shall glow, They shall in - to blos - som blow,

Win - try winds blow chill and drear, Lul - la - by, my ba - by dear.
They shall in - to blos - som blow. When the morn - ing sun shall glow.

*Con spirito*

3. Then the lit - tle flow'rs I'll prize, Then I'll kiss those lit - tle eyes,

And thy moth - er will not care, If 'tis spring or win - ter drear,

And thy moth - er will not care, If 'tis spring or win - ter drear.

502

## The Long, Long, Weary Day

*Allegro moderato*

1. The long, long, wea - ry day Is pass'd in tears a - way, The long, long,
2. When I, his truth to prove, Would tri - fle with my love, When I, his
3. A - las! if land or sea Had part - ed him from me, A - las! if
4. But he is dead and gone! Whose heart was mine a - lone, But he is

*mf*

wea - ry day Is pass'd in tears a - way, And still at eve - ning, I am
truth to prove,Would tri - fle with my love, He'd say,"For me thou shalt be
land or sea Had part - ed him from me, I would not these sad tears be
dead and gone! Whose heart was mine a - lone, And now for him I'm ev - er

*p legato*

weep - ing,When from my win-dow's height, I look out on the night, I still am
weep - ing,When at some fu - ture day, I shall be far a - way, Thou shalt be
weep - ing, But hope he'd come once more, And love me as be - fore, And say,"Cease
weep - ing. His face I ne'er shall see, And nought is left to me But bit - ter

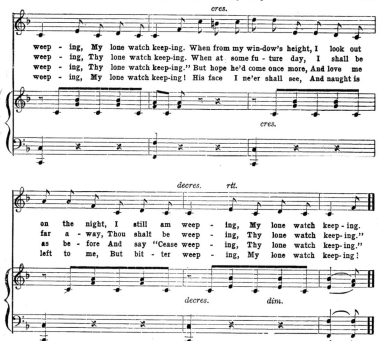

*cres.*

weep - ing, My lone watch keep-ing. When from my win-dow's height, I look out
weep - ing, Thy lone watch keep-ing. When at some fu - ture day, I shall be
weep - ing, Thy lone watch keep-ing." But hope he'd come once more, And love me
weep - ing, My lone watch keep-ing! His face I ne'er shall see, And naught is

*cres.*

*decres.* *rit.*

on the night, I still am weep - ing, My lone watch keep - ing.
far a - way, Thou shalt be weep - ing, Thy lone watch keep-ing."
as be - fore And say "Cease weep - ing, Thy lone watch keep-ing."
left to me, But bit - ter weep - ing, My lone watch keep-ing!

*decres.* *dim.*

## Blanche Alpen

CHARLES JEFFERYS  STEPHEN GLOVER

*mederato*

1. You speak of sun - ny skies to me, Of or-ange grove and bower; Of
2. You tell me oft of riv - ers bright, Where gold-en gal - leys float, But
3. Had you been rear'd by Al-pine hills, Or lov'd in Al - pine dells, You'd

*p*

## Blanche Alpen

*rall.*

winds that wake soft mel - o - dy  From leaf and bloom - ing flow'r ;  And
have  you seen  our lakes  by night,  Or sail'd in  Al - pine boat ?  You
prize,  like me,  our moun - tain rills,  Nor fear the  tor - rent swells.  It

*a tempo*

you  may prize  those far - off skies,  But tempt not  me  to  roam.  In
speak  of  lands  where hearts and hands  Will greet  me  as  I  come,  But
mat - ters  not  how drear the spot,  How proud  or  poor the  dome,—Love

sweet con - tent  my  days  are  spent— Then  where - fore leave my
tho'  I  find  true  hearts and kind,  They're  kind - - er  still  at
still  re - tains  some death - less chains,  That  bind . . . the  heart  to

Blanche Alpen

home?    In sweet con-tent my days are spent—Then wherefore leave my home?
home.    But tho' I find true hearts and kind, They're kind-er still at home.
home.    Love still re-tains some death-less chains, That bind the heart to home.

## Shining Shore

G. F. Root

1. My days are glid-ing swift-ly by, And I, a pil-grim stran-ger, Would not de-tain them
2. Should coming days be cold and dark, We need not cease our sing-ing; That per-fect rest naught
3. Let sorrow's rud-est tem-pest blow, Each chord on earth to sev-er, Our King says, Come, and

Chorus

as they fly,—Those hours of toil and dan-ger. For now we stand on Jor-dan's strand, Our
can mo-lest Where gold-en harps are ring-ing.
there's our home, For-ev-er! Oh, for-ev-er!

friends are pass-ing o-ver; And just be-fore the shin-ing shore We may al-most dis-cov-er.

# Come, Thou Fount of Every Blessing

ROBERT ROBINSON

JOHN WYETH

1 Come Thou Fount of ev-'ry bless-ing, Tune my heart to sing Thy grace; Streams of
2 Here I raise mine Eb-en-e-zer; Hith-er by Thy help I'm come; And I
3. O to grace how great a debt-or Dai-ly I'm con-strained to be! Let Thy

mer-cy, nev-er ceas-ing, Call for songs of loud-est praise. Teach me some me-lo-dious son-net,
hope, by Thy good pleas-ure, Safe-ly to ar-rive at home. Je-sus sought me when a stran-ger,
good-ness, like a fet-ter, Bind my wand'ring heart to Thee: Prone to wan-der, Lord, I feel it,

Sung by flaming tongues above; Praise the mount (I'm fixed upon it) Mount of Thy redeeming love.
Wan-d'ring from the fold of God; He, to res-cue me from dan-ger, Interposed His precious blood.
Prone to leave the God I love; Here's my heart, O take and seal it; Seal it for Thy courts a-bove.

## Happy Land

Hindoostan Air

1. There is a hap-py land, Far, far a-way, Where saints in glo-ry stand,
2. Come to that hap-py land, Come, come a-way; Why will ye doubt-ing stand,
3. Bright, in that hap-py land, Beams ev-'ry eye; Kept by a Fa-ther's hand,

Bright, bright as day. Oh, how they sweet-ly sing, Wor-thy is our
Why still de-lay? Oh, we shall hap-py be, When from sin and
Love can-not die. Oh, then, to glo-ry run; Be a crown and

Happy Land

Sav-iour King, Loud let His prais-es ring, Praise, praise for aye.
sor-row free, Lord, we shall live with Thee, Blest, blest for aye.
king-dom won; And bright, a-bove the sun, We reign for aye.

God Be with You

J. E. RANKIN, D.D.                                    W. G. TOMER

1. God be with you till we meet a-gain, By His coun-sels guide, up-hold you,
2. God be with you till we meet a-gain, 'Neath His wings pro-tect-ing hide you,
3. God be with you till we meet a-gain, When life's per-ils thick con-found you,
4. God be with you till we meet a-gain, Keep love's ban-n-r float-ing o'er you,

With His sheep se-cure-ly fold you,   God be with you till we meet a-gain.
Dai-ly man-na still pro-vide you,      God be with you till we meet a-gain.
Put His arms un-fail-ing round you,    God be with you till we meet a-gain.
Smite death's threat'ning wave before you, God be with you till we meet a-gain.

CHORUS

Till we meet, till we meet, Till we meet at Je-sus' feet,
Till we meet, till we meet, till we meet, Till we meet at Je-sus' feet, Till we meet,

Till we meet, . . . till we meet, God be with you till we meet a-gain
Till we meet, till we meet, till we meet,

# Come, Oh! Come with Me, the Moon is Beaming

B. S. BARCLAY

Italian Melody

1. Oh! come, oh! come with me, the moon is beam - ing; Come, oh! come with
2. My skiff is by the shore; she's light and free: To ply the feath-er'd

me, the stars are gleam - ing; All a-round, a-bove with beau-ty teem - ing,
oar is joy to me; And while we glide a-long, my song shall be: My

FINE

Moon - light hours are meet for love. Tra la la la la la
dear - est maid, I love but thee. Tra la la la la la

D. C. al fine

tr

la la la la la la la la la la la la. . . . . .

# INDEX

# DICTIONARY OF MUSICAL TERMS

## A

**A Ballata.** In ballad style.
**A Battuta.** In exact beat; true time.
**A Cappella.** In church or chapel style; for chorus, without accompaniment.
**A Capriccio.** As you please.
**A Deux Temps.** Two crotchets or beats in a bar.
**A Due.** For two voices or instruments; separately or in unison.
**A Piacere.** At the performer's pleasure as to time.
**A Quatre Mains.** For four hands, as a pianoforte duet.
**A Tempo.** In regular time.
**A Tre.** For three voices or instruments.
**Accelerando.** Gradually quickening the movement.
**Acciacatura.** A species of grace-note.
**Accolade.** The brace that binds all parts of a score.
**Accoppiate.** Parts joined by a brace.
**Adagio.** Slow and sustained.
**Adagio Assai.** Very slow and sustained.
**Affetto.** Emotion, feeling.
**Afflizione.** Sorrow, mournfulness.
**Air Ecossais.** A Scotch air.
**Alla Polacca.** In style of a Polish dance.
**Alla Siciliana.** In style of Sicilian shepherd's dance.
**Alla Zoppa.** In constrained, halting, syncopated style.
**Allegro.** Quick, lively.
**Allegro Assai.** Very quick.
**Allegro ma non Troppo.** Quick, but not too much so.
**Allegretto.** Cheerful, but not so quick as Allegro.
**Allegretto Scherzando.** Moderately vivacious, playfully but without haste.
**Al Segno, dal Segno.** To return to the similar preceding sign and play thence to the word *Fine*.
**Alternativo.** Proceeding alternately from one to another movement.
**Andante.** Slow, gentle, soothing.
**Andante con Moto.** Slow, but with movement, not dragging.
**Aria Buffa.** Comic song.
**Aria d'Abilita.** Song of difficult execution.
**Arpeggio.** Passages formed of the notes of regular chords, played in succession.

## B

**Ben Marcato.** Render passage or air in a clear, distinct and strongly accented manner.
**Bis.** Twice. Passage marked by a curved line under or over it to be played or sung twice.

**Bravura.** Boldness, spirit, dash, brilliancy.
**Brillante.** Brilliant, showy, sparkling.
**Brio.** Brilliancy, spirit.
**Brise.** Split into arpeggios; in violin playing, short, detached strokes of the bow.
**Buffo, Buffa.** Humorous, comic, especially as applied to an air or a singer.
**Burden.** A return of the theme of a song at the end of each verse.
**Burletta.** A musical farce.

## C

**Calore.** Warmth, animation.
**Cantabile.** In singing style.
**Cantando, Cantante.** In singing style, smooth and flowing.
**Cantata.** A vocal composition consisting of an intermixture of recitative and chorus.
**Capriccio.** Fanciful, irregular composition; caprice.
**Che.** Than, that.
**Coda.** A "tail-piece," or concluding passage
**Col Arco.** With the bow.
**Colla Parte.** Accompanist must accommodate his tempo to the leading part.
**Colla piu gran Forza e Prestezza.** As loud and quick as possible.
**Come.** As, like.
**Come Primo.** As at first.
**Come Tempo del Tema.** Same movement as the theme.
**Commodo, Comodo.** Quietly, with composure.
**Con Amore.** Tenderly, with affection.
**Con Brio ed Animato.** Brilliant and animated.
**Con Diligenza.** In studied manner.
**Con Espressione.** With expression.
**Con Fuoco.** With fire, with intense animation.
**Con Gusto.** With taste.
**Con Impetuosita.** With impetuosity.
**Con Energia.** With much energy.
**Con Moto.** With motion, actively, not dragging.
**Con Spirito.** With quickness, with spirit.
**Con Variazioni.** With variations.
**Con Velocita.** In swift time.
**Con Vivacita.** With animation.
**Contrapuntal.** In the style of counterpoint, fugal, with rich and varied parts or voices.
**Counterpoint.** The science of writing parts or melodies in combination.
**Crescendo.** Gradually increasing the tone-volume.

**D**

**Da Capo.** From the beginning, repeat from the beginning.
**Dal Segno.** From the sign, or mark of repetition.
**Decrescendo.** Gradual decreasing the tone-volume.
**Delicato, Delicatamente.** Delicately.
**Destra.** Right, right hand.
**Dito.** The finger.
**Divertissement.** Short, light composition; also airs introduced between the acts of Italian opera.
**Divoto.** In solemn style.
**Dolente.** Pathetically.
**Doloroso.** In a soft, sorrowful style.

**E**

**Energico.** With energy, force.
**Espressivo.** With expression.

**F**

**Fine.** End.
**Flebile.** In mournful style, weepingly.
**Forte.** Loud.
**Fortissimo.** Very loud.
**Forza.** With force, energy
**Fresco.** Fresh, quick, lively.
**Furioso.** Furiously, with fire, energy, intense animation.

**G**

**Giusto.** Exact, precise.
**Glissando.** In gliding manner, sweeping across the keys.
**Grazioso.** Gracefully.
**Gregorian Music.** Sacred compositions, after the style introduced into the Roman Catholic Service by Pope Gregory (about 600 A.D.).
**Gusto.** Taste.

**H**

**Harmonic Triad.** A common chord, like C-E-G, F-A-C, G-B-D.
**Hauptsatz.** The principal section of an extended movement.
**Hauptstimme.** The most prominent voice, or part; the voice or part which has the theme.
**Haut-contre.** Counter-tenor, high tenor, alto.
**Haut-dessus.** First treble, high soprano.
**Hinstrich.** An up-bow.
**Holding-note.** A note that is sustained or continued, while others are in motion.

**I**

**Il Ponticello.** In singing, where the natural tone forms a junction with the falsetto; the "break" in a voice.
**Impetuoso.** With impetuosity.
**Impromptu.** Without study or preparation.
**Innocente.** Innocent, natural, unaffected, ingenuous.
**Instrumentation.** The art of arranging music for the various instruments of an orchestra or band.

**L**

**L. H.** The left hand.
**Largamente.** Sustaining or broadening the chords or tones, ponderously, with breadth.
**Larghetto.** Time less slow than Largo.
**Larghissimo.** Very slowly and broadly.
**Largo.** A very slow, stately movement.
**Legato.** Smooth, connected, the opposite of *staccato*.
**Leggiero.** With lightness.
**Lento.** Slow.
**Lentando.** With increasing slowness.

**M**

**Main Droit.** The right hand.
**Main Gauche.** The left hand.
**Meno Mosso.** Slower movement.
**Mesto.** Pensive, sad, melancholy.
**Mezza Voce.** With moderate strength of tone.
**Mezzo.** Half, middle.
**Mezzo Forte.** Moderately loud.
**Mezzo Piano.** Moderately soft.
**Mit Begleitung.** With accompaniment.
**Moderato.** With moderation, as *Allegro Moderato*, moderately fast, not too fast.
**Molto Adagio.** Very slow.
**Molto Allegro.** Very fast.
**Mordent.** A quick trill, with but a single stroke of the grace-note (side-note).
**Morendo.** Dying away, gradually growing softer.
**Mormorando.** With a gentle, murmuring sound.
**Motet.** Composition of a sacred character in several parts: an unaccompanied anthem.
**Motive, Motivo.** Leading theme of a composition; a brief and characteristic theme.

**Musica di Camera.** Chamber-music; music in serious style, intended for performance in a house or small hall—such as string-quartets, violin sonatas, piano trios, etc.

**N**

**Nachspiel.** A postlude.
**Non Troppo Presto.** Not too fast.

**O**

**Obbligato.** Voices or instruments indispensable to the proper performance of a piece; also a part added for ornament or display.
**Opera Buffa.** A comic opera.
**Ottava.** An octave.
**Ottava Alta.** An octave higher.
**Ottava Bassa.** An octave lower.

**P**

**Parte Cantante.** The singing part, the voice or part which has the sustained melody.
**Pastorale.** In rustic or pastoral style.
**Perdendo or Perdendosi.** Gradually decreasing in speed and volume to the last note, which is nearly, if not quite, lost on the ear.
**Piu Forte.** Louder.
**Piu Lento.** Slower.
**Piu Mosso.** With more movement.
**Piu Piano.** Softer.
**Piu Presto.** Quicker.
**Pizzicato.** Plucked; played with the finger, not with the bow.
**Poco a Poco.** Gradually. By degrees.
**Poco Meno.** Somewhat less.
**Poco Piano.** Rather soft.
**Poco Piu.** Somewhat more.
**Poco Presto.** Rather quick.
**Portamento.** Gliding from one to another note.
**Premiere.** A first performance.
**Prestissimo.** The most rapid possible movement.
**Primo.** The first.

**R**

**Rallentando, Ritardando, Ritenente.** Slackening the speed.
**Rondino, Rondiletta, Rondinetto, or Rondoletto.** A short *Rondo*.
**Rondo.** A composition of several strains, with frequent return to first theme.

**S**

**Scherzando.** In a light, breezy manner.
**Scherzo.** A joke or jest; the quick movement of a sonata or symphony.
**Seconda Volta Molto Crescendo.** Much louder the second time.
**Segue il Coro.** Here follows the chorus.
**Segue la Finale.** Here follows the Finale.
**Segue Senza Interruzione.** Go on; do not stop.
**Sempre Forte.** Continuing loud, without decreasing the force.
**Sempre Piu Forte.** Steadily increasing in force.
**Senza Replica.** Without repetition. *Da capo senza replica*, play from the beginning, but disregard repeat-marks.
**Sin' al Fine.** To the end.
**Slentando.** Reducing the speed.
**Sostenuto.** Sustained.
**Sotto Voce.** In an undertone.
**Spiritoso.** With spirit, animation, energy.
**Staccato.** Short, pointed, detached; the opposite of *Legato*.
**Stark.** Loud.
**Syncopation.** A displacement of accent, either by having a rest on a strong beat, or by tying a strongly accented tone to a weaker.

**T**

**Tasto Solo.** Played without chords.
**Tempo Giusto.** In exact time.
**Tempo Primo.** In the first or original time.
**Tenete Sino Alla Fin del Suono.** Keep keys down as long as sound lasts.
**Tenuto.** Sustained; held for the full time-value.
**Tutti.** All voices or instruments, or both.

**V**

**Variazioni.** Variations of an air or theme.
**Veloce.** In rapid time.
**Vivace.** With animation.
**Volta.** Time, turn; as *prima volta*, the first time; *una volta*, once.
**Volti Subito.** Turn the leaf quickly.

# CLASSIFIED INDEX

Under this head will be found the songs in the alphabetical index, which precedes this. In this index the same song will often appear in two or more classes; because in its history it has been found popular under circumstances not originally contemplated by its composer. Thus Dixie appeared originally as a negro minstrel song, became popular as dance music, and eventually was played by military bands North and South during the great Civil War. Bonny Eloise, a sweet little ballad, mingled its strains with the rhythm of dancing feet all through the winter of 1860-61, and then (like "The Girl I Left Behind Me" in the English Army) became the last greeting of hundreds of volunteers to the loving hearts they left forever. Other compositions have been accepted by fraternal and collegiate singers for so long that they are also a part of the recognized melodies, sung at fraternal and collegiate gatherings.

It has been also considered best to recognize this fact, because some have sent songs in in one class and others the same in another, in either of which its popularity has been recognized.